THE BUILDINGS OF
ROMAN BRITAIN

DATE DUE F

GUY DE LA BÉDOYÈRE

TEMPUS

First published Batsford 1991
This edition 2001

PUBLISHED IN THE UNITED KINGDOM BY:

Tempus Publishing Ltd
The Mill, Brimscombe Port
Stroud, Gloucestershire GL5 2QG

PUBLISHED IN THE UNITED STATES OF AMERICA BY:

Arcadia Publishing Inc.
A division of Tempus Publishing Inc.
2 Cumberland Street
Charleston, SC 29401
1-888-313-2665

Tempus books are available in France, Germany and Belgium
from the following addresses:

Tempus Publishing Group	Tempus Publishing Group	Tempus Publishing Group
21 Avenue de la République	Gustav-Adolf-Straße 3	Place de L'Alma 4/5
37300 Joué-lès-Tours	99084 Erfurt	1200 Brussels
FRANCE	GERMANY	BELGIUM

British Library Cataloguing in Publication Data.
A catalogue record for this book is available from the British Library.

ISBN 0 7524 1906 4

Typesetting and origination by Tempus Publishing.
PRINTED AND BOUND IN GREAT BRITAIN

Contents

List of illustrations

Text figures

Colour plates

Foreword

This book was originally published in 1991, and was generously praised for its treatment of a subject scarcely touched in Romano-British studies, apart from individual studies of buildings. Nothing has been produced on the subject since. It has been unavailable for a number of years but it has been drawn to my attention by a number of students and museum curators that the book has proved extremely useful ever since it first appeared. So, it has been a great pleasure to prepare a second edition for Tempus and I would like to express my thanks to Peter Kemmis Betty for inviting me to do so.

In order to recast the book in a different format, and also in view of increased reproduction costs for photographs sourced from museums, some of the original illustrations have had to be deleted, but the colour section has been extended. Where enhanced versions of the original drawings were produced for other books, these have been substituted. It has not been possible to make significant revisions to the text, but a number of minor corrections and alterations have been introduced. The bibliography has been updated with a selection of recently published papers and books.

The only significant text casualty has been the removal of the appendix covering some relevant ancient inscriptions recording buildings in Roman Britain. I have normally substituted a reference to *The Roman Inscriptions of Britain*, abbreviated *RIB*. At the time of writing a new corpus taking into account discoveries since 1955 is still in preparation. So, in those cases I have referred the reader directly to my *Companion to Roman Britain* (Tempus 2000) where that work features an illustration and description. This book, indicated *Companion* in the text, has a full chapter dealing with building inscriptions, so it is hoped that the reader will forgive being directed to that source for the information.

Guy de la Bédoyère
Welby 2000

Map of Roman Britain showing the location of sites illustrated throughout the book. The column capital is from the site of the basilica at Silchester. Grid references for other sites mentioned in the text can be found in the bibliography

Introduction

This book is an innovative experiment in drawing together as many different types of Romano-British buildings as possible and to reconstruct many of them on paper. Unfortunately, with very few exceptions the buildings of Roman Britain are not amongst the most impressive historical monuments this island boasts. For the most part the surviving examples form disappointing chunks of shapeless masonry (**colour plate 1**). Even the remains of villas with their colourful mosaics present a challenge to the most inspired imagination. The fact is that not a single Romano-British building has survived even nearly intact, though this is not uncommon elsewhere in the former Empire (**1**).

In the fifth century Britain gradually drifted out of the sphere of classical influence. During this period a great deal of change took place and by the eleventh century England had emerged as one of the most influential Christian states in Europe. The growth of towns and the small distances involved meant that it was virtually impossible for ancient settlements to rot in peace — Roman settlements like York were built over or the stone was carried away, as at Verulamium and Silchester. Only the walls of towns, which survived into the Middle Ages, and the military buildings of the remote west and north, stood a reasonable chance of surviving as recognizable ruins.

But to judge the architecture of Roman Britain from crumbling stumps of flint and tile is unfair. The Romans were responsible for the first major buildings to be built in Britain. Many public buildings would have borne comparison with the medieval cathedrals. The contrast with pre-Roman Britain is particularly important — houses are known but there is no evidence for any sort of ordered architecture, or building programmes. The material culture of the Mediterranean world was well known to the wealthy members of tribes in south-east Britain. They enjoyed imported luxury goods and stored their wealth in silver and gold but the cultural borrowing went little further. In many ways the buildings of Roman Britain represent the most radical feature of a new age because they symbolize not just the concept of cities, civic identity and local government but also the more generalized spread of wealth amongst the population expressed in more robust housing. Religious cult centres were consolidated with the building of temples, which were rare before 43.

The ruin of Roman Britain has made the province easier to understand. For example, the dereliction of the third-century fort at Richborough allowed the extensive excavations which have revealed much of its past. It would be inconceivable to damage a house in Herculaneum for the sake of what might lie underneath. Equally no one would consider demolishing Westminster Abbey for the sake of the Saxon abbey beneath. But ruined Roman buildings can sometimes be judiciously removed in part to reveal not only the construction sequence but perhaps also a late Iron Age roundhouse beneath. When modern development makes destruction a certainty then there is no reason not to trace a

1   *The capitol at Sbeitla (Sufetula) in Tunisia. Some of Roman Britain's public buildings will have survived in this form as late as the early Middle Ages. However, intensive urban growth, a large population and demand for stone from the Saxon period onwards has guaranteed that now only fragments remain*

site's history at all its stages. So it has been possible to learn far more about the buildings of Roman Britain than would ever have been possible had they been much better preserved.

Excavation since the late 1700s has revealed that Roman Britain was a place rich in buildings of all kinds. On one hand the island was very far from being a centre of classical architecture — there were no Pantheons for instance — but its towns were bigger than some of its medieval counterparts and some of the villas were remarkable for their complexity. There were also some astonishing structures like the triconch hall at Littlecote (**144**). However, few have been completely excavated and naturally attention has always been drawn to the more dramatic examples, for example Bignor (**colour plate 2**) and Lullingstone (**colour plate 23**). Building developments in modern towns have led to occasionally dramatic discoveries like the temple of Mithras in London and also a wealth of evidence for Roman civic public buildings. In most cases these urban buildings have to be analysed from fragmentary traces of walls. This may be frustrating but at the same time provides a stimulating basis for piecing together the known components into a coherent whole.

The excavation of buildings discovered in open land is a more leisurely process. But even after several years of careful digging the building and its associated features rarely form more than a ground plan. Of course, people do not live and work in ground plans and trying to interpret the structure as a building with form and the history of its development is far from easy. Visualizing its original appearance can be even more difficult, and depends on understanding which parts of a building existed at the same time and trying to reconcile what has been found with intelligently imagined walls and roofs.

This book is an attempt to try and give *form* to ground plans and ruins. Of course we will never know for certain what Romano-British buildings looked like but this is no justification for sometimes ignoring the fact that all the ground plans recovered are the skeletons of buildings which once had walls and roofs. Reconstructions on paper are often attempted now but the fact that very few reports of excavations known to the author include contour maps with the plan, along with elevations of surviving remains against the Roman ground level, shows how little serious attention is paid to recording the evidence of the structure itself in a comprehensive format. It is even quite rare to include photographs illustrating the site within the landscape. This is really quite remarkable when one considers how many pages are usually given over to recording dozens of pot rims and other finds, or providing a meticulous record of mosaic panels and fragments of painted wall-plaster.

These omissions can occasionally make it extremely difficult to make sense of the excavator's description, of particular regret when the site no longer exists. And, occasionally, assertions are made about a building's original appearance without experimenting with different alternatives. Orthographic projections based on the ground plan can show some ideas to be very unlikely, while at the same time suggesting alternatives. Charting falls of roof tiles would give invaluable information about the likely layout of roofs but even this apparently obvious record is hardly ever made, or at least published. Alan Sorrell, famous for his artistic reconstructions of Romano-British settlements, bemoaned these shortcomings some years ago and it is sad that so little note has been taken. The authors of recent reports of excavations at the temple in Bath and the *forum* site in London are to be congratulated for paying so much attention to recording the structural details.

So how should one attempt to show a three-dimensional building in two dimensions? For the most part the drawings in this book use the techniques of orthographic projection, which are discussed in more detail in Appendix 1. This does have the disadvantage of creating an unreal world of parallel lines and right angles. The truth of course is that buildings work because they have parallel lines and right angles (amongst others) — it just so happens that they do not look to the eye as if they do. So when reconstructing a building we have to begin with the unreal world because that shows us if the structure we are imagining can be reconciled with the plan we have found. This does not mean that the reconstruction is right but that it is possible; a problem with beginning with an artistic interpretation is that one can unwittingly ignore a detail of the plan, making the restoration a technical impossibility. Orthographic projections force one to take note of the consequence of every feature of the plan.

The range of buildings in Roman Britain was considerable, running from the most basic kind of rectangular strip house to the basilicas. This book sets out to reconstruct as many different types as possible, though obviously this involved great selectivity, and inevitably there will have been omissions. A bias has been adopted towards buildings which are structurally interesting and distinct, and/or published in accessible form and/or which can easily be visited today.

This book is based on a concise general text; the illustrated buildings are accompanied by extended captions in order to make them as self-contained as possible, thereby saving the reader from having to trace a single building's history through numerous references in the index. Places are referred to with the names in common usage — thus Verulamium and Vindolanda appear throughout for St Albans and Chesterholm. Naturally there are examples of buildings assignable to more than one category. In recent years it has been suggested that some of the great 'villas' such as Chedworth were actually cult centres, designed to house pilgrims visiting nearby temples, though of course it may have functioned in both capacities. A conservative approach has been adopted here simply because it will be easier for the reader to find something where he expects to find it, though it is hoped that as much note of modern thinking and different points of view has been taken as possible.

Even so, it is very important to be realistic about our interpretations of ancient buildings and the limitations imposed on us — we have very little positive evidence and debates about the use of some curious buildings, like Littlecote's hall, are based on very limited material. The tendency to place too much emphasis on the iconography of a mosaic, or the design of a ground plan, is quite understandable but all too often these arguments become accepted as facts when in truth we often simply do not know. Sometimes it is suggested that, say, abandonment of a particular site may be linked to known historical events such as the repercussions following the defeat of Clodius Albinus by Septimius Severus. Albinus, governor of Britain, competed with Severus for the Empire in 196/7 and it may well be that his supporters were dispossessed. While it may be possible, with reservations, to suggest a link between a general phenomenon found at a number of sites and such an historical event, it is quite misleading to associate any one site with the event unless there is much more specific evidence in the form of inscriptions or literary evidence which refers to the site in question. These are very rare, for example Tacitus' description of the burning of London, Colchester and Verulamium during the Boudican Revolt.

Although a number of the sites mentioned can be visited today it is always worth bearing in mind that much of the inspiration behind this book is to be found in France, Italy, on the fringes of the desert in North Africa, and in western Turkey. Nothing in Britain now can compare with a cool *atrium* of a house in Herculaneum in Italy, or the majestic capitol at Sbeitla in Tunisia (**1**) — but the purpose of this book is to show that this was not always so, to provoke discussion about a subject which has often been ignored and to give a little life to stumps of walls.

Considering the debate currently taking place about the future of architecture in modern Britain, not least the controversy over the Millennium Dome, it seems particularly appropriate to recall a period of intensive new building which was both functional and often inspired. We may never be able to stand in the sunlight and look across the temple precinct at Bath or fly low over Verulamium in high summer (**colour plates 12 & 24**) but we can at least imagine what may once have been.

1 Construction techniques

Introduction

Hardly a single Romano-British building survives in a form recognizable to the men who built it. This makes it difficult to try and understand how a building was erected and the techniques used to create a durable structure. The archaeologist is usually confronted with the pitiful remains of a building likely to consist of no more than wall footings and remnants of the superstructure, though fragments of roof tile usually abound. If he/she is lucky the superstructure will lie where it fell and the walls will bear traces of plaster. In unusual circumstances the walls will stand to a significant height, for example at Beauport Park in East Sussex. At this remarkable site, buried by a collapsing slagheap, the whole roof was found in pieces in and around the bathhouse (**42**). Waterlogged or burnt conditions may even preserve traces of organic components, such as rafters or the frames from wattle and daub walls.

But in most cases the building will have been reduced to a mere ground plan, usually by centuries of stone-robbing and ploughing. If the building was made entirely of timber this will have long since rotted away and only aerial observation followed by careful excavation of the bedding trenches and post-holes is likely to reveal anything of its form. Re-using stone from Romano-British buildings was regarded as a convenient alternative to quarrying from the later part of the Roman period up until modern times (see chapter 7).

Despite the disappointing lack of impressive surviving evidence we have a reasonably good idea of what many Romano-British buildings must have once looked like. The extraordinary towns of Pompeii and Herculaneum in Italy are probably the best examples but there are many other sites with very well preserved ruins not only in Italy, but also in France, Spain, North Africa and Turkey. Although there may have been regional styles of architecture and building design one of the remarkable features of the Roman world was its relative uniformity. So we can often be reasonably confident about what a building looked like, especially when its plan identifies it as an example of a well-known stereotype, like a theatre or a basilica.

Selection of sites and the planning of buildings

Surveyors

There were various reasons for why particular sites were selected as suitable plots for buildings. Agricola, governor of Britain from 78-84, was said by Tacitus to have had a remarkable eye for suitable ground on which to build a fort (*Agricola*, 22). This was a

2   *Depictions of buildings and surveying equipment*
   a. Drawing of a pharos *(?) on a tile from London. The tile seems to show a cross-section of a stepped tower. It may be a drawing of something else entirely, perhaps a cross-section of a basilica, a finial, or even a component from a heating system like a boiler.*
   b. Drawing of a house (?) on wall-plaster from the villa at Hucclecote.
   c. Wall painting from Trier (Germany) showing a country house with towers and colonnaded portico.
   d. Bronze norma *(mitre/set square) from the construction level of a second-century building in Canterbury. It bears the name G(aio) Cu(...) Valeno, 'for Gaius Cu.. Valenus' and was probably used by a joiner (after Hulse). Architects and surveyors would have used similar, but larger, examples.*
   e. Groma, *used for laying out the axes of a right angle*

comment on his tactical judgment, rather than his ability as an architect. He would have been advised by a military surveyor, *mensor*, such as Attonius Quintianus attested on a lost altar to Mars Condates from the fort at Piercebridge, county Durham (*RIB* 1024). Many towns, such as Verulamium or Wroxeter, grew up around early forts themselves sited close to a native settlement. In other cases the fort alone provided the stimulus by acting as a market on one of the new roads — for example Cirencester, and London, a city which almost certainly grew up around an early fort guarding the crossing over the Thames. Subsequently some of these towns received official status and were properly laid out when the fort was given up. In the countryside rural houses of early Roman date are often found to have been built over pre-Roman roundhouses and similarly rural temples are often found on sites which had clearly previously functioned as the focus of a native cult, even if no earlier 'temple' had been involved. Obviously in such cases surveyors played no part in the choice of location, though they may have been used to lay out the new building.

Surveyors were men educated in arithmetic and geometry and were often slaves or freedmen. They worked with various pieces of equipment such as the *groma*, a device for sighting straight lines by suspending two pairs of weighted lines (**2e**). In this way the right angle of an insula or the direction of a road could be set by looking across one of the pairs of weights at an assistant in the distance. As such it resembled a modern theodolite. In addition the surveyors would have used measuring instruments based on units of feet, *pedes*, and a mitre/set square, *norma* (**2d**).

Surveyors were mainly responsible for laying out land on which buildings were to be erected. Normally this happened on new sites where forts or towns were planned. Vegetius described how the surveyors measured out the ground for the tent-parties and allocated the soldiers to their individual quarters (*epitoma rei militaris*, iii.8). In such cases it was important that the correct amount of land was allocated for individual buildings and that the plots were laid out in the correct relationship. In practice this was flexible though all towns and forts conform to fairly similar patterns. In forts for example surveyors started from a central point in front of the headquarters, also called the *groma*. At Inchtuthil the headquarters building was disproportionately small but the surveyors had correctly allowed a much larger area (**18**). Presumably the building would have been reconstructed on a larger scale if the fortress had remained in occupation. Similarly the surveyors had allowed space for the commanding officer's house but this was never built. Military surveyors were not always reliable: building in a new province was likely to be unpredictable, particularly when it concerned forts being erected in the front line under military and political pressure. The Neronian legionary fortress at Usk in south Wales seems to have been abandoned by *c.*75 in favour of the site further south at Caerleon, possibly because it turned out that Usk was prone to flash floods, something evidently unforeseen. At Easter Happrew in Scotland the curious diagonal Flavian fort plan has been attributed to poor surveying.

Most of the major Romano-British towns show evidence for regimented planning of blocks and public buildings. In general it seems that sites were chosen for military, religious, social or geographic reasons rather than the specific conditions of a particular plot. This is hardly surprising and certainly reflects the writings of the first-century BC architect Vitruvius. He described the priorities for siting a public building as 'general convenience and utility' (I.7.1). Silchester and Verulamium are the best examples because the sites have never been significantly built on in later periods. However, local factors often created eccentricities. At Verulamium the street grid was complicated by the approach of Watling Street from London at an angle. One of the results was the unconventional 'Triangular Temple' (*see* **120**). Minor towns were not usually laid out in this way and grew up haphazardly along the line of a main road, like Kenchester in Herefordshire. The substantial town of Water Newton seems to have been a product of the very successful Nene Valley pottery industry; it, too, developed irregularly around a road, in this case Ermine Street, the main route to the north.

The Flavian Fishbourne 'palace' was laid out on a site previously occupied by military buildings and the so-called 'proto-palace' but the new building was so large that extensive levelling was necessary. Soil was moved from the western half of the site and used to build up the eastern side. The eastern part remained lower but instead of a slope, two terraces had been created with the west wing slightly higher than the rest of the structure. This can be seen in 119. The building's early date and complexity makes it certain that surveyors had been used to plan out and organize the site.

Academic debates exist about the basis of measurement used on different sites because the inaccuracies, both in the original laying out and in modern plans, found at different places makes it difficult to be certain what the original scheme was. It has been argued recently that Silchester and Caerwent were laid out on a basis of units called *pedes Monetales* (Walthew, 1987), used to lay out the insula and the buildings within them. These units were 2.21m (7ft 3in) in length, though a half unit 1.1m (3ft 9in) was also used. This is made even more complicated by the fact that some places, for example Silchester, were apparently re-surveyed on slightly different alignments. Traces of the original plan survive in the orientation of earlier buildings. At the fort of Gellygaer in south Wales it appears that the various fort buildings were measured out on multiples of five or ten Roman feet, a Roman foot (*pes*) being 0.296m (about 11 modern inches).

Architects

Surveyors worked closely with architects, and may even have been employed by them. We know the names of a few architects who lived in Britain, such as Amandus, *arc(h)itectus*, who erected an altar to Brigantia at Birrens, though we know nothing of his work (*RIB* 2091). Another, called Quintus, dedicated an altar to Minerva at the fort of Carrawburgh on Hadrian's Wall and was probably a soldier (*RIB* 1542). Like the surveyors they were educated men and would have used some of the same equipment. Even so the architects of major public buildings seem sometimes either to have lacked access to civic records (if they existed) or were remarkably careless in their preparatory work.

The basilica at Cirencester was built of high quality masonry in the last quarter of the first century, but curiously the site chosen lay partly over the ditches of the earlier fort. The fort had been abandoned as late as the 70s so it seems odd that either the architect was ignorant of the ditches' existence, or the possible consequences of building on top of them. In any case the basilica had begun to subside by the middle of the second century. Even the major basilica in London was built over filled-in brick earth quarries with similar results (**59 & 60**). More peculiarly the second-century basilica and forum at Wroxeter were built on the site of unfinished public baths, simply demolished to make way for the new project. A new set of baths was built in the adjacent insula. The reasons are unknown but may have been connected with problems over water supply. At Colchester the theatre was apparently built over the levelled eastern defences of the Claudian legionary fortress though too little is known about the theatre to know if this had any disastrous results.

All these examples suggest a strange lack of co-ordinated long-term planning, perhaps because there was a lot of administrative pressure to erect public buildings swiftly — we are uncertain, but even at Bath the late vaulted cover building for the sacred spring created apparently unforeseen problems with the huge weight of the vault despite the provisions which had been made for the cover building for the Great Bath (**11 & 12**). This haphazard approach to some major building projects seems also to have occasionally prevailed in private, or small-scale, projects. The early, circular temple at Wanborough seems to have partially collapsed within 50-60 years of being built in the late first century. The ambitious *frigidarium* at Lufton (**97**) needed propping up with substantial buttresses when it began to subside. The temple at Nettleton had to be strengthened internally to support a similar structure and eventually collapsed possibly because the precautions found necessary at Lufton were not adopted (**134-5**). The villa at Great Witcombe was built on an unsuitably steep hillside right over a spring, though this may have been for religious reasons (**114-15**); thereafter the owners seem to have been preoccupied with keeping the house in serviceable form. At Littlecote the fourth-century Orphic hall was built partly over an earlier road. Eventually subsidence occurred and one of the apses seems to have been damaged (**144**).

An interesting and related topic is the extent to which buildings were maintained. There are many military inscriptions, and some from other sites, which commemorate the restoration of buildings which had been allowed to deteriorate completely (if we can take them at face value). An example is the slab from Birdoswald dated to 297-305, recording the rebuilding of several buildings including the headquarters and the commandant's house (*RIB* 1912). As it happens most of these date from the third century and as far as the military ones are concerned probably result from the general lack of military activity in the period, as well as a taste for commemorating events. But it seems strange that a temple of Isis in London could have been allowed to decay in this way, especially as it was important enough to be rebuilt by the governor or his deputy (*Companion, 167, fig. 65*). Similarly at Caerleon, a temple dedicated to Diana was restored by a legionary legate in the mid-third century (*RIB* 316). At Bath a cryptic and incomplete inscription appears to record the repair and repainting of an unspecified structure in the temple precinct (*RIB* 141). There is also the restoration of a *principia* at the imperial estate(?)/villa at Combe Down (*RIB* 179). Whether these are more generally representative of a lack of investment in maintenance, particularly of official buildings, we cannot be sure. On the other hand they may be yet more examples of structures that had not been well-designed in the first place.

These various examples suggest that many Romano-British architects belonged to the 'suck it and see' school of thought, contrasting with the popular image of Roman building as the product of competent planning and techniques. In other words if the building started falling down it was either patched up or abandoned. If it didn't fall down there wasn't a problem. If correct this suggests that successful projects were as much a result of luck as design. The great majority of simple ordinary buildings would have been designed by the owners themselves more or less as they went along, erected perhaps with help from neighbours or locally hired labour. In most cases the building would have belonged to a stereotype adapted to local circumstances and requirements with various alterations taking place as the project progressed.

Although this must have been true of ordinary houses it may even have been true of substantial public buildings. Most major Romano-British public buildings, especially the basilica and forum, are all very similar and often derive from military prototypes (compare **30** and **63**). This raises an interesting point if we assume that many early major Romano-British public buildings were designed by military architects, or people trained by them. Such men would have been accustomed to working on virgin sites, or consolidating in stone an earlier timber fort. They may not always have fully appreciated the kind of structural problems arising when erecting massive masonry buildings on previously disturbed land. However, this does not explain the lack of foresight found in private or religious projects such as Lufton, Littlecote and Nettleton.

Needless to say we have no actual plans of Romano-British buildings. Vitruvius said that it was essential for an architect to be able to draw so that he could communicate his ideas effectively. He also describes the preparation of ground plans, elevations and perspective as well as the conception of new ideas through a flexible approach to specific problems (I.2.2). Some copies of plans, carved in stone, have survived from other parts of the Empire, for example a mausoleum and attendant buildings at Perugia in Italy, but are very far from being accurate blueprints of the intended projects because the proportions of the various elements do not match the stated measurements. However, they must have served as guides, aided by the sketching of buildings 'on site' perhaps by the architect in order to help him explain his intentions to the workmen. A tile found in London may be one of these. It seems to bear a sketched cross-section of an unspecified building. This has been identified as a *pharos* which is certainly a possibility (**2a**). It may also represent the cross-section of a basilica, or something else entirely — perhaps a stone finial, or even part of a pump or similar hydraulic system. A scratched representation of a building on plaster from the house at Hucclecote in Gloucestershire seems to represent a two-storied house with a gabled roof. The upper storey seems to have square windows and the lower storey seems to have two arched entrances. However, the illustration is clearly incomplete (**2b**).

We have practically no example of a single Romano-British architect who we can associate with a specific structure. Building inscriptions generally record the emperor, governor, community or private individual who commissioned the project. But at Beauport Park in East Sussex a remodelling of the bathhouse in the early third century seems to have been carried out by a man called Bassus or Bassianus under the orders of the *vilicus* (director) of the ironworks. Bassus is described as a *curam agens,* which means he was in charge of the work in hand. So he was probably responsible for designing the extension to the bathhouse (**42**). He was an architect or builder of poor quality despite his almost unique status of having escaped ancient architectural anonymity. His extension is of conspicuously poor work when compared to the neatly laid stones of the earlier part of the building.

From an archaeological point of view all these points raise a number of problems. It would be unwise to make assessments on the probability of there having been an upper storey, or other architectural complications, on the basis of the thickness of a stone footing or depth of a foundation as it is quite obvious that this sort of theoretical application was not applied, or if it was it was quite likely to be wrong. We rarely have any evidence for the extent to which timber had been used in a wall, and obviously a largely timber wall would have required less in the way of foundations. So one house might have had an excessively thick wall without an upper storey and another might have had an upper storey built on an inadequate wall and foundations. This did happen and one need only mention how the new gable end of the house at Meonstoke fell down (**96**) probably because of inadequate foundations or bonding to make the point. Had there been more time it would have probably been propped up with buttresses.

One important point worth considering is that the poor survival of Roman buildings in Britain makes it very difficult to be certain whether they were ever actually finished. Medieval cathedrals often took centuries to finish and it may well be that some major Romano-British buildings were never completed, making discussions about whether the structures were viable or irrelevant. The headquarters building at the legionary fortress of Caerleon had a huge basilican cross-hall (**29**). Some of the foundations and wall-footings have been located but the whole area was covered over with a thin layer of packed soil and no remains of columns were found even though the positions of their bases were. Of course it could have been comprehensively demolished but fragmentary traces of the superstructure might have been expected. With public buildings the problem of local money may have had an even more significant effect on construction projects. These could have easily lasted longer than the patience, fortunes or lives of their benefactor(s). From an archaeological point of view such situations are almost impossible to identify and the details are lost in the untraceable machinations of Romano-British local politics and finance.

With so little specific evidence it is not easy to draw general conclusions about Romano-British architects and surveyors. Possible examples of poor planning or design are not isolated and the impression is of a provincial profession occasionally out of its depth. There were obviously many reasons for this and it will never be possible to isolate those complicating any one instance. But we only have to consider the kind of problems befalling modern buildings to know that poor planning, hasty construction, shortage of money and the use of inadequate materials are usually behind most buildings which prove structurally unsound. However, it would be unfair not to point out that many of the simpler (and not necessarily smaller) Romano-British buildings exhibit no evidence at all for subsidence or collapse resulting from an inherently unstable design, or unsuitably prepared ground.

Timber

It is almost certain that the vast majority of buildings in Roman Britain were made of timber, all or in part. This is based on the fact that timber, at the time, must have been far more readily obtainable than building stone. It would have been felled locally and would have required a minimum of effort to convert into fort buildings, dwellings and even public buildings like the first basilica at Silchester (**58**). The availability of suitable timber may even have helped dictate the distribution of buildings, particularly country ones but we have no idea of the extent of initial deforestation and subsequent forestry management which took place in Roman Britain. It has been calculated that the fortress at Caerleon

3 *Early daub and timber wall types (after Crummy but adapted), based on mid-first-century walls excavated in the legionary fortress at Colchester (c.43-7).*
a. Daub and timber wall. A mortar plinth provided a footing, a layer of timber provided a level base for the wall of sun-dried bricks. The surface was then rendered and could be plastered to provide a perfectly adequate, if not particularly strong, wall which could be painted.
b. Wattle and daub internal wall made out of a timber frame laced with wattles and packed with daub and then rendered and plastered

would have required the equivalent of 150ha of woodland (Brewer, 1987, 16; about seven times the area of the 20.5ha fortress; 495 x 420m), though obviously maintenance and rebuilding would have used up even more. A writing tablet from an early well on the site records that some men were concerned with the collection of building timber (*materia*). Presumably as the province developed stocks of properly seasoned timber would have been built up, though during the early stages of military building such long-term considerations would have been ignored. Wood was prepared either by sawing or splitting the trunks to make planks and posts. Later on a new problem may have emerged. At the New Fresh Wharf in London examination of quayside timbers suggested that substantial exploitation of mature trees during the second century had created a shortage of supply. By the late third century the quay builders were obliged to turn to younger trees. If correct this gives us some idea of the massive scale of Roman use of timber.

Archaeological evidence of timber buildings is usually relatively poor — remains of such buildings are almost always confined to post-holes and sleeper beam trenches — but many buildings, which appear to be made of stone, may have only had stone footings to inhibit rot. Even so very few first-century buildings in Britain seem to have had any stone at all. Only in the second century and after did it become commonplace to consolidate a structure in stone. Verulamium is an excellent example: it took a major fire in *c.*155 to provoke the townspeople into building stone houses, or at least with stone footings.

Buildings made entirely of timber were generally secured to the ground in one of two ways. They are found most frequently in early military sites, because these were often occupied for a short period of time before being abandoned. On longer period sites where later stone buildings were erected on the same plots it can be difficult to identify traces of earlier timber structures. In the simplest method the upright posts which formed the frame were inserted straight into post-holes which were packed to make them secure. The building's superstructure was then nailed or pegged on and around the timber uprights. The iron nails used could be quite substantial, for example 30cm (one Roman foot) in length. The use of prefabricated components would have hastened the whole process. The early military granary at Fishbourne is a very good example of this and the archaeological product is a pattern of post-holes. Sometimes the waterlogged remains of the base of an upright may remain in the hole or even as no more than a 'ghost' of discoloured soil. Unfortunately they tell us nothing of the superstructure. The mid-first-century granaries at the fortresses of Usk and Inchtuthil were built with the more complicated method. In this case a series of trenches were dug into which sleeper beams were laid (**35**). These horizontal beams were designed to form the base for the uprights inserted into holes designed specially to receive them. Likewise there is no information about the superstructure because the only product of archaeological excavation is the sequence of sleeper trenches. A remarkable recent discovery in London is the almost complete floor and parts of the walls of an early second-century timber warehouse (**156**). We can be sure that carpenters were skilled men who used precision equipment, much of which has not changed up to modern times. The mitre square from Canterbury (**2d**) has been interpreted as the possession of a skilled joiner, Gaius Cu... Valenus, who was probably preparing timber on the site of a second-century domestic structure (*RIB* 2433.19).

Whether or not the footings were of timber or stone timber walls must have been made up of a series of uprights between which horizontal beams were inserted or laid across. This created a timber frame filled either with wattle and daub, timber, brick or stone. Timber framed walls filled with brick can still be seen at Herculaneum in southern Italy. Here the unique conditions of being buried under a wall of boiling mud and lava carbonized the wood. The careful excavations of modern times have shown that upper storeys were often built in this way. The structure is lighter and stronger as a result though obviously normal weathering must have meant that such buildings would have needed considerable periodic repairs. While this technique must have been used in Britain it is more likely that the timber framed buildings of Roman Britain would have had wattle and daub fillings in the walls. Fortunately the circumstances of the Boudican Revolt in 60 have left well-defined burnt layers at London, Colchester and Verulamium from the sack of each settlement. This has preserved the footings of wattle and daub walls (**3**). Waterlogged deposits can preserve wattle and daub as well. Vitruvius was very critical of wattle and daub because of its instability and inflammability. He considered it only as an expedient solution to a lack of time or money (II.8.20) and emphasized how vital it was to build the wattle and daub on a raised base in order to prevent damp which would rot the timber frame and cause the wall to sag and crack its plaster skin.

The overall impression of such structures must have resembled the half-timbered houses, still a common feature of Britain and northern Europe. Apart from wattle and daub the other most likely walling would have been planks of timber. The reconstructed granary at the first-century fort of the Lunt, near Coventry, was re-erected in this way. The effect is similar to the 'clapperboard' technique, still visible on some eighteenth- and nineteenth-century houses in England, particularly East Anglia and Kent.

4 *Carved stone removed from a quarry at Fallowfield Fell, near Hadrian's Wall about four miles east of Chesters fort. It bears the inscription [P]ETRA FLAVI CARANTINI, which means 'the rock of Flavius Carantinus' (RIB 1442). The stone has been removed to Chesters museum*

Stone

Building partly or entirely in stone did not become commonplace in Roman Britain until the second century. It was not only durable and practical but also the only viable means, along with concrete, of building walls strong enough to support vaults. It was also the most desirable medium for constructing elaborate buildings of any type, for example classical-style temples and basilicas. The practice of enjoying baths heated by furnaces made stone an essential material for bathhouses. There are a number of rural sites where a bathhouse has been located but no house, suggesting that the latter was built of perishable materials — a risk which could not be taken for baths (for example Baston Manor, Hayes in Kent).

Stone was quarried locally wherever possible, and sometimes inscriptions are found which confirm that the quarry was worked in Roman times (**4**). Foundations are not always examined closely in excavation but they probably varied extensively depending either on the height of the building or the experience of the man who was building it. Normally a trench was dug and filled with rubble courses set in some sort of cement. These foundations might be narrower than the walls they supported as in the house at Plaxtol (**90**), or they might be wider. Where the land was damp, or the walls were to be built to a considerable height, then stone foundations might be laid on top of a timber raft which was itself set on piles driven several metres into the subsoil. This may sound rather unreliable but it was a very well established technique and is usually found under major fortifications, for example the late riverside wall in London (**155**), or the Saxon Shore fort at Pevensey (**48**). Where a building was set into a hillside the slope might be cut back and the stone set directly onto the surface, for example at the Huggin Hill baths in London

5 The baths at Huggin Hill, London during excavation. The huge complex of public baths was terraced into the slope down to the Thames. On the right of this view a substantial wall can be seen abutting directly onto the slope which has been cut back to create two levels

which were terraced into the slope leading down to the river (**5**).

Evidence of attempts to restrict the effects of rising damp and rain passing through porous masonry are extremely rare. Hypocaust systems may have helped dry walls, and indeed the purpose of the system may have been as much to combat condensation as to heat rooms. However, hypocausts were not as common as is sometimes popularly imagined and were in any case usually confined to bath suites. A building at 25-6 Lime Street in London put up after *c.*125 had a cellar built at least 1.6m (5ft) below the surrounding ground level. Three rows of roof-tiles (*tegulae* — see **9**) had been mortared vertically to one of the exterior walls in what has been interpreted as an attempt to create a barrier against damp (see London in bibliography for chapter 4). Even if it was effective no other examples are known from London so the technique cannot have been very widespread.

There were two basic methods of building in stone in the Roman period. Masonry construction involved the use of accurately sawn and placed blocks of stone. Their weight made mortar unnecessary and it was extremely durable. However, it required a great deal of unskilled effort to transport stone to the site and a great deal of skilled effort to erect the building. The unfinished remains of a stores building at Corbridge (**6**) give an idea of what this could involve. Concrete construction, *structura caementicia*, was much better suited to Roman Britain where it was usually based on mortared rubble. This formed the core of a wall faced with small blocks of stone or brick. A few courses of the faces were built first and the rubble core poured in. When this had set the height of the faces was raised and more rubble core poured in, and so on. The facing and the core can be clearly seen in Hadrian's Wall at Poltross Burn (**7**). As the wall's height increased it was supported with wooden scaffolding set into putlog holes. These can be seen in the 'Old Work' at Wroxeter and in the 'Mint Wall' at Lincoln (**62**) but few surviving Romano-British walls are high enough to show this. However, Vitruvius pointed out that rubble construction, however beautifully finished, was not durable (I.8.8). If the facing stones became

6 *Unfinished masonry at Corbridge, Northumberland. Part of a substantial building, possibly a store, which may have been built during the late third century but which was never completed. Although the blocks have been dressed on the sides lying against other stones their faces are still rough*

displaced then the internal core is exposed and as the cement bonding decays so the rubble begins to break up. This is why Romano-British buildings cannot be exposed to public view unless modern consolidation of the core and facing has been undertaken.

It does seem to have been general practice, as elsewhere in the Empire, to use rectangular or square tiles as levelling and bonding courses, as quoins for corners and to create a frame for openings (**8**). The effect of this was to use the tiles almost as a kind of frame filled with stone. This, combined with cement or concrete used as pliable filler, made up for irregularities in the stone. In this way flint nodules could be used as facing stones in substantial walls, and is particularly evident in city walls in south-east England, for example at Silchester and Verulamium. Even in these cases the facing stones were worked to create a relatively smooth surface but such a useful commodity was readily carted off in the Middle Ages and few traces of the old surface survive. It was not always necessary to use tile. Hadrian's Wall was built entirely of stone. Although the width varied according to the zone and period in question the Wall was made up of a core of concreted rubble with sides of dressed stone.

The external appearance of many stone walls may have been quite different from that popularly imagined. Recent work on Hadrian's Wall has suggested that the curtain was rendered and whitewashed. At the temple on Maiden Castle traces of external rendering and painting were found. This may have been far more common than we will ever appreciate and it may be that Romano-British towns and houses resembled modern

7 *Hadrian's Wall at milecastle 48 (Poltross Burn). The Wall's facing stones can be seen in contrast to the rubble core. This particular section also shows where the milecastle's wing walls (left of centre) had been built to 'Broad Wall' specifications (see chapter 2). The foundation for the Wall had been prepared for the same gauge but when the Wall was actually constructed on this stretch plans had changed and it was being built to the new 'Narrow Wall' width*

Mediterranean settlements in having rendered and brightly painted walls. Unfortunately the British climate has destroyed most of the evidence.

Roofing

Although the shattered fragments of roof tile are one of the most obvious clues to locating a Romano-British building little is known about how roofs were constructed. Roofs were obviously essential but they create certain problems. Firstly they had to be strong but as light as possible; secondly the weight had to be distributed so that it was directed down through the supporting walls. Most tiles were made of fired clay but in some areas where the stone was suitable slates made of stone could be used instead. Slate or Cotswold limestone was ideal. Many buildings must have been thatched, especially the outbuildings on villa estates and the more basic houses. However, the only evidence for this is a lack of tiles in amongst the building's debris, and of course in any one individual case this may be because the tiles had been removed for re-use.

There has been a great deal of debate about exactly how the tiles were secured to the roof. The same tiles are in common use in Mediterranean buildings today. Figure **9** shows how a modern Italian roof is constructed. It has the interesting effect of both solving the problem of tiles lacking nail holes and explaining part of Vitruvius' description which is otherwise difficult to understand.

8 *Tile arch inserted in the masonry wall of the commandant's baths at Binchester, built by the* numerus Concangiensium *(a low status auxiliary infantry unit). The arch was one of a number which helped circulation of warm air beneath the floors of the fourth century bathhouse*

It was possible for a decorative effect to be created by using tiles of different colours, achieved through the use of different clays and different firing conditions. At Lullingstone, Kent, the second-century house was roofed with red tiles occasionally interspersed with yellow tiles. At Piddington, Northants, the *imbrices* (curved roof tiles) were over-fired to create a deep blue colour. They were laid over yellow *tegulae* (flat roof tiles). This roof was supported by plastered columns painted red and purple-brown. This reminds us that the ancient world's appreciation of garish colour schemes was much stronger than surviving remains usually imply.

Many tiled roofs may have covered and concealed vaulted roofs, though this would generally have been confined to bathhouses where the warm and damp air would have had a destructive effect on roof timbers (**41, 76**). Tile was also used in the vault at Beauport Park which covered one of the warm rooms. Large fragments of the vault lay on the floor where it had collapsed and it was possible to see that the central row of keystones had been flanked on either side by a row of tiles. The bathhouse at Chesters used tufa sections in the vault which created voids and thus saved weight (**10**). Vaulting did mean that the lateral walls had to be substantially stronger in order to withstand the forces. The Great Bath at Bath shows this to good effect (**11, 12**) and shows just how much reinforcement work had to be done even though extensive use had been made of weight-relieving voussoir tiles.

Windows and doors

Romano-British buildings must have had windows but hardly any survive either *in situ*, or in fragments. The Beauport Park and Chesters bathhouses and the town house at Colliton Park, Dorchester, retain window sills (**13**). The Dorchester house's window had collapsed

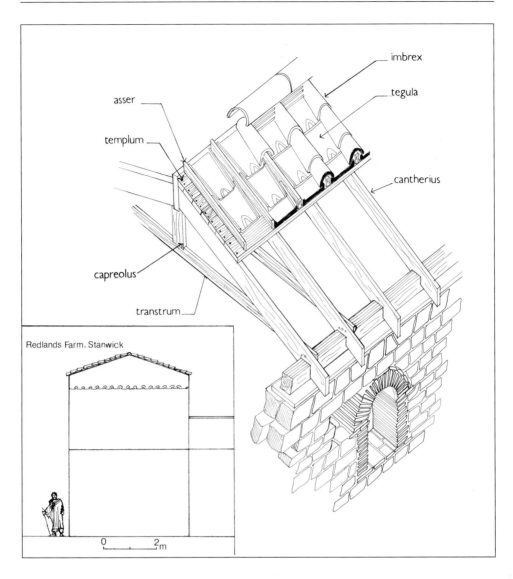

Labels on diagram: imbrex, tegula, asser, templum, cantherius, capreolus, transtrum

Redlands Farm, Stanwick

0   2m

9   *Diagrammatic view of a Roman tile roof. This diagram is based on and adapted from a modern Italian roof illustrated in Barry (1980, fig. 183). The exact details of the construction of Roman roofs in Britain are unknown for obvious reasons. However this version makes sense of the Vitruvian description and also explains why it was not necessary to secure every tile with nails. The problem concerns the upper strips of wood (asseri). Vitruvius describes these as simply overlying the layer of* templi *and consequently they seem rather superfluous. This modern Italian roof shows how the* asseri *were laid at a distance from one another in order to create channels for the* tegulae. *The tegulae were wedged in and consequently it would not have been necessary to nail each one in — particularly as the* asseri *would have expanded when damp. The joins were covered in mortar and the* imbrices *laid over. A ridge of* imbrices *was laid along the apex of the roof, any gaps being filled with mortar and pieces of broken tile*

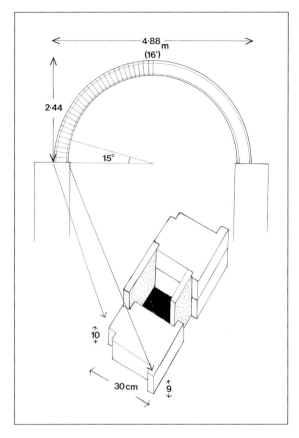

10 *Vaulting at the bathhouse, Chesters fort, Hadrian's Wall. The vault was made out of a series of ribs of solid, shaped blocks. Each rib was connected to its neighbours with flat blocks sitting on shoulders cut into the solid blocks thus creating voids to lighten the vault. By using the measurements of the blocks and the known diameter of the room it is possible to reconcile the vault with the room. It can be seen that the vault blocks were less wide than the wall. Therefore it may be that the external wall (on the left; the right wall abuts another room) rose higher to support a pitched roof above the vault*

11 *Lower portion of a reinforced pier of the Great Bath at Bath (see **colour plate 24**)*

12 Cross-section of the Great Bath at Bath, Avon (after Cunliffe, but adapted). The Great Bath was 22m (72ft) long by 8.8m (29ft) wide and was built in its original form in the late first century. At this period it has been assumed that the bath had a pitched roof supported by a colonnaded arcade with two storeys (right). However this created long-term problems with rotten wood because of the predominantly warm and wet atmosphere created by the thermal waters of the spa. Eventually, by the late second century at the earliest, the building was completely re-roofed, this time with a barrel vault. The weight and thrust was far too great for the existing piers and consequently they were substantially thickened (left). The surviving stumps show this very clearly (11). The side-walls were equipped with additional piers to help absorb the thrust. The vault itself was made of hollow box-tiles (to save weight) with a concrete skin capped with tiles. It may very well have had a pitched roof to protect it against wind and rain

into the house but it could be partially reconstructed and shows that the stone was moulded to take a wooden frame for the glass, splinters of which were found about. The collapse of the gable end of the house at Meonstoke has preserved brick-arched windows which had been blocked up at a later date (**96**) and the collapse of Duncan's Gate at Colchester has preserved part of another (**82**). On the northern frontier round-headed windows were often created by carving a semi-circle into a single piece of stone. This is how the gate at South Shields has been reconstructed (**28, colour plate 3**). The depictions of buildings from Hucclecote and Trier though seem to show square windows (**2**). Although we also have sections of iron window grills from other sites (for example Vindolanda) the truth is that we have no idea of how common windows were. Too many may have been considered a disadvantage in houses which were designed to be warm and comfortable, too few would have made expensive artificial lighting necessary. But we can assume that glass would have been essential for the heated chambers in a bathhouse, while shutters and grills were probably more usual for other windows.

The only surviving evidence for a door is usually a space in the wall. With a single exception all Romano-British doors had perished before discovery. When the vault in the headquarters building at Chesters was excavated in the nineteenth century the door was found in place. Made of oak it was strengthened with iron bands and studs but it rapidly disintegrated on exposure to air. Sometimes sections of the door frame are found but this is generally only when the frame was made of stone. Many houses at Caerwent had stone sills and at Great Witcombe a complete frame, made of four single pieces of stone was found. Stone sills have recesses in them for the door pivots and these show if the door was single or double-leaved. Timber frame members very rarely survive but sometimes an impression of a timber sill can be found in wall cement as in the recent excavation of a house at Plaxtol in Kent.

Decorative features of Romano-British buildings

Amongst the most interesting aspects of Romano-British houses are their decorations. Many have yielded traces of wall plaster but this is rarely preserved well enough to allow reconstruction, and in any case a large number of the houses were excavated before the techniques had been developed. More important are the mosaics because enough are known to make it possible to have some idea of their frequency and origin, and to see how they might reflect or dictate a building's form. This is such a huge subject that it would be quite impossible to do more than just consider a few general points here.

Mosaics and tessellated flooring

Villas and town houses seem hardly to have existed in the first century beyond the very simplest types of buildings (see chapter 4). Correspondingly very few mosaics are known from the period though the large house, like Fishbourne (the 'proto-palace', which preceded the better known Flavian house) and Eccles in Kent, were decorated with mosaics as early as the 60s. These were simple monochrome geometrical designs, reflecting the wider tastes of the period: better-preserved contemporary examples are known from Pompeii and Herculaneum. They were probably installed by professional craftsmen from the continent.

Throughout the period simple tessellated floors, made up of small pieces of stone or tile, are fairly common. Normally they were uniformly red or simple geometric patterns and were ideal for corridors or houses owned by the less wealthy. An alternative was *opus spicatum* where narrow rectangular tiles were laid in a herringbone pattern. This seems to have been particularly durable. The cheapest option of all was *opus signinum* where crushed tile and brick was mixed with concrete to create flooring with a red-brown hue. At Verulamium this first appears *c.*100 but much later on it was occasionally used to patch damaged mosaics once of the highest quality, for example the Seasons mosaic from Cirencester (see below).

In the second century the better-appointed town houses seem to have been fitted with

13 Reconstructed window recess in the south wall of a room in the town house at Colliton Park, Dorchester, Dorset. Glass from the window itself was found within the room. The wall is made of flint nodules cemented together but around the window larger pieces of roughly dressed stone consolidated the opening

mosaics and tessellated floors more as a matter of course and this suggests a developing Romano-British tradition of the art. Verulamium and Colchester have produced the largest number of examples and stylistically the mosaics were based on geometric backgrounds and panels containing representations of animals, fantastic or natural, human beings, divine or mortal, or inanimate objects like vases. Colour was now commonly used. The panels may have been prefabricated and chosen from stock by the customer. The Verulamium examples tend to be rather restrained whereas some of the panels found at Cirencester show that some Romano-British mosaicists of the late second century were inspired artists of the highest order. The head of Dionysus as Autumn in the Seasons mosaic from Dyer Street is one of the most vital mosaic portraits from anywhere at any time, despite having been crudely repaired with *opus signinum*. Although town houses had mosaics at this period there is comparatively little evidence for them in the countryside and only about 20 are currently known, for example at Boughspring near Chepstow and Great Witcombe, both in Gloucestershire, and Brislington in Avon.

Few Romano-British mosaics have been attributed to the third century but by the fourth the elaboration of a number of villas seems to have stimulated a revival (**colour plate 23**). Students of the subject have been particularly fond of trying to identify regional 'schools' based on designs and the topics depicted. Interesting though this is such theories are necessarily based purely on the products and we really cannot distinguish the products of one workshop from the works of another though geography and distance make it likely

14 South-west gate at Lincoln showing the re-use of masonry. The gate was built in the early fourth century but was substantially redesigned later in succeeding decades to include two projecting towers. Part of the north tower's plinth included a section of carved entablature, possibly from a temple. The carved stone now visible is a cast of the original

that designs and topics might tend to be regional. This is as likely to reflect the customers' tastes as those of the craftsmen. The wealthy Romano-British seem to have been fond of classical mythological topics, while at the same time tolerating errors of composition and content. The market may have been made up of customers anxious to present an appropriately fashionable and sophisticated classical image, but who lacked the knowledge (and suppliers) to make sure their requirements were executed. Certainly, contemporaries in Gaul like the poet Ausonius mocked the Britons for their provincial crudeness.

'Influence' is as likely to come through the medium of demand as it is through those who supply it — this applies equally to architecture in this context — a mosaicist interested in staying in business would have made what his customers wanted; style and subject matter can be easily imitated. Probably the most interesting are the remarkable mythological series from Brading in the Isle of Wight, and the Orpheus mosaics from Barton Farm near Cirencester and Woodchester. These are highly complicated geometric designs using a number of stock components combined with naturalistic animals and humans. Content and execution varies considerably. The villa at Bignor has a particularly dramatic series of high-quality fourth-century mosaics (**colour plate 2**), while lesser pavements often have significant errors in how the panels and tesserae have been laid out.

The kind of mosaics referred to above were the most expensive and would certainly not have been the kind of decoration most Romano-British would have taken for granted, any more than they would have expected to live in large courtyard houses. Even for those who did, mosaics rarely covered more than a very few floors, the remainder being consolidated with simple red *tesserae* or *opus signinum*. There would probably have been rugs or carpets as well but naturally these do not survive.

Very few mosaics are known from non-domestic contexts in Britain. One of the rare military examples is from Caerleon, found in the second-century headquarters building. However, it was laid in a single small room in the north-east range and the design is a very simple geometric one surrounded by an equally simple scroll. The fourth-century temple of Nodens at Lydney had a mosaic depicting a marine scene and cryptic inscription recording its funding from temple offerings and laying under the supervision of one Victorinus who may have been an interpreter of dreams (*RIB* 2448.3). It is an equally unusual example though rather more elaborate in design. These rare instances mean that mosaics in Roman Britain can only really be studied in the villas and town houses.

Wall-plaster

The walls of any house with even limited pretensions would have been rendered with plaster. Those who could afford it would have paid for the walls to be painted with designs, probably in rooms with mosaic floors. Public buildings would certainly have been extensively painted. Whereas many mosaic floors are known from Britain, painted wall-plaster is much rarer and is usually so fragmentary that it is extremely difficult to restore the original design.

Wall-plaster was normally built up in layers graduating from coarse layers bonding the plaster to the wall to a fine skim providing the painting surface. In Roman Britain two or three coarse layers around a centimetre in thickness normally provided the base. Plaster was derived from lime and sand as it still is. Rough stone surfaces were ideal but wattle and daub, or tile surfaces, needed keying first. Plaster from the fourth-century house in Colliton Park, Dorchester (**106**) had traces of reeds on the reverse and these may have formed part of the backing required for ceiling plaster, though this is not certain. The skim was achieved by using powdered calcium or powdered marble; the latter was unlikely to be used in Britain for obvious reasons. It seems that the main background colours were painted on before the plaster had dried, as the drying process created a smooth surface on which to paint the more detailed elements of the design. In order to make the whole process easier plaster was sometimes laid in sections. Unfortunately, we know nothing of how Romano-British wall-plaster artists operated, or even the name of a single one.

With limited resources available, archaeology has obviously only concentrated on the more exciting compositions and it is clear that the affluent Romano-British were able to afford competent artists. In the first century it was much less common, reflecting the early state of the province's development. However, the Flavian house at Fishbourne (**109**) and another house of similar date at Boxmoor in Hertfordshire are amongst a small number of examples. Not surprisingly they followed a well-established basic Roman layout which divided a wall into three horizontal zones: the lower dado (not more than about 80mm/2.5ft in height); the main section which was divided into vertical panels containing the most elaborate scenes or topics (around 2m/6ft in height); and a narrow upper which created a border with the ceiling. The main section is invariably the most interesting because it usually incorporated smaller panels depicting mythological figures engaged in some activity or a motif, alternatively they might form part of a larger scheme involving fantastic architecture.

Ceiling designs were more two-dimensional in concept but often no less complex and they must have been even more difficult to execute satisfactorily. Generally they involved repeated sequences of motifs contained within square, circular or polygonal panels. It is probably safe to assume that floors, walls and ceilings were often decorated with a theme based on a single concept but it is unusual to recover the remains of a single panel, let alone a whole scheme.

Other decorations

The only other kinds of decoration installed in Romano-British buildings were stucco (decorative plasterwork) and carved stonework such as balustrades (**113b**) and columns. Not surprisingly both are rare, stucco particularly because it is so prone to fragmenting. Many houses have produced traces, but it may have been much more widespread than we can now easily appreciate. Towns like Pompeii and Herculaneum show that stucco was commonplace in first-century Italy, decorating ceilings and walls in all kinds of buildings. It was particularly suitable for decorating the internal surface of vaults. Fishbourne is one of the few places to show that it was also used occasionally in Britain.

Ornamental stonework is better known. We can be confident that extensive use of it was made in public buildings and major religious buildings, for example the temples at Colchester and Bath (**122**, **124**). London has produced a large number of fragmentary traces, suggesting that ornamental stonework was widespread in the province's capital. Various pieces have been recovered from recent excavations along London's riverfront including fragments of columns and capitals. Other major towns have produced more substantial pieces of stonework almost certainly from major public buildings like the basilica or forum. Ornate carved stone capitals have been found at several sites, for example Silchester, Cirencester and Caerwent. At Bath the recovery of a very large quantity of the carved stonework from the temple and its precinct gives us a very good idea of its original appearance. Most of these provincial pieces would have been carved locally from stone quarried in the vicinity. We even have the names of a few of the Romano-British craftsmen, such as Sulinus, *scultor*, on an altar from Bath (*RIB* 151). Such ornamentation even extended to the northern frontier where forts seem to have been decorated with appropriate figures like a figure of Mars from Housesteads on Hadrian's Wall, carved in a niche. It probably once stood in the headquarters.

As far as private houses are concerned we have really very little evidence, except for stone columns but again these tend to reflect local availability of stone. The houses at Bignor, Gadebridge Park, Keynsham and Chedworth are amongst those which have yielded remains of columns, balustrades or cornices, but like mosaics they were probably the preserve of the rich rather than a commonplace fitting. Columns were normally turned on lathes but where the stone was not of good enough quality to allow this they might be built up of stone or tile discs and covered with moulded cement and plaster before being painted, as at Piddington. Roof-finials, made of stone or fired clay, were

15 Hypocaust at Rockbourne villa, Hants. This is a unique example of a heated floor standing on pilae *made of curved roof tiles,* imbrices. *The room was built as part of an extension to the villa house around the first half of the third century*

designed to act as attractive terminals, probably at the apex of a gable and have been found at several other sites, for example Dewlish, Llantwit Major and Rockbourne. Some of these were made of fired clay and normally had triangular cut-outs and trimmings made with finger-pressed frills. The villa at Piddington has produced fragments of at least 15, suggesting that they may have been much more common than hitherto suspected.

Very few Romano-Celtic temples have produced ornamental stonework. The temples at Bath (**colour plate 24**), Nettleton (**colour plate 26**) and Corbridge are exceptional in this respect. The problem is that large pieces of stone have always been prone to robbing, even in the late Roman period when it became common to remove stone and use it for new defensive structures. The west gate of the lower town at Lincoln, built in the fourth century, was found to contain a particularly ornate piece of a cornice that had obviously been removed from another building (**14**), possibly a temple of classical form.

But stone is difficult to transport and unless it was available very locally it was more convenient to use it sparingly but effectively as veneers or inlays secured to a brick or concrete core. This applies particularly to exotic coloured stone not found in Britain. London has produced numerous examples of exotic stonework, for example porphyry from Egypt and Sparta (Greece), and marbles from various sites in the Mediterranean as well as Purbeck in Dorset. Similar fragments have been gathered from the temple precinct at Canterbury. However, while examples are common, most of them are no more than

16 Pila *in the commandant's fourth-century baths at Binchester, Durham. The stacks, at a little over 1m (3ft 5inches) in height, are unusually tall but exceptionally well-preserved*

chippings or fragments and give us very little idea of how the material was distributed, and whether it comes from private as well as public buildings. The Neronian 'proto-palace' and the later Flavian palace at Fishbourne has produced some of the very earliest evidence for the use of stone in this way, though it is an exceptional assemblage. Numerous sections of marble mouldings, pieces of *opus sectile* (flooring made up of various coloured stone shapes like squares and triangles) and traces of masons' debris were recovered.

Hypocausts, water-supply and baths

The hypocaust system of heating is a feature so commonly associated with Roman life that it is rather easy to assume that it was far more widespread than it actually was. The principle is very simple and is described so frequently that it only needs a brief summary here. Hot air from a furnace was channelled under the floors of rooms and up through the walls, escaping out of the roof. The cavity under the floor was either created by supporting the floor on tiles (**15, 16**) or by building channels into a solid floor (**17**). Hot air from the furnace, which was invariably a small external structure, usually entered through arches which might also carry the heat to an adjacent room (**8**). The air was carried through special hollow tiles in the wall.

The most common use of hypocaust systems was in bathhouses in order to create the correct temperatures in the warm room, *tepidarium*, and the hot room, *caldarium*. Public bathhouses could involve huge floor areas supported on tiles, for example at Huggin Hill in London (**77**). The furnaces also heated water for the hot and warm baths. Depending on the circumstances water was collected locally from rainwater, springs or wells, or it was supplied to the building from a public reservoir sited on higher ground, itself fed by aqueducts. The water was contained in a cold lead or stone tank from where lead or wood pipes with bronze taps carried a supply to a large bronze boiler supported above a furnace with huge iron beams. The furnace naturally made a bathhouse an enormous fire risk so it is not surprising that many baths were built away from villa houses or forts (this was not always the case — integral baths are known at a number of villas, and some military baths were built within the fort). For the same reason they were built of stone. The plumbing arrangements are known from intact systems in houses in and around Pompeii and

17 Hypocaust in Room N1 at Fishbourne palace. The heating was being added to this room around the end of the third century when the whole building was destroyed by fire. The hypocaust, built of upturned roof-tiles in a room in the north wing, had never been fired and no floor had been laid above it though abandoned heaps of mortar suggest it was soon about to be. Note the four channels directing heat from the centre of the room to the four corners where vents would have been sited to allow it to escape up through the walls

Herculaneum. However, very little evidence apart from lead pipes has survived in Britain because the materials were so readily re-usable. But at Chedworth (**113**) a number of massive iron bars were found in the northern baths which must have been used to support boilers (though they had been displaced by the final period); most of the other examples known have also been found in bath buildings, for example at Catterick. The largest weighs 230kg (484lbs) and is 1.61m (5ft 4in) long. Once heated the water was carried to the baths in more pipes. The circulating hot air in the wall cavities helped to keep it warm.

But apart from these hypocausts are comparatively unusual and if fitted, like most of the luxuries associated with 'Roman villas' such as mosaics, they were generally confined to a small number of rooms. In practice most rooms would have been heated by braziers. In addition unless the function of the room(s) is otherwise beyond doubt it is always a possibility that the underfloor heating channels were actually designed for the less luxurious purposes of drying clothes, fabric and/or grain rather than the wet and cold Romano-British. They may also have helped combat rising damp. It would have been hopelessly impractical to try and heat most public buildings but the enigmatic 'tower' at Stonea (**66**) does seem to have been fitted with a hypocaust and so was one of the tribunals in the basilica at Caerwent.

2 Military buildings

Introduction

Britain was a frontier province of the Roman Empire. It began that way and remained so. Throughout the period there were about 30 legions though this number varied. The nominal strength was about 5000 citizen legionaries, divided into 10 cohorts of 480 men (though for some of the time the first cohort was 800-strong) plus officers. Three legions were permanently in Britain, though between 43 and the 70s there were usually four. They were variously dispersed into legionary fortresses, or vexillation (detachment) fortresses.

Auxiliary troops, raised in the provinces, were divided into cohorts of infantry, cohorts of infantry with a unit of cavalry, or cavalry wings. The size of the unit was based on the legionary cohort with nominal strengths of 500 and 1000. In practice, the actual numbers varied a great deal according to the nature of the unit, and the numbers detached on other duties. But the result was that auxiliary forts were a great deal smaller than legionary fortresses. The exact numbers in Britain are unknown, but the total was probably equivalent to the legions, making an overall garrison of 30-40,000 men, depending on the period.

Of course these troops had to be accommodated, fed, provided for and equipped. Not only that but they had to be defended whether this was in a permanent fort or temporary, perhaps even overnight, quarters. As an insecure, hostile and recalcitrant province for much of its early life Britain experienced a considerable amount of troop movement. So there are many examples of military buildings and defences. These range not just from early Claudian forts to Hadrian's Wall and the Antonine Wall, but include substantial legionary fortresses, the late forts of the Saxon Shore, signal towers on the coast, marching camps and a whole host of other conventional forts. There were a number of different construction techniques and it is as well to be aware that as far as the Roman army was concerned turf, earth, timber and stone were all perfectly suitable.

Monumental inscriptions are relatively rare in Britain. Shortage of suitable stone, fashion, literacy, destruction and reuse are all possible reasons. However, the army was responsible for a disproportionate amount of the 2500-odd which are known. Although most of these are imperial and religious dedications, or tombstones, they include a number which record military building activity. Often the buildings to which they refer are long lost, but they help to build up a picture, not only of the type of structures which the army used, but also the need to repair and restore these facilities over the several centuries the Roman army was in occupation. Despite the military bias to inscriptions recording buildings, and the triumphant celebration of completing the work, there is little architectural detail beyond bald descriptions of the structures. Just one slab, from Moresby, records the success of completing a *culmen*, meaning a gable or projection (*RIB*

799). Many of the known texts belong to the early third century and record the restoration of structures, often *a solo* 'from the ground up'. In such cases the original building work had gone unrecorded, or the relevant inscription was removed and destroyed at the time of the repair work.

British weather, agriculture and stone-robbing have combined to level many Roman forts, but the large numbers known and the very considerable effort expended in excavation and analysis has produced an unparalleled body of evidence. Moreover, the uniformity of army habits means that much of the knowledge gained from Britain about Roman military building is relevant to the Empire as a whole. In general, apart from size, there is no need to distinguish between legionary and auxiliary military building techniques. Almost all forts might serve for either, or even both, depending on the circumstances. The forts on Hadrian's Wall were built by legionaries but occupied by auxiliaries. Only legionary fortresses were built by legionaries for their exclusive use.

Forts and their buildings (first to early third century)

Types of forts

The Roman fort was really a military settlement. It was a self-contained unit where troops could be fed and sheltered. Siting was important (see chapter one and **19**): a fort had to be secure but close to communications for supplies. Forts were not the same as camps. A camp was essentially an overnight bivouac — normally a simple rectangle of mound and ditch built as large as was necessary to accommodate a unit in tents, and levelled the following morning or within a few days or weeks. Many have been identified in Britain, usually from aerial photography, but they are not 'buildings' in the true sense of the word.

Roman forts were much more permanent establishments though in practice 'permanent' might mean five years or 250 years. The fort is distinguished from the camp by having much more elaborate defences and also in having internal buildings. From the first century to the early third century — the main period of military activity in Britain — they were designed as variations on a very basic format found throughout the Empire. The only differences tend to be those of scale and sophistication as a comparison between the plans of the legionary fortress at Inchtuthil, Elginhaugh and Housesteads show (**18-20**). Apart from the defences the main features are the headquarters building, the commander's house, the granaries, and barracks. Most forts had a hospital, stables, ovens, latrines and baths. While examples of all these buildings are known from many sites in Britain relatively few are well-preserved, well-studied and visible today.

Defences, ramparts and gates

During the first century most forts were built in Britain with turf and timber ramparts, broken only by timber gateways. The archaeological evidence is usually slight but where burning has taken place or the site is waterlogged there may be more remains of timber. In general ramparts may survive as gentle mounds, if at all, and gates are usually only identifiable as arrangements of post-holes. Only a few sites are visible on the ground today, for example at Hod Hill in Dorset.

18 Plan of the Flavian legionary fortress at Inchtuthil, Perthshire (after Richmond), c.83-7, probably built by and for the XX legion Valeria Victrix. This well-known plan exhibits a number of peculiarities which means that it cannot be regarded as wholly typical of a legionary fortress. But as it was occupied briefly it does offer a snapshot of Roman military organization and logistics. It had stone defences but contained only timber buildings because it was so short-lived. The headquarters building (HQ) is unusually small. A space has been set aside to the east of the headquarters building for the legate's house, unexecuted. The ten barracks and five houses to the west seem to represent the enlarged first cohort. By the end of Vespasian's reign (69-79) the first cohort was apparently enlarged so that it contained five double centuries of 160 men each (800), rather than six centuries of 80 men (480). Consequently there were only five centurions, hence the five houses (instead of the normal six). Granaries are marked G; the workshop W; and the hospital H

In the simplest form a turf rampart with sloping sides supported a walkway, probably fronted by a timber parapet. More elaborate versions, called 'box ramparts' (**22**), involved an array of planks and beams used to 'lace' and strengthen the turf. The most interesting site to visit is the mid-first-century fort at the Lunt, Baginton, near Coventry where experimental reconstruction in the 1970s has highlighted long-term problems, such as rotting timbers and sagging of the ramparts. However, labour-intensive repair work, uneconomic in today's terms, would have been quite acceptable to the Roman army which was being paid anyway and enjoyed unlimited access to local raw materials.

Timber gateways are rather harder to understand simply because a pattern of post-holes supplies no information about the superstructure. The simplest timber gates were supported on four or six posts between a break in the rampart, for example the south gate at the Claudian fort on Hod Hill, Dorset. They may have supported a tower as well, or perhaps simply a bridge for the rampart walkway. The reconstructed gate at the Lunt fort, Baginton, was based on representations of timber gates shown on Trajan's Column, a source which also suggests that towers may have been roofed. More elaborate plans would have formed the basis for double-portalled gates equipped with towers, and in some cases were recessed, for example the south-east gate at Great Casterton (**23**). The gates themselves were probably made of timber posts and beams, plated with iron against attackers trying to fire them. Fragments of iron sheathing were found on the site of a gate at Fendoch. The gates swung on pivots, and were closed against raised thresholds. The Lunt reconstruction was based on representations of gates on Trajan's Column, a source which also suggests that pitched roofs might have been used. Interval and angle towers were used along the ramparts and at the corners of the fort to provide extra observation posts and artillery platforms. They are usually represented by much simpler patterns of post-holes, for example at Elginhaugh (**19**), and are not associated with breaks in the rampart.

Stone defences in Roman Britain belong mostly to the second century and later though it would be quite wrong to give the impression that turf and timber had become obsolete. Some evidence from Trajan's Column suggests that stone gates may actually have had timber superstructures though artistic licence or error may be responsible. A number of stone fort gates and portions of walls have survived in Britain to a reasonable height but none supply conclusive information about roofing and parapets. The well-preserved Severan north gate at the fort of Bu Njem in Libya appears to have had crenellations. Crenellations also appear on various walls depicted on Trajan's Column. A collapsed section of the fort wall at Wörth in Upper Germany showed that the walkway was on average 4.5m (15ft) above ground level. It was marked by a projecting chamfered course of stone. The parapet appears to have been 1.6m (5ft) high and was equipped with crenellations. The legionary fortresses may have had elaborately carved stonework in the defences; recently substantial and ornate cornice stones have been found in the fortress wall at Chester.

Stone defences were frequently added to forts already built with turf and timber. The simplest way of incorporating the stone was to cut away the front of the turf rampart and replace it with stone facing. New forts had walls which were built of rubble cores and which were faced on either side. Once completed the wall was reinforced with an earth bank built up against the internal face. Earth banks were not used on Hadrian's Wall or later forts (see below). At Gellygaer the Trajanic defences were built of two stone walls separated by a narrow void filled with earth.

Military units responsible for building ramparts counted the number of feet they had built and sometimes recorded the work on an inscription, either as a matter of pride or for quality control. At Carvoran, *c*.136-8, a century under the charge of one Silvanus 'ramparted for 112 feet' (*RIB* 1820), while at Bainbridge *c*.205-8 the VI cohort of Nervians built 'with irregular stonework' something which was probably the rampart (*RIB* 722).

Units equipped with artillery sometimes built special ramps up against the earth banks. At the Claudian fort of Hod Hill these took the form of chalk slopes next to both gates. Not many other examples are known but at High Rochester inscriptions record the building and repairs of masonry platforms in the early third century (*RIB* 1280, 1281). These are the only dated Romano-British examples and it may be that they represent a new defensive policy in the third century. However, it is not possible to be certain because artillery platforms were always built separately from walls and ramparts to prevent recoil pressure from damaging the defences.

The most informative remains of gateways are to be found on the northern frontier, especially the west gate at High Rochester (**24**), and the east and south gates at Birdoswald (**25, 26**) but also at Housesteads (**27**) and South Shields (**28, colour plate 3**) — all these forts belong primarily to the second and early third centuries. A number of reconstructions of the west gate at Housesteads were prepared a number of years ago, showing this type of gateway with crenellations and rooms above the portals. They may be correct but it is equally likely that the modern rebuilding of the west gate at South Shields is equally likely. The most obvious difference is the use of gabled and tiled roofs, for which there is a certain amount of evidence from Trajan's Column. It is also possible that the same gate had different superstructures at different times.

No doors survive but holes in flagstones show that they swung on pivots, probably made of iron (**25**). The doors were inserted by sliding the pivot through a channel cut in the floor stone. Once the pivot had dropped into the specially carved hole the channel was filled with lead and the door could then swing without sliding out of position. These pivot holes can be seen at a number of gates. The four main gates were normally twin portal though in many cases, especially on Hadrian's Wall, one of the portals was subsequently blocked up. Single-portal gates were normally used for subsidiary gates, or those which were likely to have less traffic passing through, for example the west gate at High Rochester (**24**) which overlooks a steep slope while the main road, Dere Street, passes the fort to the east.

As with timber and turf forts the defences were augmented with angle and interval towers along the ramparts. They seem to have been simple stone towers attached to the internal face of the wall and were probably designed as observation posts and shelter. Sometimes the ground floor was used to house an oven.

In general, up until the reign of Antoninus Pius (138-61), stone gates and interval or angle towers were built flush with the defences. This can be seen particularly clearly at Birdoswald and Housesteads (**27**). However, from then on it became increasingly common to use projecting gate-towers. Whether this marks a change in tactics or a move towards a more defensive posture overall is not certain. Nevertheless the effect was to

*19 Plan of the Flavian turf and timber fort at Elginhaugh, near Edinburgh (after Hanson). The fort is at least big enough (3 acres) to have housed an auxiliary infantry, or infantry and cavalry, cohort of about 480 men (six centuries of 80 soldiers) plus officers. The purpose of all the timber buildings is not known and it is possible that the garrison was a larger one. The buildings were indicated by sleeper trenches and post-holes. A 2.4 acre annex lay to the west for protecting stores, and perhaps horses. The fort seems to have been occupied for around a decade and then deliberately dismantled, around the same time as Inchtuthil (**18**)*
a. Commandant's house
b. Headquarter's building
c. Granaries
d. A stone building of unknown purpose, possibly a workshop where fires would have made timber hazardous

create more easily defended individual gates, for example the west gate at Brecon y Gaer. By the beginning of the third century it was also becoming common to do away with square gate-towers and build semi-circular projecting towers. This became especially marked in the Saxon Shore forts (see below and **48**).

Gates were particularly suitable for embellishment and decoration. Normally they carried inscriptions which described who had built the gate and when. One of the most explicit comes from at the south gateway at Risingham, an outpost fort on Dere Street, north of Hadrian's Wall, and records the rebuilding of a 'gate with walls' built *c.*205-8 (*RIB*

20 *Plan of the auxiliary fort at Housesteads, built c.122-6 in the central sector of Hadrian's Wall. The forts were added after the initial phases of construction. The former line of the Broad Wall foundation (**50**), and the site of turret 36b, are marked by the dotted line, though the peculiar position of the north-east angle tower suggests that the Narrow Wall curtain was not actually built until the fort was in place. The first garrison was the* cohors I Tungrorum *though the fort was probably built by legionaries*

1234). A few years later in *c*.223, a 'gate with towers' was repaired at Vindolanda (*RIB* 1706). These are elaborate examples — earlier inscriptions were less specific, such as the Trajanic inscription of 107-8 from York which almost certainly came from the south-east gate (*RIB* 665). It is consequently less certain that they come from a gate unless there is a specific reference to it. Gates might also be decorated with sculptures. The east gate at Housesteads bore a relief depicting Victory. These carvings and inscriptions were probably painted and the whole gate itself might have been rendered or whitewashed.

Fort buildings

The internal buildings of Roman forts of the first, second and early third centuries follow very standard plans, though with considerable variation in detail. Nevertheless it is quite possible to discuss them as general types because most of the differences are usually in scale.

*21 View of the fort at Housesteads on Hadrian's Wall looking north. The fort is often illustrated with aerial photographs but this view shows how the commanding stronghold straddles a ridge. The Wall itself lies on the far side where the ground falls away steeply. On the slope below the fort to the south lay the civilian settlement (*vicus*). The Military Way joined the fort at the east gate on the right-hand side after crossing the Knag Burn*

Headquarters

As with the Roman town the most important building was the administration centre. It is no coincidence that the civil forum and basilica bears much resemblance to the military headquarters building (*principia*), especially in a province where troops may have contributed to civic development. The *principia* consisted of a square or rectangular courtyard with an ambulatory and offices on three sides. On the fourth side, opposite the entrance, was the covered cross-hall, behind which lay offices and shrines for the unit's standards, sometimes including a strong-room dug into the ground. In cavalry forts a forehall seems to have been built along the front of the building, parallel with the cross-hall on the other side, for example at Brecon y Gaer. These may or may not have been roofed but would have allowed the mounted troops to parade, and perhaps perform drill.

As such an important building the *principia* was probably the most architecturally ambitious structure in the average Roman fort. The surviving pieces of column from the *principia* at the legionary fortress of York show that it was monumental — the columns from the cross-hall were just under 7m (22ft) in height. Unfortunately none of the legionary fortresses have yielded much evidence for their *principia* except for the Flavian fortress at Inchtuthil. However, the internal buildings here were built of timber and the *principia* seems to have been disproportionately small. No doubt it was built in haste as an essential facility with the intention of replacing it when time allowed (**18**). It was only 42 by 45m (138 by 148ft), compared to 74 by 100m (243 by 328ft) at Chester and 66 by 94m (217 by 308ft) at Caerleon (**29**); though this may never have been finished), but space permitted a building 66 by at least 69m (217 by 226ft).

Caerleon's *principia* is not visible today but other examples can be seen at Housesteads,

22 Military defences (a-g after A. Johnson). All these types might be used at any time in Roman Britain up to the late second century though a-b were the most common in the late first century. In structural terms the problem was to prevent the earth or rubble rampart collapsing outwards under its own weight — each type represents a different solution to the same problem. Choice would have been dictated by habit and availability of raw materials, especially timber. In the third and fourth century military defences were built as free-standing masonry walls, creating different problems for the builders

a. Single turf revetment

b. Double turf revetment

c. Double turf revetment with rubble core, enabling a vertical face to be constructed

d. Double turf revetment with timber lacing for stability

e. Single timber revetment (e-f were not commonly used in Britain)

f. Double timber revetment

g. Clay rampart with stone foundation

h. Stone revetment with earth bank

23 Reconstructed isometric view of the timber south-east gate of the auxiliary fort at Great Casterton, Leicestershire. The gate was a double-portalled example, flanked by towers and was recessed behind the ramparts. It was built c.60-70 as part of new south-east defences which reduced the fort's size. As the plan consists solely of post-holes there are many possible ways of reconstructing such a gate

Chesters and Vindolanda (**31-33**). The *principia* served a number of practical purposes. It provided open and covered assembly areas, rooms for storage and administration, and a strong room where the unit's standards, valuables and money could be safely locked away. At Chesters the steps leading down to the sunken chamber and also the vaulted roof can still be seen (**32**). When the Chesters vault was excavated its oak and iron door was found in place although it soon disintegrated. The central room of the rear range of rooms behind the cross-hall was called the *sacellum*. Containing the strong room it lay on the main axis of the building, facing not just the entrance to the *principia* but also the main

24 Single-portal west gate at High Rochester, Northumberland, an outpost fort first built in timber in the late first century but not consolidated in stone until the mid-second century. The field wall and blocking to the gate are modern. The north jamb survives to the height of the springer for the arch

entrance to the fort. The standards formed the focus of the various rituals which took place in the military calendar (*fasti*), including worship of the gods, the imperial cult, the *genius* of the unit and the very standards themselves. These rooms were secured with low stone screens into which iron grills were inserted (**33**).

Headquarters buildings were particularly suitable for architectural embellishment. The date of construction or dedication was recorded on a monumental inscription, though few survive. One from Rough Castle on the Antonine Wall states that the fort *pri[nci]pia* had been built by the VI cohort of Nervians in a text datable to the period 139-61 (*RIB* 2145). Carved reliefs decorated the building, perhaps on either side of the entrance. Carved reliefs from the *principia* at Housesteads, depicting a Victory poised on a sphere and Mars, are amongst the few surviving examples though their exact original position is unknown. The *sacellum* at Corbridge contained a relief of Hercules killing the Hydra, assisted by Athena. Hercules was popular amongst soldiers for obvious reasons and this piece of sculpture emphasized the religious associations of the *principia* in a military unit's life. A fragmentary slab of the early third century from Reculver records the dedication of a shrine in the *principia* (see *Companion*, 121).

25 *The south twin-portalled gate at Birdoswald fort on Hadrian's Wall looking across the east portal. Note the pivot hole for one of the east portal's gates in the right foreground beside the base of the arch*

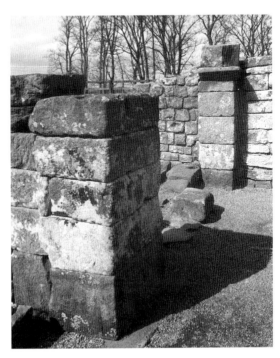

26 *The east gate at Birdoswald fort on Hadrian's Wall, one of the best preserved military gates in Britain. In the foreground is the centre support for the twin arches and beyond is the north jamb which survives to the springer of the arch*

27 *Twin-portalled west gate at Housesteads (isometric reconstruction after Child, but adapted). Built c.122-6. The superstructure is purely hypothetical but this reconstruction shows a version where the whole gate is of a single height capped with crenellations and a flat roof*

Accommodation

Most of the average fort's area was taken up with accommodation in the form of barrack blocks. In rare cases a fort with a special function might differ — the Severan period fort at South Shields was adapted to house a very large number of granaries to support Septimius Severus' campaign in Scotland (209-12). Almost every fort had a house

*28 Reconstructed west gate at the fort of South Shields. Dates of the stone defences here are still uncertain but it has been suggested that the first stone fort on the site, including this gate, was built around the mid-second century. Height and roofing are speculative (see also **colour plate 3**)*

(*praetorium*) for the commanding officer and his family; legionary fortresses had individual houses for the six military tribunes (one *tribunus laticlavius* and five *tribuni angusticlavii*), the camp prefect (*praefectus castrorum*) and the five centurions of the first cohort as well.

Legates' houses are not known in great detail from Britain. At Inchtuthil an area had been left aside next to the *principia* but no building had taken place by the time the fortress was dismantled *c.*86/7 (**18**). However, many examples are known from smaller forts. They differ from most Romano-British houses by being built in Mediterranean style: inward looking they consisted of four continuous ranges of rooms built around a rectangular courtyard (**105**). The best surviving example can be seen at Housesteads where this plan was adapted, despite being terraced into the hillside on which the fort was built. At South Shields an example dating to the fourth century has only been uncovered relatively recently and is a remarkable contrast with the dereliction observed at forts on Hadrian's Wall in the same period.

Occasionally such houses enjoyed the addition of a private bath-suite, for example at Chesters, but in general the houses were modest by civil standards (especially in later centuries) though some have produced traces of window-glass and wall-plaster. The officers' and centurions' houses at Inchtuthil show that these were modelled on similar but smaller and more modest plans.

The barracks, *centuriae*, as implied by their ancient name, were built to occupy individual centuries of soldiers. In practice for infantry this meant 80 men plus centurions and a handful of 'non-commissioned' officers. The 80 men were divided into ten groups of eight, the 'tent-parties' (*contuberniae*) and this is reflected in the minimum of ten parallel pairs of rooms which appear in most barrack blocks. The centurion and his assistants occupied the block at the end of each barrack — in legionary fortresses the assistants would have occupied a pair of rooms each, making 14 parallel pairs (**34**). The building grew directly out

29 Principia *at the legionary fortress of Caerleon (isometric reconstruction). The great hall was about 64m (210ft) long by 25m (82ft) wide but excavation revealed no traces of superstructure despite the existence of column bases and substantial foundations. It may therefore have never been completed. Its intended form is a little difficult to understand because of a very wide gap between the columns in the centre of the two arcades supporting the nave roof. This has been resolved here by restoring the building in cruciform shape. Such a form has the advantage of focusing attention on the main shrine of the legion's standards which were contained in the* sacellum. *At either end of the hall there would have been a raised tribunal where the legion's officers could preside over administrative and disciplinary matters*

of the layout of tents in a marching camp and served the purpose of making sure that when on the march every soldier knew where he would pitch his party's tent in relation to the whole unit. Cavalry barracks were slightly smaller and were probably designed to accommodate two *turmae* (64 men) in eight pairs of rooms plus extra space for the officers. Although they must have been cramped, evidence from the early first-century timber legionary barracks at Colchester shows that internal walls may have been plastered, some rooms had hearths, and drains were placed in the street outside the barracks.

As basic functional day-to-day structures, barracks did not feature widely in inscriptions. Only two from Britain are known. Barracks were built at Bainbridge in 205 by the VI cohort of Nervians, while between 255-60 at Caerleon, the seventh cohort of II legion *Augusta* rebuilt theirs (*RIB* 334). The latter is one of the latest dated military inscriptions from Britain.

30 The principia *at Housesteads (isometric reconstruction), based on the plan of the building currently visible which dates from the third century. The colonnade around the forecourt was later walled up, either to strengthen the building or perhaps to provide more weather-proof storage space*

Stables

Stables are difficult to identify from archaeological evidence though the large number of auxiliary cavalry regiments stationed in Britain makes it certain that many forts contained them. Some of the structures which appear to be barracks, but lacking some internal divisions, may have accommodated horses though any simple building of unspecified purpose may have served. The most likely supporting evidence is the presence of internal drains. Drains would have helped to create a dry, and more hygienic, environment. Such drains have been identified at Brough on Noe, Ilkley and Halton Chesters, but they were not essential and have not been found in some other forts which certainly had auxiliary cavalry garrisons. Other possible evidence might take the form of wear on flooring, for example at Hod Hill. A number of forts on the Antonine Wall have been found to have enclosures attached to one side. Their purpose is unknown and while they may simply have been used as storage areas they may also have been used to corral horses.

Drill hall

The *exercitatoria baselica* [sic] *equester*, cavalry drill hall, is only known in Britain on an inscription from Netherby. The text states that the project had been begun 'a long time ago', and was completed under Severus Alexander in 222 (*RIB* 978).

31 Cross-hall of the principia *at Housesteads looking south. Note the steps leading up to the hall on the left and the arch bases within the hall*

32 Strong-room vault in the principia *at Chesters. Steps in the foreground lead down to the vault in which the unit's standards and valuables would have been stored*

56

33 Stone screen in the principia *at Vindolanda. The rooms at the rear of the* principia *contained the standards when they were on display. Access to the rooms was restricted with stone screens and iron grilles*

Granaries

A hungry army is a useless army and the logistics of supplying Roman troops with enough to eat were well-organized. Granaries (*horrea*) appear in every fort. As we have already seen some forts might be almost entirely given over to them in order to act as supply-bases, as at South Shields. Their importance can be seen from the inscription found at Benwell on Hadrian's Wall, which records a granary built by the fleet, *Classis Britannica*, in the fort's earliest phase (*RIB* 1340), *c*.122-6. Further along the Wall, in 225 at Greatchesters, a granary was restored (*RIB* 1738).

Granaries presented three major problems to their builders: controlling the effects of damp and rodents, and withstanding the lateral forces created by the grain itself as it settled. Military granaries were normally rectangular, though there was considerable variation in size depending on the needs of the garrison. Timber examples were built either on posts inserted into the ground or inserted into sleeper beams laid in trenches. The posts allowed air to circulate freely below and helped prevent rodent attacks (**35**). Stone granaries were rather more imposing. Usually the floors, either of timber or stone, were laid on dwarf walls or pillars which created a series of air channels; granaries with solid floors, for example at Caerhun, may have been adapted for other purposes. Air was allowed in through narrow ventilator slots with mullions. The best surviving example can be seen in the east granary at Corbridge (**36, 37**) which retains the dwarf walls, flagstones and ventilator slots.

Access to a granary was by a loading platform or steps, usually beneath a covered portico. Platforms, indicated by slots or postholes, meant that grain could be transferred from a wagon straight onto the raised floor. The timber granary at the mid-first-century fort of the Lunt was reconstructed with a platform running beneath a portico, with steps

34 Early first-century timber barracks at Colchester, c.43-7, probably built by the XX legion. A number of recent excavations have identified traces of timber, wattle and daub barracks which were subsequently used when the fortress was given up. The axonometric reconstruction is based on plans of the southernmost barracks on the Culver Street site, adjacent to the ramparts and south gate, using details from other contemporary barracks in the fortress. The narrower building is a single block, the wider is two barrack blocks back to back. Each barrack block was about 69m (226ft) long and had a large room for the centurion at the east end, and 14 pairs of rooms for the ten groups of eight legionaries and other 'non-commissioned' officers. Some of the rooms had hearths and while traces of drainage gullies have been found in front the verandahs are hypothetical

at either end. It is not known exactly how the grain was stored but as most stone granaries were equipped with substantial buttresses it seems likely that grain was poured into bins which lay alongside the walls. It was quite usual to build granaries in parallel pairs, for example at Housesteads and Corbridge (**20**, **37**), probably for convenience and to help support one another.

35 Timber granary at Inchtuthil (isometric reconstruction). The presence of a covered loading area is implied in the two very large post-holes found at the end. The other posts were set into sleeper beams laid in transverse trenches. Evidence for at least five others was found. About 83-7

Hospital

The hospital (*valetudinarium*) was sited in the central part of the fort. The principles of construction seem to have been access and seclusion. The product in its most elaborate form was a series of concentric rectangles of wards and corridors built with double walls. The corridors allowed access to the rows of wards on either side. The ranges and corridors might even be separated by spaces in order to reduce noise levels. This can be seen particularly clearly from the plan at Inchtuthil (**18, 38**) though the only visible example now is the auxiliary hospital at Housesteads. This is a rectangular building with four ranges of rooms around a corridor and a central courtyard. The fort at Fendoch had an even simpler example where two parallel ranges of rooms were separated by a central corridor.

It should be borne in mind that unless specific evidence in the form of surgical equipment is found the identification of such buildings is very uncertain in forts. The buildings may have been workshops and/or storerooms and unless another building within the fort (for example at Inchtuthil) can be assigned to these purposes, then a firm identification cannot be made. Only in the legionary fortresses where the most sophisticated versions were built can the plan be regarded as conclusive evidence.

Workshop

The Roman army consisted of small, independent, self-contained units. It was absolutely essential that each unit could service and repair its equipment and facilities. Many forts have yielded evidence for workshops (*fabricae*) though as we have seen with hospitals identification is not always certain but the workshops are more likely to contain evidence of the activities which went on. Typically these are hearths or traces of smelting. Sometimes, as at Inchtuthil and Elginhaugh where the forts were abandoned, the metal goods like nails were sealed in pits to prevent them being of use to the enemy. The design of the buildings seems to have been a range of rooms around a central courtyard (**39**).

Considering the need for ventilation and the claustrophobic effects of low roofs in a hot and noisy atmosphere the workshops probably had quite high walls. Some of the rooms may have been open to the sky.

Armoury

Not identified anywhere as a specific structure, the *armamentaria* is only known from an inscription found at Lanchester (*RIB* 1092). The text records the building's restoration under Gordian III (238-44), in a period when many auxiliary units recorded their activities on inscriptions. It may have been effectively the same as the workshop, *fabrica* (see above).

Latrines

The most outstanding example of Roman toilet facilities in Britain is at Housesteads (**40**). The remarkable latrine was sited in the south-east corner and was built early in the fort's life. It underwent considerable alteration but the basic design remained unchanged. The latrine was fed by two supplies of running water from several different tanks and cisterns, built at higher levels. Some of this water was provided for washing and more water carried waste away out of the fort from beneath the seats in the latrine. A centurion's quarters at Chester was equipped with a lead-lined latrine of early first-century date. Relatively few traces of similar buildings have been found at forts elsewhere in Britain though provision for hygiene must have been made everywhere.

Bathhouses

Bathhouses were usually built outside forts but in the case of legionary fortresses substantial *thermae* were erected within the central area, for example at Exeter and Caerleon (**41**). It made good sense to site such a fire risk outside, especially if the fort was a small establishment. The two best-preserved military bathhouses are at Beauport Park in East Sussex (**42**) and at Chesters on Hadrian's Wall (**43, colour plate 4**), but only the latter is currently accessible. The fragmentary remains of the bathhouse outside the fort at Ravenglass in Cumbria include some of the highest upstanding walls of any Roman building in Britain (**169**).

All these examples vary from the basic design of the Roman bathhouse but they conform to the general theme. The structure had to be durable and was often quite sophisticated, for example at Caerleon. At Chesters the bathhouse possessed a latrine, a changing room and a complicated series of rooms. Set into the slope below the fort it was strengthened with buttresses. The bathhouse at Beauport Park, while a modest building, possessed two vaults and had undergone substantial alterations (**42**). It may have been associated with a nearby fort, but if so, the fort has remained undiscovered.

A curiosity of the military bathhouse is the number of inscriptions which record their construction or restoration. Around ten such inscriptions have been recovered from Britain, at least twice as many as record the *principia*, and this seems to be the case elsewhere in the north-west. Other military structures are mentioned on even fewer, if at all. The reasons may be connected with pride at having the facility, and the need for stone throughout which made inscriptions possible and rendered the whole structure (including the inscription) liable one day to reuse, and thus preservation.

36 *Stone east granary at Corbridge (isometric reconstruction). Two stone granaries have been found
at this site, dating to the third century (see **37**). Sections of the floor and the remains of the
ventilation slots in the side walls survive. Column bases and steps on the street front show that
each had covered porches. The large buttresses give an idea of the kind of lateral forces (from the
settling grain within) which were anticipated.*
*Below: cross-section view shows the under-floor channels, ventilated by air which entered through
the ventilation slots which contained a mullion to restrict access from larger animals and rain*

*37 Granary and fountain at Corbridge. This view shows the front of the granary reconstructed in **36**. Note how years of repairs in antiquity raised the level of the road above that of the column bases. Similarly years of knife sharpening(?) or washing wore down the walls of the fountain*

Arenas

The Roman military arena (*ludus*) was very similar to the civic amphitheatre (see chapter 3). Several are known from Britain and are usually described as amphitheatres despite having a slightly different purpose. The two best-known are at the legionary fortresses of Caerleon (**44**, **45**) and Chester because they were partially built of stone and have therefore survived comparatively well, making them impressive monuments for public display (though half the Chester arena remains buried). Not all forts had permanent arenas though one has been identified near the auxiliary fort at Tomen-y-Mur in north Wales.

Typically a military arena was sited just outside the fort walls and provided seating for most of the garrison. It would have been used for weapons training and public displays of fighting skills. The niche in the side of the arena at Caerleon may have been dedicated to Nemesis (Fate) who was associated with gladiators so it is probably safe to assume that the garrison was also entertained by matched pairs. The recently discovered amphitheatre in London lies well within the city walls but also lies adjacent to the Hadrianic fort in the north-east part of the settlement. It may therefore have originally been a military arena, perhaps adopting a civilian role in later years. The Neronian auxiliary fort at the Lunt, Baginton, has revealed traces of a unique circular building identified as a possible horse training arena, *gyrus*. This was a circular arena, 34m (112ft) in diameter, contained within

38 Perspective reconstruction of the hospital, valetudinarium, *at Inchtuthil looking north-east. The building consisted of four wings with concentric ranges of rooms built around a courtyard. The inner range of rooms did not continue around the west wing. The outer range was made up of a series of groups of rooms. Each group was accessible only from the central range, which seems to have been one long corridor. The inner range was a further series of rooms. Each concentric range was separated by a gap and the reason for this was probably to create as much peace and quiet as possible. About 83-7*

the fortifications; in fact the fort walls were built on a twisted path in order to go round the gyrus. The identification is by no means certain and an alternative possibility is that it was a stockade for prisoners.

Temples

A number of inscriptions record the presence of shrines and temples in and around forts. Some of these are discussed in more detail in chapter 5. However, the actual buildings themselves are practically unknown with the exception of the extra-mural temples of Mithras at Carrawburgh, Housesteads, and Rudchester, and of Antenociticus at Benwell (**141-3, 146 & colour plate 28**).

Other buildings

Most fort plans conform to a recognizable pattern and the buildings are generally stereotypical. At the legionary fortress of Chester, established in the late first century probably by the II legion *Adiutrix Pia Fidelis*, a building was begun which has defied

39 Workshop, fabrica, *at Inchtuthil, looking north-west. This seems to have been a courtyard building with a portico. The reconstruction has been made deliberately high on the assumption that the need to disperse noise and smoke would have made low roofs unacceptable. The building contained a pit into which more than a million nails and other pieces of redundant ironwork were sealed, following withdrawal of the Roman forces. About 83-7*

interpretation. Known now as the 'Great Elliptical Building' it was based around a 9 by 14m elliptical courtyard with a central pool and a series of radial chambers following the ellipse, resembling the substructures of an amphitheatre. The ellipse was inserted into a rectangular external wall and the whole building sited next to the fortress baths. It was abandoned during construction and left derelict for around 150 years when it was completed on a slightly different design.

No other such building is known anywhere in the Roman world. It may have been for displays of horsemanship (see cavalry drill hall above), or the 12 chambers may have contained statues of the principal Roman gods and goddesses. Another suggestion is that they had some sort of role to play in provincial government. It was not the only unusual feature of Chester, which was around 20 per cent larger than York and Caerleon at the time it was laid out. The *principia*, for example, was associated with an unparalleled enclosed courtyard, 160 by 60m in area. Like the Elliptical Building, its purpose remains unknown.

40 Latrine at Housesteads looking south-east across the fort. Tanks which supplied washing and flushing water can be seen at upper left and lower right, connected by channels to the latrine. Note the commanding view from the fort across the land to the south

Later forts

All the fort buildings discussed above refer to the buildings belonging to the period of conquest in the first century, consolidation during the second century, and re-conquest in the early third century. Thereafter, following a period of peace, military strategy in the Western Empire became wholly defensive. This can be seen particularly clearly in the building of town defences on the continent. In Britain the old forts continued to serve, often with significant amounts of repair work because the long peace in the middle years of the third century had allowed many forts to literally fall into ruin (for example, *RIB* 1912).

With the growth of a maritime threat to the southern and eastern shores a new phase of fort building began. The sequence is complicated and poorly dated but the result was the system of forts of the Saxon Shore, the *Litus Saxonicum*. As monuments a few of these forts are amongst the most impressive remnants of Roman Britain, particularly at Richborough, Pevensey and Portchester but this applies entirely to their massive curtain walls and bastions (**46-9**). Of their internal buildings very little is known because with few

41 Flavian fortress baths at the legionary fortress of Caerleon in elevation. The drawings show the main block of vaulted halls which served as the cold, warm and hot chambers. The western facade (above) overlooked a swimming pool installed in the 80s in the adjacent courtyard. A covered exercise hall was certainly planned and begun but like the great hall of the headquarters building (29) it may never have been finished

exceptions these appear to have been built of timber. The remains of some of the forts were adapted by castle builders in the Middle Ages (for example, at Portchester and Pevensey) and consequently post-Roman activity has tended to destroy details of these timber structures. Only a single wall-stump remains of the fort at Bradwell-on-sea in Essex; Dover is known from fragments of walls and bastions identified in recent years; Walton Castle near Felixstowe in Suffolk disappeared over a cliff many years ago; and Brancaster's stone walls have been entirely robbed out.

Despite variations in detail the forts all share a location on or near the coast, though suitable high ground was exploited if available. The earliest forts seem to have been those at Reculver and Brancaster. Their plans resemble those of the more traditional 'playing card' forts of the northern frontier zone and Wales. Even so such archaeological evidence as exists suggests that while Reculver may have been built by *c.*225, Brancaster could be as much as 50 years later. In fact the main series of forts seem to belong overall to the period *c.*260-300. The others differ radically from earlier Roman military tradition by lacking internal berms, i.e. the walls were freestanding, and in possessing colossal projecting bastions, some of which were solid masonry. These reflected developments in artillery

42 *Bathhouse at Beauport Park, near Battle, East Sussex (axonometric reconstruction). Despite being located in the congested south-east of modern Britain it was only discovered in 1969, having been buried during the Roman period by a landslip of industrial slag. The bathhouse formed part of a large settlement concerned with the extraction of iron ore. The fact that majority of the bathhouse's roof tiles bear the stamp of the* Classis Britannica *suggests that detachments of the fleet were involved. This may seem curious but it is worth noting that Bodiam, which lies a few miles to the north, was originally the site of a large inland harbour. Despite that, no fort or other official building has been found.*

The bathhouse itself survives largely intact having lost only its roof and upper walls. Even so much of the roof was found collapsed in and around the building. There were two distinct periods: Period 1 early second century, Period 2 late second, early third century.

*The drawing, looking north-west, shows the bathhouse in its final extended form with the additional changing room and hot room. A wooden tank a few metres south-east supplied the building. See **43** for ancient names to these rooms*

A = Period 2 changing room

B = vaulted warm rooms

C = hot rooms

D = cold plunge

E = Period 1 furnace (disused)

F = Period 2 furnace

In later years the bathhouse seems to have been used as somewhere to live by people who knocked an entrance through the apsed room, and one of their dogs was found amongst the pilae *of floor-supporting tiles* machines, which had become larger and more powerful (**48, 49**). Not only did the defences have to be strong enough to support them but upheavals within the Empire had also made it more likely that a Roman fort would be assaulted with Roman military equipment. Some of the forts show that plans changed during building. Burgh Castle was built with round corners, an internal earth rampart (probably) and the external bastions were added during the process of construction. This is clear from the fact that the bottom parts of the towers are not bonded to the walls though the upper courses are. Similarly, at Richborough, one of the towers was added after the walls had been built. Here there is clear evidence of the walls being built by separate gangs (**47, colour plate 5**).

Unfortunately, apart from Reculver, no inscriptional evidence has survived to indicate who built the forts and whether they formed part of a concerted policy to build a chain of coastal defences. The Reculver inscription appears to credit the building of a shrine in the *principia* to the governorship of one Quintus Aradius (?) Rufinus. His name is otherwise unknown in Britain but, if he was governor, the building might have taken place in *c.*225-30 (see *Companion*, 121 and figure 43). This does not help date the main sequence of forts and arguments have tended to hinge on coin evidence but this is not particularly conclusive.

Stephen Johnson has presented a convincing argument in favour of the Emperor Probus (276-82) being responsible. In 276 Gaul was overrun by barbarian tribes and subsequently

*43 (opposite) The bathhouse at Chesters (axonometric reconstruction). Shortly after their discovery in the 1880s John Collingwood Bruce described the baths as a 'large and lofty range of buildings'. Built into the slope below the fort the baths lay close to the west bank of the River Tyne. Movements of soil down the slope covered the building from view, and preserved it, until 1885 in a similar manner to Beauport Park (**42**). Its history is extremely complicated and the letters used to identify the rooms follows the scheme used by MacDonald (see bibliography). Some of the rooms were vaulted (**10**)*

A = apodyterium (changing room) — note the niches, perhaps for storing clothes.

N = a vestibule

K = frigidarium (cold room)

L = early cold bath

J = later cold bath

E = laconicum (dry-heat room)

I = tepidarium (moist warm room)

H = second tepidarium, with buttresses to support the building against the downward slope to the river.

F & G = caldaria (moist hot rooms). G contained a number of tufa and tile components which have been identified as parts of a vaulted roof. Ribs of tufa were connected with two rows flat tiles to create cavities between each rib, thus saving weight.

M = latrine

Furnaces were sited next to B's north wall, and by G's, and H's south walls

many of the cities and towns received new defences. The Saxon Shore forts, which, it should be added, have counterparts on the Gaulish coast, may have been part of this grand strategy of concerted defence. The existing forts at Reculver and Brancaster (?), which presumably represent earlier less concerted efforts to resist a growing maritime threat, were incorporated into the new scheme. Burgh Castle, already under construction, was adapted to the new style of military architecture paralleled in town walls and forts alike.

The system was not confined to the shores of the English Channel and the North Sea. Late forts are known at Cardiff and Lancaster and military enclosures have been identified on the Isle of Anglesey. None are closely dated and it is possible that like Pevensey they represent supplements, added during the fourth century as the need arose. Pevensey differs from the other Saxon Shore forts in having an irregular plan. The evidence of a single coin beneath a bastion has been used to suggest that the fort was added in or after the mid-330s. Unfortunately the late Roman military document, the *Notitia Dignitatum*, is both too late and too inaccurate to help us understand in detail how these forts were operated. The *Notitia* seems to be based on information of troop dispositions in *c*.395 with various updates for the next 40 or so years incorporated, but not necessarily excluding out-of-date information.

Most of the names on the list can be matched with known sites but one, *Portus Adurni*, creates a problem. It either represents Portchester or Walton Castle, or an unknown site. Whichever is right leaves us with the problem that we have at least one more fort than the *Notitia* lists. The debate is an inconclusive one because the evidence does not exist to resolve it. While the forts may eventually have been incorporated into a cohesive system we cannot say when that was; it seems changes of plan had taken place all along — perhaps one of the forts had been abandoned by the time the *Notitia* was drawn up. There is also the role of the usurper Carausius (286-93) to consider — it seems likely from archaeological evidence that Portchester was put up during his rule, and it has even been argued that the main sequence of fort construction was his responsibility in an effort to defend his new empire from a Roman invasion.

The archaeological evidence is poor so we can only see the forts as broadly belonging to a late third-century imperial initiative to defend the north-west provinces from a maritime threat. There is no specific evidence to attribute them to any one emperor, or any particular threat — the history of the period shows that threats had existed intermittently for some decades and as a result there were already some fortifications available. Subsequently changes were made where necessary but none of these ideas detract from the fact that these late forts belong to a new style of military thinking. These were not Agricolan forward camps, or forts designed to hold hostile passes in

44 (opposite) Arena (ludus, at Caerleon, Isca, fortress of legio II Augusta from the late first century until the beginning of the fourth.

a. Plan of the arena (after Wheeler). The building was built in the late first century (Period 1) in an area to the south-west of the fortress walls, cut in part from a low slope. It was based on earthen banks, created from soil dug from the arena. Wooden seats were laid across the banks and these were revetted by stone wall. During the Hadrianic period the structure was repaired and more buttresses added (Period 2) but thereafter it was allowed to deteriorate. At the beginning of the third century it was repaired and remained in use until the late fourth century. There were eight entrances, the main ones being at the ends of the long axis. The entrances on the short axis incorporated small chambers, the easterly example adding a small shrine. These two entrances supported ceremonial seating (omitted in the reconstructions to show the substructure). There were four small additional entrances. The arena was drained by a culvert running its full length. The area of the arena, relative to the seating, is large and its should be borne in mind that this was primarily a military structure, not a civic amphitheatre and should be more accurately described as a ludus. Seating capacity is estimated at around 5,500 individuals, roughly enough for the entire legion.

b. Reconstruction of the amphitheatre (after J.A. Wright). This shows the walls as being completely of stone. However they may actually only have served as footings supporting a timber revetment for the earthen banks

mountainous territory. Instead they were designed to secure the coastline by acting as strongholds for units able to defend themselves with an array of artillery. We have no evidence for any of the forts being involved in a campaign but the general growth and development of rural lowland Roman Britain in the third and fourth centuries suggests their existence may have contributed to a sense of security.

The forts of the Saxon Shore were not the only military provisions made during the later period. As we will see the northern frontier of Hadrian's Wall required extensive rebuilding in the fourth century and a number of signal towers were built on the north-east coast. The legionary fortress at York had its western defences extensively remodelled during the fourth century. Originally built for the IX legion *Hispana* in *c.*71 and later it had emerged as the military and civilian capital of northern Britain. It was also the place in which Constantine I, the Great, was declared emperor. Around this time the section of wall overlooking the river Ouse was augmented with a series of polygonal towers. These may have been designed to make the fortress as impressive as possible in accordance with its new status as headquarters of the *Dux Britanniarum* (Duke of the Britons). The *duces* were regional commanders of frontier troops appointed initially either by Diocletian (284-305, who instituted the system) or Constantine I (307-37). The west corner tower has survived to an impressive height of 5.8m (19ft) with a medieval superstructure. Known as the 'Multangular Tower' it has 10 projecting faces based on a plan of 14 faces. The other four faces are omitted to allow access to the tower from within the fortress. Supported on a concrete raft and piles it would have had internal floors of wood but its original height is unknown.

45 *The amphitheatre at Caerleon today looking north through the south entrance. Note how much lower the ground level of the arena was — this created flooding problems and eventually the main entrances had to be blocked up*

Frontier Works

At no time during the Roman occupation of Britain did military control extend over the whole island. During the reign of Domitian (81-96) and Septimius Severus (193-211) considerable advances were made into Scotland but these were never consolidated. As a result the frontier always lay within the island. Like elsewhere in the Empire the second century was a period in which these frontiers were made permanent. In Britain this policy resulted in the walls of Hadrian (117-38) and Antoninus Pius (138-61) the former of which is amongst the most famous of all Roman construction works at any time. They belong to a more general range of Roman frontier works, particularly those in Germany, though Hadrian's Wall in particular forms a uniquely coherent group of buildings and military works.

Although Hadrian's stone Wall had a much longer life than the earthen Antonine Wall both projects were similar in concept and form. Unfortunately we have little evidence for the reasoning behind the walls — we are told that Hadrian was the 'first' to build a wall in order 'to separate the Romans and barbarians' (*Scriptores Historiae Augustae, Hadrian,* xi.2). This seems to have followed from a general inability of the Roman army to control effectively northern Britain during the reign of Trajan (98-117). Following the abandonment of Agricola's northern conquests by Domitian in *c.*86/7 Roman policy in Britain becomes very difficult to understand because we have no literary or epigraphic references available until Hadrian's reign. This incidentally highlights the inadequacy of archaeology under such circumstances and, realistically, we have to accept that the beginning part of the second century is something of a 'dark age'. A number of military installations between Corbridge and Carlisle appear to belong to this phase. They may have formed a frontier zone based on the east-west road now known as the Stanegate though whether they were conceived as such is quite another matter. If so Hadrian's Wall may have been designed as a re-working of the idea, based on an actual wall. By the reign of Antoninus Pius it had apparently failed because another war was fought following

46 *Saxon Shore fort at Richborough, Kent. The Saxon Shore forts present a number of archaeological and historical problems. Richborough was one of four forts built in fairly close proximity to one another around the east coast of Kent. Construction of the fort, shortly after c.273, involved destroying all the other structures on the site (see **79**). The original garrison is unknown but by the late fourth century* legio II Augusta *seems to have been based here. The fort was built with integral circular corner bastions and square interval towers but a number of irregularities in detail (**47**, and **colour plate 5**), plus a misaligned ditch show that changes took place during building work.*

a = section through the ditches and wall

b-c = bastion design

d = plan of the site (the east wall and part of the south have been eroded away)

which Pius 'built another wall, this time of turf' (*SHA, Antoninus Pius*, v.4). But we should always be wary of attributing these projects to specific events — they may represent political and military responses to more general situations.

Hadrian's Wall

Unfortunately Hadrian's Wall has acted as a convenient source of building stone for centuries and much information has had to come from the more remote central sector, which is the only part in a reasonable state of preservation (albeit heavily restored). Most of the eastern section lies under modern Newcastle-upon-Tyne and the Military Road

47 *North wall of Richborough fort. To the left of centre the join between two sections of wall built by different gangs can be clearly seen because of the styles of stonework. To the right is the simple north postern gate*

48 *West gate of the Saxon Shore fort at Pevensey. Originally the gate bastions would have been joined by arched portals. The projecting gate bastions illustrate the radical changes in military architecture towards a more overtly defensive posture. Pevensey seems to be later in date than most of the Saxon Shore forts and was probably built towards the middle of the fourth century*

built between 1752 and 1757. However, a century of study and excavation has produced a coherent picture of the Wall's development revealing the most important aspect of the system: radical alteration of the original plan and reconstruction throughout its history (**50, colour plates 6-11**).

Hadrian's Wall was begun about the year 122, following the emperor's visit to Britain. Whether Hadrian played a significant part in its design or not is unknown. Considering

49 West wall with bastions at Portchester. Standing almost to original height because of mediaeval repair work this is the best-preserved section of Roman military defences in Britain. The crenellations which can be seen near the second tower are probably post-Roman work

his interest in architecture it is not improbable that the scheme was based at least in part on his ideas. It seems to have been conceived as a stone wall 10 Roman feet (about 3m) broad with a forward ditch (**colour plate 7**) separated by a berm about 20 Roman feet (6m) wide (**50b**). This wall was called in antiquity a *vallum* (rampart), not to be confused with the additional ditch and mound feature now called the Vallum (see below). An inscription from near Turret 26b records the erection of 113ft of *val(lum)* (*RIB* 1445).

The stone curtain ran from a bridge on the Tyne at Newcastle, *Pons Aelius*, running westwards to the River Irthing at Willowford. From this point the Wall was continued westwards in turf to Bowness-on-Solway. The stone wall, as planned, is now usually described as the 'Broad Wall'. The total length was around 76 Roman miles (111km).

Inscriptions indicate that the units responsible were detachments of the II, VI and XX legions which built approximately five mile units. Differences in the way the Wall was built correspond with these and it seems that there were two basic methods now known as 'Standard A' and 'Standard B'. Standard A consisted of a single course of large stones above the foundations followed by an offset, and is associated with the II and VI. In Standard B three or four smaller courses preceded the offset and is associated with XX (**50a**). The Wall had milecastles every Roman mile and turrets (or perhaps more accurately described as signal towers) every third of a mile in between (**50c-h, 51-5, colour plates 9-11**). These measurements were adhered to sometimes with a perplexing disregard for tactically disadvantageous locations, but careful surveying has shown that quite significant variations in distances were allowed. For example milecastles 37 and 38 are separated by a distance of 0.99 of a Roman mile, 38 and 39 by 0.94 of a mile, and 39 and 40 by 1.11 miles. The main forces of auxiliary units were located behind the Wall at forts already in existence on the east-west Stanegate road (for example at Vindolanda). The system of milecastles and turrets, but no Wall, continued some way down the Cumbrian coast. Recent excavations have suggested that where necessary additional structures were incorporated. At Peel Gap, between turrets 39A and 39B, a tower was added to fill a gap. Other recent work at Denton Burn suggests that the Wall curtain may have been whitewashed. If so its original appearance may have been rather different than that popularly imagined.

By 124, several radical alterations had been introduced. The sequence is very complicated and minor details need not concern us here. Unfinished sections of the stone wall were now built on a narrower gauge. The new design is known now as the 'Narrow Wall', and though usually said to be eight Roman feet wide there is actually considerable variation, sometimes to less than seven feet wide. Standard A and Standard B continued in use. The change of policy is manifest in the fact that the foundations and some milecastles and turrets had already been prepared for the 10ft Broad Wall, and the change in thickness is quite clear at a number of sites (**7**). Rather more significant was the decision to build 12 forts on the Wall itself, in some cases involving the demolition of existing turrets, for example at Chesters and Housesteads. The new forts were sited around seven Roman miles (about 10km) apart. Each was to be garrisoned by an auxiliary unit and were built either up against the Wall's south side, or projecting in part to the north — this depended on local conditions (**21**). The reason must have been that the older forts to the south were simply too far away to allow a speedy response to an incursion, and possibly because it was easier to supply the frontier garrison when it was concentrated into a single zone.

At around this time the so-called Vallum was added (**colour plate 8**). This was a ditch flanked by mounds running south of the Wall, and helps explain this inaccurate name. *Vallum* means 'rampart', but the conspicuous remains of its mounds led to the belief in early studies that this was actually the frontier. The name has stuck, despite the fact that the Roman army would have (and did) apply the word *vallum* to the curtain itself.

Although the ditch to the north of the Wall was sometimes dispensed with when it was made superfluous by precipices the Vallum was constructed almost regardless of the local landscape. Just how regardless can still be seen at Limestone Corner where colossal pieces of the local stone were hacked out to form a ditch. They still lie where they were hauled and form a vivid reminder to an age of explosives and power drills of the power of disciplined muscle. At Down Hill, near the site of milecastle 21, the Vallum runs like a switchback over the hill despite the fact that the ground drops steeply away immediately to the south. In general the Vallum lay around 120 Roman feet (about 33m) behind the Wall but this varies very considerably depending on the terrain (**50**). It thus created a 'military zone' with the Wall. Crossings were built at each fort and this suggests that the Vallum was also devised as a means of funnelling trans-Wall traffic into easily policed channels. The Vallum sometimes diverts to go round forts demonstrating that it was either contemporary or later. However, at Carrawburgh, the Vallum lies beneath the fort and was filled in showing that this fort was added later in order to fill the long gap between Chesters and Housesteads.

In the east the Wall was extended to the fort of Wallsend where it ran down into the River Tyne. In the west the stone forts had been built into the turf wall but this was itself subsequently built in stone, probably under Hadrian. At Birdoswald, which had projected north, the new stone wall was re-aligned to meet the fort's north wall, thus placing the whole fort south of the Wall. In essence this was the completed form of Hadrian's Wall. In time the purpose of the components altered — gates were blocked up, others were opened (for example at Knag Burn by Housesteads) and the Vallum was given crossings throughout its length. Much of the dereliction identified on the Wall resulted from the time when the Antonine Wall was in use. It needed so much repair in the early third century and later that some post-Roman chroniclers believed Septimius Severus had built the Wall from its foundations. The long period of peace during the third century also contributed to decay.

Much space has been given to discussing the strategic intentions behind Hadrian's Wall and the tactical plan behind the various components. The fact that the Wall was altered during construction implies that its purpose changed according to circumstances — it is thus hopelessly simplistic to try and attribute the Wall's construction to a single idea. There were probably many reasons. The Wall must have provided a psychological boost not just to local inhabitants who wished to become peaceably Romanized, but also to the population further south. Likewise it must have appeared as a potent statement of Roman power to those beyond the Wall to the north. It cannot have really been intended as an absolute barrier because outpost forts to the north, for example at Bewcastle, indicate that Rome regarded land immediately to the north as under her control. In any case a determined 'raider' would have had little difficulty in scaling the Wall if he so desired. It is rather more likely that the Wall and its various crossing points made it possible to supervise local movements. From a military point of view the forts and milecastles may well have enabled a swift response to incursions and it seems an unavoidable conclusion that the various turrets and milecastles were designed to make observations and communications easy. However, it is worth remembering that the Wall garrison of about 5,000 men was dispersed along the whole length. Consequently the number of men available in any given area was limited to a few hundred. If this was effective then it seems that the scheme was designed more to deal with small-scale skirmishes rather than major invasions.

All these are possibilities and the Wall was probably designed to deal with them all; it is not strictly necessary to see the Wall as purely a response to a pressing military crisis. Where the plan seemed inadequate it was altered and in time the Wall probably became so integrated a part of military routine and local civilian life that its original intention was largely forgotten. There is no doubt that Hadrian's Wall was an astonishing project. It is the kind of ancient structure that invokes modern incredulity, particularly with regard to cost. This is quite irrelevant. Hadrian's Wall cost nothing at all. The materials were free and the soldiers were being paid regardless. It made no difference to the Imperial treasury whether they fought wars, sharpened their swords or built walls if that seemed a good idea at the time. This makes it easier to understand why Hadrian's Wall was more or less abandoned 20 years after it was built.

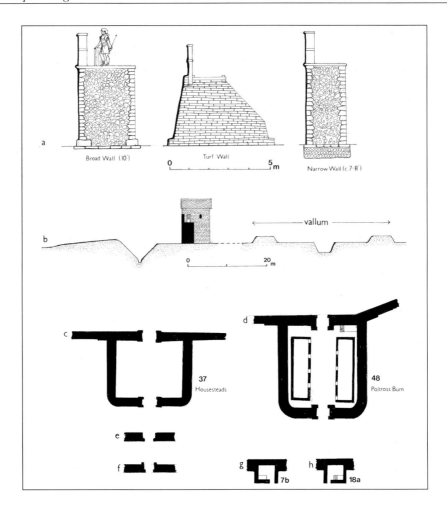

50 Hadrian's Wall.

   a = The different methods used to construct the Wall. Initially the Wall was designed to be built in c.121 as the Broad Wall in the eastern sector and turf in the western. After c.124 unfinished stone sections and the turf sector were completed as the Narrow Wall (though the turf alignment was not always followed, for example in the vicinity of Birdoswald). The stone wall was built with two different foundations as shown here — however these were used for both the Broad and Narrow Walls depending on different units responsible for construction.

   *b = Cross-section of the Wall with forward ditch and vallum to rear. The Vallum's distance behind could vary quite considerably depending on local terrain (**colour plate 8**).*

   c-d = Milecastle plans (37 and 48). Milecastles have been given modern numbers starting from the eastern end of the Wall.

   e-f = Other types of milecastle gates

   g-h = Turret plans (7b and 18a), built about every 1/3 mile between milecastles. The numbers of turrets follow those of the milecastles, thus turrets 7a and 7b are the next two turrets west of milecastle 7

51 Milecastle 48 (Poltross Burn) looking north showing the remains of the flight of steps which led up to the wall-curtain. It is possible though that they only led up to a low flat platform on which a ladder stood. This would have had tactical advantages had the curtain been scaled by an attacker because a ladder could be swiftly removed

The Antonine Wall

The Antonine Wall runs between the Firth of Forth and the Firth of Clyde in Scotland, about 160km (100 miles) north of Hadrian's Wall. It was built by the early 140s and was permanently abandoned in the 160s. There may have been several reasons: a new emperor or governor needing a new reputation; idle soldiers; the tying up of too many troops in the numerous garrison posts of Hadrian's Wall; the difficulty of supplying the remote central sector forts.

The new frontier was closely modelled on its predecessor but was built entirely of turf. This does not appear to have been the original plan because the fort of Balmuildy, one of the earliest on the frontier, was built of stone and was prepared with wing walls of stone. This suggests that a stone curtain had been intended, but the plan was altered after the project had been begun.

The most obvious advantage the new frontier had was its length. It is only 37 Roman miles (59km) long, or around half the length of Hadrian's Wall. The use of turf should not be interpreted as an economy measure employed under duress because Roman frontiers were usually built of turf. Like Hadrian's Wall the new wall had a forward ditch but this was separated from the wall by a broader berm 20-30 Roman feet (7-9m) wide.

Unlike Hadrian's Wall forts were associated with the new frontier right from the very beginning. They were interspersed with fortlets but there is no positive evidence for a regular series of turrets. These strongholds are distinctive for their slightly irregular plans and considerable variation in size. This may be explained in part by the idea that some of

52 North gate of milecastle 37 during repair work looking north. The survival of the springers makes it possible to restore the arch and therefore a minimum height for the wall (see **colour plates 10,11**)

the forts were built before the Wall, and some after, perhaps having discovered that the original provision was inadequate. At any rate the forts and their capacity mean that the total garrison cannot have been very much less than that on Hadrian's Wall. In military terms this means there were twice as many men per mile of frontier than before. An important tactical difference was that the Antonine Wall appears to have had no equivalent to the Vallum on Hadrian's Wall. This is curious because the Vallum was built with such diligence that this suggests it was regarded as an indispensable component of the frontier.

The Walls as buildings

The Antonine Wall was abandoned permanently by the 160s and that thereafter Hadrian's Wall served as the northern frontier. More details of their fascinating history can be best pursued by reading Stephen Johnson's, and Breeze and Dobson's excellent summaries of the archaeology, and the most recent edition of John Collingwood Bruce's handbook, edited and revised by C. Daniels.

We more are concerned here though with the building of the Walls and their associated structures. No part of Hadrian's Wall stands to full height today and nor has it done in recorded times. One of the highest sections, at Hare Hill, still stands to 3m (10ft). However, the surviving lower part of a flight of steps at the milecastle of Poltross Burn (MC 48) suggests, if extended at the same angle, that the walkway on the rampart within the milecastle was 4.8m (15ft) from the ground (**51**). The remains of the north gate at milecastle 37 (**52, colour plates 10-11**) support this. This does not mean that the Wall itself was this high, or even that it was the same height throughout its length. However, assuming that a parapet existed to protect patrols, the Wall must have presented a face of around at least 5-6m (17-20ft) high to the north. It is likely, but not certain, that the Wall had crenellations. The Rudge Cup, a small bronze vessel, is decorated with what appears to be a stylized representation of the Wall with crenellations and may be a souvenir of a visit. No collapsed upper sections of the Wall have been found but occasionally bevelled stones do turn up in fallen masonry. These may have capped crenellations.

The material used was mostly local sandstone and a number of quarries have been identified in the vicinity of the Wall (**4**). The facing stones were crudely dressed and laid

*53 Reconstruction based on milecastle 37 (Housesteads) (see also **colour plates 10, 11**). Changes of ground level have been ignored for simplicity. Milecastle 37 is a 'short-axis' milecastle and a fragmentary inscription shows that it was built by the II legion Augusta (RIB 1634). The inscription was probably identical examples found at milecastle 38 (RIB 1637-8), which state that building took place under Hadrian during the governorship of Aulus Platorius Nepos. Milecastle 37's claim to fame is that it retains its north gate up to the first springers on the two arches (**52**). Reconstructions of milecastles frequently show the gatehouse as projecting from the wall of the milecastle. In this particular case it is evident from the surviving remains that only the massive blocks of the door jams project — the rest of the gatehouse was flush with the flanking walls. Subsequently the north gate was narrowed and some of the partial blocking is still visible on the site. In fact the ground falls away so steeply to the north that this gate must have been useless except for foot-traffic, though narrowing of milecastle gates seems to have been a general phenomenon*

in horizontal courses on a stone foundation. About two courses were laid and then the core, a mixture of rubble, clay or mortar, was poured in. Another two courses were laid, more core poured in and so on (**7**). In order to relieve pressure from water forming ponds in natural dips or depressions, drains were built into the structure. Similar arrangements also allowed streams to run under the Wall. Recent archaeological work on the Wall has produced evidence to suggest that whitewash and/or a hard white lime mortar may have been used to cover the whole curtain, perhaps in order to make the frontier conspicuous from a distance.

Milecastles were miniature forts attached to the south face of the Wall and were equipped with sheltered accommodation (**53, 54, colour plates 9-11**). Most had gates in their north and south walls, making it possible to cross the Wall, but there are exceptions.

*54 The remains of milecastle 39 ('Castle Nick') looking east. Unlike milecastle 37 (**52-3**), this milecastle lacks any evidence for monumental gate masonry and is associated by some with the VI legion, though there is no inscriptional evidence to support that. Castle Nick was built to Narrow Wall specifications, but excavation has shown that a Broad Wall foundation for the curtain had been laid here on a slightly different alignment before the Narrow Wall superstructure was erected*

Turrets were even simpler and were not equipped with gates through the Wall (**55**). The turrets probably had at least two floors, the upper of which was reached either by ladder or wooden stairs. Normally the turrets were recessed into the Wall though additions, like that at Peel Gap (see above), were just tacked on to the existing curtain. When a turret was demolished the wall recess was filled in. These structures all served the important purpose of allowing access to the walkway on the Wall itself. However, the milecastles and turrets were also built along the southern shores of the Solway Firth to extend the system, albeit without the actual wall curtain.

As with forts discussed earlier there is no evidence at all for the roofing of the milecastles and turrets. Traditional reconstructions show these with crenellations in the manner of a medieval castle. It has been argued that the lack of roof-tiles from Hadrianic destruction levels is evidence for crenellations. But there is no specific evidence for crenellations either and in any case it would have been perfectly feasible to roof the buildings with perishable materials like wooden shingles. As with the forts it is not entirely easy to accept the idea of flat roofs in Britain. These posts were presumably intended as observation bases. If so it is logical to assume that a dry, comfortable soldier is more likely to do his observing than a wet, cold one. Quite apart from personal comfort is the problem of structural maintenance of flat-roofed buildings, particularly in such exposed places. Gabled or pitched roofs on turrets and milecastle gates are more likely to have been

55 *Hadrian's Wall, turret 18a (Wallhouses East). This turret, when excavated, was in an
exceptional state of preservation and retained a ladder platform though height and roofing remain
conjectural. They may have resembled the reconstruction shown in **56** of a timber signal tower
with an external gallery but the Wall probably served this purpose (assuming it had a walkway
along the parapet, but even this is not certain)*

a = Cross-section west to east showing the ladder platform and access to the upper floor
b = The same, externally, showing ground-floor access
c = Cross-section south to north
d = The same, showing the curtain itself in cross-section

suitable. The general evidence from Trajan's Column is that timber superstructures of
gates might be flat-roofed but the majority of stone structures and free-standing towers
portrayed seem to have had pitched roofs. It is quite possible that the turrets may have
resembled the signal towers described below in having external wooden platforms, in
which case they would have been a little higher than reconstructed here (**55, 56**).

The turf Walls were built differently. Although the western sector of Hadrian's Wall
was eventually replaced in stone the new curtain did not always follow the same course.

56 *Timber signal tower at Beattock Summit, Lanarkshire (isometric reconstruction). One of a series of towers this site is represented by only four post-holes and a shallow encircling ditch so there is little obvious evidence for its original appearance. However signal towers are portrayed on Trajan's Column and they appear to have had an external gallery which would have served, not only as a look-out platform, but also as a support for a brazier*

This has allowed examination of the turf version. It was made of cut turfs sometimes laid on a cobbled base 20 Roman feet (6m) wide. Its height is unknown but in order to have been effective it would have needed to be around 3m (10ft), probably supporting a timber palisade. The Antonine Wall was built on a cobble base 14 Roman feet (4.5m) wide. The continuous stone base increased stability, facilitated drainage and probably meant that with parapets the wall was at least as high as Hadrian's. Either this followed a lesson learned, or there was better planning. There was nothing particularly unsatisfactory about using turf; the technique is fast and durable — parts of the Antonine Wall are still visible today — and it was the normal method of building Roman frontiers.

Signal towers

An organized army is dependent upon communications. Hadrian's Wall and the Antonine Wall provided a fairly rigid system of linear communications with the various turrets and milecastle towers incorporated into the structure. Signal towers were also built in isolation, though in a series, and they formed a vital component of military communications. For example a sequence of ten, averaging less than a mile apart, are known from eight miles of road between Perth and Strageath.

Signal towers were generally built of timber because this was the quickest and most efficient way. Consequently the archaeological evidence is limited usually to post-holes and ramparts. However, a number of square timber signal towers appear on Trajan's Column. These provide the basis for the reconstruction of the Beattock tower (**56**). The design was simple and presumably effective. The tower supported an external gallery and

57 Signal tower at Scarborough restored in elevation. A series of these towers were built along the Yorkshire coast in the late fourth century. They were probably designed to warn against sea-borne raiders from northern Europe. All the examples known seem to have consisted of a tower surrounded by a walled courtyard and an outer ditch. They may have resembled later Norman keeps

a brazier and was defended by a palisade and ditch. The remains of a tower's circular surrounding rampart and ditch can still be seen at Bowes Moor, four miles west of Bowes in North Yorkshire. Trajan's Column shows that a palisade of stakes capped the rampart.

Not all towers were timber. A square stone tower at Pike Hill on Hadrian's Wall pre-dated the system. The Wall was diverted to incorporate it and turret 52a lies less than 200m to the west showing how it lies 'out of sequence'. It lies at an angle of 45° to the wall because it was aligned with a series of signal towers and forts.

Much later in Roman Britain's history it proved necessary to defend the eastern and southern coasts with the forts of the Saxon Shore (see above). Subsequently it also proved necessary to augment coastal defences with much more elaborate signal towers. These are better described as signal stations and really amount to small forts. In fact, during the first century, coastal fortlets were built for signalling, for example at Martinhoe in Devon, containing accommodation for a century of troops (about 80 men) and an outer fortification for the beacons.

The late fourth-century stations were much more elaborate and involved an outer ditch, and a stone wall for the compound which contained a stone tower possibly up to 30m in height (100ft). A series is known from the east Yorkshire coast and they seem to have been built in or after 369. An inscription from Ravenscar specifically describes the station as consisting of a *turrem et castrum*, 'tower and fort' (*RIB* 721). The site at Scarborough is probably the best known and can still be seen in part today though the height of the tower as reconstructed (**57**) is purely hypothetical; the large piers suggest a substantial building, perhaps resembling a Norman castle keep but without the corner towers. Occupation seems to have lasted into the fifth century.

3 Public buildings

Introduction

P1 → bd for law + order.

All organized communities need administrative centres. In the relatively sophisticated government of the Roman world this was true not just at imperial level, but also at provincial and local level. The Roman state had to delegate its power through local communities because ancient transport and technology was so primitive that it would have been impossible for it to function otherwise. So in Roman Britain we find that many of the settlements we call 'towns' contained a public hall (*basilica*) and associated market place (*forum*).

P2 → bd for ostentation ment

Public life was more than just provincial and civic administration. The Roman world contained many monuments to past events, local pride and ostentation such as triumphal arches, theatres and circuses. Inscriptions and documents from all over the Empire show that imperial initiatives, civic governments and private individuals were all responsible for public buildings. The letters of Pliny the Younger to Trajan, written while he was governor of Bithynia and Pontus are very instructive. The evidence from Britain is, however, particularly sparse — the majority of surviving building inscriptions from Britain record military and religious structures. For example, only the Verulamium and Wroxeter forum-basilica complexes have produced inscriptions and even these do not specify the actual buildings. None of the known civic amphitheatres, baths, theatres, walls or gates has produced an inscription. One stone from Brough-on-Humber records a theatre stage, *proscaenium*, donated by an aedile some time between 140-61, but the building itself is unknown (*RIB* 707).

City funds were derived from imperial grants, local taxes on trade and rents on civic property as well as from cash paid by local magistrates in return for their offices. Sometimes buildings were erected at the expense of a single man or family. Although town governments had employees who must have contributed to the labour required for public buildings it would be wrong to think in modern terms of costing because of the availability of forced labour. We might even include the army in the latter because soldiers were being paid regardless of what they actually did with their time, and may well have been obliged to participate in civic building works as part of the policy of Romanization. On the other hand it may be that some towns actually could not afford these projects, causing ruinous financial problems for their communities — our total lack of detailed knowledge leaves this as pure speculation.

ROMANIZATION

It is certainly quite wrong to imagine that all Romano-British towns had fully functioning public buildings in the second century — evidence from North Africa (where far more inscriptions have survived) shows that work could go on for decades or more. The famous Agricolan inscription from the forum at Verulamium (see *Companion*, 117) might only belong to an early stage of a project that could have stretched on till late in the second century absorbing large quantities of the town's money (**colour plate 12**) (though it is fairly certain that the state made a contribution), and perhaps explaining why the theatre was not erected until after *c.*155 on a site apparently reserved for it long before.

A few other inscriptions supply us with factual information about these public buildings but they are usually tantalizingly vague or incomplete. We also have Tacitus' reference to Colchester's possession of a senate-house and theatre by the year 60. Beyond that we have only the stumps of walls, reconstituted ground plans and guesswork to base our reconstructions on. It is impossible to know what the different parts of public buildings were used for even if one can be certain about what was a forum or a basilica. A description of rooms in a basilica as municipal offices is no more than an educated guess, and we really cannot extrapolate any information about how any particular town was governed or administered from such remains in the absence of any epigraphic or other verbal evidence. This is not going to change but the remarkable amount of building activity which has gone on in Britain over the last couple of decades has affected all of Britain's towns to a greater or lesser degree. So many towns have Roman origins that much new information about the structure of ancient public buildings in Roman Britain has emerged, even if most of the new evidence is fragmentary.

Basilica and forum

In practice the towns with a forum and basilica were the provincial capital, the *colonia* (settlements of Roman citizens), and the administrative capitals of the tribal cantons, for example Silchester. There seems little doubt that these buildings were derived directly, in architectural terms, from the headquarters buildings of the military forts. This is an important distinction and it would be wrong to imagine a Romano-British forum on the lines of the much earlier surviving example at Pompeii in southern Italy. Here the forum is an elongated piazza with temples and arches at either end; the basilica forms an appendage to the south-west corner of the forum. Nevertheless the collective function was the same: to act as the centre of local government, administration, trade and commercial activity.

The basilica and forum was also an important expression of civic pride and display and it must be that these buildings individually represent the largest and best the local community could afford (or thought they could afford), though there may have been a certain amount of state assistance and patronage. Consequently there is a fair amount of variation in scale — contrast the basilica in London with that at Caerwent for instance — but we can only guess at the variation in decoration and adornment. The plans of these buildings look a little Spartan but originally they would have been surrounded by statues of emperors, local worthies, military heroes and gods and goddesses, quite apart from carved stonework, wall-paintings and marbled veneers. The forums were thriving markets — the late second-century fire at Wroxeter was followed by demolition covering the collapsed remains of abandoned stalls, and preserving their stock. These included pottery (Romano-British mortaria and Gaulish samian) and whetstones though obviously

58 Flavian timber basilica at Silchester (isometric reconstruction). Missed by Victorian excavators this early basilica lay beneath the later stone version. It seems to have been built in the 80s replacing an even earlier rectangular timber building with a portico, perhaps a market, up by the 50s or 60s. Apart from the entrance which split the main hall in two the timber basilica seems to have been conventional in form with a nave and two aisles

perishable commodities left no trace.

As we saw in chapter 2 the *principia* was the administrative centre of the Roman fort. It consisted of a hall, in front of which was an open area surrounded on the other three sides by an ambulatory and a range of rooms. The Romano-British civic equivalent of this building was usually rather larger, though size varies, but it is quite possible that either the architects were ex-soldiers or on loan from the army, or that architects in Britain derived

59 Reconstruction of the Hadrianic basilica and part of the forum at Gracechurch Street, London, built c.120-150 but the evidence is so sparse that no greater precision is possible. It was aligned on the approach to the bridge over the Thames and roads in the vicinity were given a new layout. The basilica was certainly a very substantial building. Late Roman churches which still stand show that the height should be roughly equivalent to the width of the nave and one aisle which for this building was about 24m (79ft). The gaps between the piers are known and these suggest an arcade of the dimensions shown which corresponds very well with the suggested height. The hall was about 150m (492ft) in length. The apse is shown free-standing here but in fact it may have been incorporated into the hall in which case the external appearance would have been entirely rectangular.

No traces of the decoration of the building have been recovered apart from fragments of painted wall-plaster. It is certain that there must also have been various architectural embellishments such as detached columns and capitals, decorated cornices, inscriptions and statuary. The well-known bronze bust of Hadrian is likely to have come from here

their ideas from what they saw around them in military forts. Verulamium's forum is usually considered an exception because of the three temples and side entrances (**colour plate 12**) though in fact it only differs in detail and the general plan is fairly conformist. Unfortunately we have relatively little information about when such buildings were put up. We know that the Verulamium forum had apparently been dedicated by the year 79, and that the forum at Wroxeter had been built by 130-1 (*RIB* 288). Archaeological investigations have indicated that the second-century basilica at Silchester overlies a timber predecessor dated to the 80s, as at London (**58**).

London was the capital of Roman Britain. We do not know this for a fact but it is a more than reasonable supposition because the town was the biggest in the province and its Hadrianic basilica was also the largest. We also know that the post-Boudican *procurator provinciae Britanniae*, Julius Classicianus, was buried in London. The site of London's basilica has been the subject of a number of intermittent excavations since the nineteenth century. Only a small portion of its plan has been recovered but by extending known walls a very reasonable complete plan has been drawn up.

London had two consecutive basilicas and forums built on the same site but the first pair was much smaller and simpler. It seems to belong to the mid-Flavian period and probably represents part of official policy to reconstruct Britain after the Boudican Revolt of 60. Its scale is surprisingly small, smaller in fact than contemporary structures in cantonal capitals in Britain, for example at Silchester. Perhaps it was an expedient project, designed to get a working building into commission as fast as possible, as may have been the case with the *principia* at Inchtuthil (**18**). At around 5,500m² (59,000 sq ft) it was very unassuming in comparison to the replacement built around, and finally over, its predecessor covering nearly 30,000m² (323,000 sq ft) in the process. The later building must have been a particularly magnificent construction, which may have taken decades to build (**59-60**), if it was indeed ever finished. We know nothing about its date except that a coin of Hadrian in excellent condition found sealed in the mortar implies that building work was underway by the end of his reign and after. Of course it could have begun much earlier, and ended far later but it is tempting to associate its inception with Hadrian's known visit early in his reign, particularly as Hadrian is known to have promoted civic development elsewhere (see Wroxeter above). The truth is that we do not know if he was involved but its function was evidently to act as the centre of provincial administration and justice.

The great basilica of Roman London consisted of a hall about 35m (115ft) wide, and about 150m (492ft) in length, oriented roughly east-west on the long axis. Its north-south axis seems to have been aligned on the road running downhill to the bridge across the Thames. The hall was divided into two side aisles, separated from the central nave by two rows of brick piers. These probably supported arches, possibly embellished either with pilasters or detached columns. We cannot know the height of the nave, but by taking the parallels of similarly designed early churches which are still standing we can assume that it was approximately equivalent to the sum of the diameter of the nave and one aisle; in this case about 27m (89ft). The roof was tiled but whether this was supported by vaulting, or timber rafters, we do not know. At the east end of the building was an apse with a raised floor level, used by the presiding magistrates. There may have been a similar apse at the west end. On the northern side of the building there was a row of rooms running off the north aisle, and beyond that a further row. These would probably have been used as offices, and perhaps for the storage of the government and judicial records.

Unfortunately the limited excavations on the basilica site have yielded no evidence for elaborate architectural decorations in the form of carved columns and capitals, cornices and architraves (**60**). However, in this case it is certainly safe to assume that they must have been there, and were carried off or broken up in later centuries. It would be unthinkable for this colossal and prestigious building to have been built merely of plastered brick —

60 The north-east part of the Hadrianic basilica of London by Leadenhall and Gracechurch Streets under excavation. The wall in the foreground is the north wall of the complex and the walls in the background running at right angles represent internal divisions. The site has since been destroyed to make way for a modern building

some fragments of painted wall plaster have been found. The end of the London basilica is, like everything else in Roman Britain, an enigma. The remains of some of the walls are fairly substantial but they formed no part of later, medieval, buildings. The fact of course is that that building had a specific function that became redundant once provincial and civic government came to an end. Structural problems may have played a part because the building, like a number of major Romano-British buildings, was put up on ill-prepared ground (see chapter 1).

Almost all the basilicas of Roman Britain seem to have been similar to the London example. The only difference is that they were without exception smaller. Lincoln's was

forum + basilica declined in imp. with ascendancy of Augustus.

91

61 Axonometric reconstruction of the forum and basilica at Lincoln. Excavations have identified traces of the structure at various locations, and extension of known features makes it inevitable that the 'Mint Wall' (62) must be a surviving part of the basilica's north wall. The proportions are relatively small-scale and it seems that the basilica also lacked a north aisle

exceptionally small, surprising given the city's status as a colony (**62**). Some have been excavated in their entirety, for example the Silchester basilica, now entirely under grass. This building is particularly interesting because recent excavations, designed to make up for the shortcomings of Victorian archaeologists, have shown that the masonry second-century building was preceded by a wooden version, put up in the 80s. The stone building was modest by London's standards and was only 82m (269ft) long, by 17.5m (57ft) in width (**66**). It had two apses but only one aisle, separated from the hall by a single row of columns about 8.6m (28ft) in height. However, the even smaller basilica at Caerwent resembles London more closely but was only 50m (164ft) long and 20m (66ft) wide (**63**, **colour plate 1**). Even this modest and comparatively remote example of classical architecture had columns embellished with ornately carved Corinthian capitals, and painted wall-plaster. None of the Romano-British basilicas are now visible apart from the north wall of the basilica at Lincoln. Known for years as the 'Mint Wall' only recent

62 *The 'Mint Wall' in Lincoln, now identified as the north wall of the basilica surviving to a remarkable 21m (70ft) in length and 5.5m (18ft) in height. Putlog holes in the wall were probably for scaffolding during construction. The lack of windows seems strange but if this was the basilica's north wall then there may have been practical reasons for this*

excavations in the city centre have shown that it formed part of the civic centre (**62**).

The basilica was always built in association with a forum (**colour plate 12**). This was a much simpler building and consequently there is little variation in the basic plan. The forum was an open square or rectangle surrounded on three sides by covered and colonnaded ambulatories. The ambulatory normally ran along a central row of rooms, which were probably shops, on the other side of which a further ambulatory formed the external part of the building. The ambulatories were only broken by entrances or, rarely, temples (**63**). The fourth side was crossed by the basilica which itself had civic offices to the rear. Vitruvius said the forum's size should reflect the number of local inhabitants, neither being too small to be useful nor so large that it looked like an empty desert (V.1.3).

The evidence available seems to suggest that there were two periods in which towns built their administrative centres. The first was during the Flavian reconstruction of Roman Britain. However, the buildings were on a modest scale and it was only after the second decade of the second century that the towns began to embark on more extravagant projects. The later history of these monumental building complexes is not very clear. That London and Cirencester suffered subsidence has already been mentioned. There are a number of cases where later churches seem to be associated with the sites, for example in London, Lincoln and Verulamium. Even the great hall of the *principia* at York now lies

63 *Isometric reconstruction of the basilica and forum at Caerwent (see **colour plate 1**). One of the smallest of all the civic administrative centres in Roman Britain this building was built on a similar model to most of the other, much larger, examples. It only had an external portico on the south side and instead of having apsidal tribunals at either end of the basilica there were simple rectangular rooms, though one of these was heated. Despite its modest scale it had columns with carved stone capitals. At a late point in its history the west range of offices or shops in the forum had a temple-like building inserted into it*

beneath the great medieval minster. It is quite possible that the basilicas served a Christian function in their later years and the religious associations of the sites continued, even once the basilicas had crumbled. In several cases churches were founded on the sites. At Lincoln the church of St Paul-in-the-Bail was founded in the old forum. Its early history is obscure but some of the associated burials seem to date back to the fifth and sixth centuries. However, the Romano-British basilicas probably decayed because in the fifth century and later the technology, skill and will needed to maintain them simply no longer existed. As the biggest and most complicated buildings the basilicas and forums were the least likely to be maintained, especially as their administrative purpose had disappeared.

Other market buildings

While the forum functioned as the main centre of urban commercial activity it could sometimes be supplemented by a separate market building known as the *macellum*. These were not apparently very common in Britain but this may reflect a difficulty of interpretation; examples have been found at Cirencester, Leicester, Verulamium (**64**) and

Shape of building is telling of urban contemporary life.

Wroxeter and it seems inevitable that any reasonably sized town would have outgrown the facilities afforded by its forum. Of course there would have been shops like those in Insula xiv at Verulamium (**102**) arranged along a street front, but markets were essential for non-residential traders such as farmers or merchants. At Pompeii the *macellum* not only contained shops and booths for changing money but also a shrine and meeting place for the priests of the imperial cult. Unfortunately we cannot be certain whether the Romano-British examples were public or private but their central locations makes it very likely that they were civic projects provided as a supplementary facility.

Official residences and other monumental buildings

The governors of Roman Britain were each officially known as a *legatus augusti*, which means literally 'the emperor's delegate'. He was usually a man of high social rank, a senator who had almost certainly commanded a legion earlier in his career. He was assisted by a procurator, usually of equestrian status. The governor lived in and worked from what we would describe as a palace. Assuming that London was the official capital of Britain for most of the period we are concerned with it was also the most likely site for the governor's palace.

A building, which lies partially beneath Cannon Street Station in London, is thought a likely candidate for a palace but no evidence has been found which makes this certain. A number of stamped tiles indicate it was an official building. The plan (**65**) is very incomplete, defying meaningful reconstruction, but there seems to have been a very substantial building set in terraces by the Thames including an ornamental garden with a large pool overlooked by a large hall. Around the garden were ranges of rooms. The better preserved remains of the so-called governor's palace at Aquincum in present-day Hungary show a series of 'state rooms' opening off a corridor with the rooms and baths of the private residence to the rear. Unfortunately the remains of the London building are so fragmentary that it is impossible to be sure of its original appearance. A number of massive walls have been recorded in the vicinity during various building operations since the nineteenth century. However, the jaunty layout of the rooms which are known in better detail makes it impossible to integrate them all into a coherent plan.

What is certain is that the building was massive. The whole complex was about 130m (426ft) long from north to south. The hall was over 24m (80ft) long and over 13m (43ft) wide. Other circumstantial evidence suggests that there were colonnades and a bath suite as well as the various rooms, garden and pool. Underlying deposits do not post-date the late first century so it seems reasonable to conclude that this was yet another in the series of monumental buildings erected in Roman Britain during the Flavian period. Of its subsequent history little is known but it was evidently mostly ruinous by the late Roman period because dumps of late Roman rubbish lay in a number of the rooms. The terracing of the building probably also meant that there was some kind of substantial water gate or wharf on the riverbank. The Huggin Hill bath complex is only about 300m (1000ft) to the west and it is possible that a number of major public buildings were strung out along the riverbank.

*64 Macellum at Verulamium (final phase — fourth century; axonometric reconstruction). The site
was a long-lived one and it lay immediately across Watling Street from the theatre. It was built in
the first century on a much larger plan with two rows of nine 'shops' facing one another. By the
second century it had been reduced in size to two rows of five shops. More reconstruction work
followed in succeeding years and by the later fourth century it had been remodelled with a
monumental facade. Whether it was roofed like a basilica, or open as shown, is unresolved*

There are a small number of monumental buildings whose purpose remains unknown.
The enigmatic complex of structures in the Fens at Stonea in Cambridgeshire includes a
building with such massive foundations that it has been assumed that it must have been a
tower (**66**). It had an apse, was heated and seems to have had a hall and gallery attached to
it. It was built in the Hadrianic period but interpretation is extremely difficult because it
falls into no familiar category and, apart from the surrounding buildings, stands in virtual
isolation. It has been suggested that the building commemorates an early battle against the
Iceni but this is obviously quite uncertain and in any case by *c.*200 the building had been

65 Plan of the so-called 'governor's palace' at Cannon Street, London (after Marsden). This remarkable building is only known from tantalizing traces and seems to have consisted of a main hall with ornamental garden as well as a series of surrounding ranges of rooms and wings. It was built in the late first or early second century and was terraced on three levels on the slope down to the Thames where there would probably have been a substantial watergate and wharf. More recently it has been suggested that the baths complex at Huggin Hill to the west may actually be the palace of the provincial governor. Both sites are associated with tiles stamped for the provincial government: P P BR LON ('procurator of the province of Britain at London'). By the late fourth century the site was derelict though there may have been casual occupation of the ruins

completely demolished. Another possibility is that it was a facility for overlooking the surrounding area which is of course very low-lying — there are few villas in the region and it has been suggested that, following drainage, the Fens were operated as an imperial estate which would have been managed by a procurator. Alternatively it may have provided a convenient landmark in a comparatively featureless landscape. It may have

66 *Tower at Stonea Grange, Cambridgeshire. This enigmatic site was discovered in 1980 and involves extensive traces of settlement in the Cambridgeshire Fens. The most remarkable building is what appears to have been a monumental tower with colossal foundations. Built in the Hadrianic period it had an apse, a hypocaust, a flanking corridor and attached hall. It may have been a purely commemorative building (following the defeat of Boudica?), a kind of land-locked lighthouse for guidance in a comparatively featureless landscape, or even a central administrative and observation post for what may have been an imperial estate. However, by c.200 the tower had been demolished*

served all or none of these functions. Perhaps even more remarkable is the monumental winged building of palatial proportions on the edge of the Fens at Castor, near Peterborough. Like the Stonea tower it seems curiously displaced in such a comparatively remote area of the province and it is tempting to interpret it as the headquarters of an imperial estate (**67**).

The history of Roman Britain in the early fifth century and the subsequent decay of a Romanized form of life is very obscure. One possibility is that the towns continued to function for several decades with some sort of centralized local authority. At Wroxeter careful excavations have revealed a series of timber buildings erected on the site of the baths *palaestra*. One of these is sufficiently large to suggest that it was of some importance (**68**). Its purpose is entirely unknown but it may be that it was either an administrative centre or even the headquarters of a man who was a local leader. This is not a purely fanciful idea — such evidence as exists (and this includes the Arthurian legends) suggests the gradual emergence of regional kings or chiefs.

Amphitheatres and theatres

The semi-circular classical Roman theatre (used for plays or religious displays) or elliptical amphitheatre (used for gladiatorial contests or military displays) could be something of a

1   *The basilica at Caerwent during excavations. Although substantial traces of the building remain, it was only excavation which exposed them to view*

2   *Mosaic from Bignor villa, west Sussex, depicting a matched pair of cupid gladiators. A secutor, armed with a short sword and shield, fights a retiarius, armed with a trident. The scene forms part of a floor in the apsidal room at the north-west corner of the villa and was laid during the fourth century*

3   *The reconstructed Antonine west gate of the fort at South Shields, Tyne and Wear in north-east England*

4   *Remains of the military bathhouse at Chesters fort on Hadrian's Wall looking north across one of the hot rooms. The structure's exceptional state is due to its being cut into a slope. Post-Roman erosion filled the ruins. See **43** for further details*

5   *The north wall at the Saxon Shore fort of Richborough, showing a clear junction between working parties from the different styles of masonry used*

6   *A short section of Hadrian's Wall rebuilt at the fort of Wallsend. The crenellations and height are hypothetical*

7   *Hadrian's Wall at Limestone Corner (just east of the fort at Carrawburgh). The Wall is beneath the modern road here but the remains of Roman stoneworking can be seen with the forward Wall ditch. The blocks, laboriously hauled out, have been abandoned by the Wall builders who evidently gave up at this spot*

8   *General view east just south of Hadrian's Wall near milecastle 42 showing the rearward Vallum ditch and mound complex stretching into the distance. The Wall ran along the crags to the left. The Vallum was constructed regardless of the terrain, unlike the forward ditch (**colour plate 7**)*

9 *Hadrian's Wall and milecastle 42 at Cawfields. The milecastle's gateways and plans suggest it was built by the II legion* Augusta *(see **colour plates 10, 11**)*

10 *The north gate of milecastle 37 on Hadrian's Wall as presently displayed. The arch stones have been partially restored. Overgrowth has obscured details of the gate jambs (see **52**)*

11 *A view of Hadrian's Wall milecastle 37 as it might have appeared in the second century.*
Painting: author

12 *Reconstructed view of the basilica and forum at Verulamium looking north-west. In the distance*
the theatre and its adjacent triumphal arch can be seen. The town's defences run along the ridge to
the left and the whole site lies on the east-facing slope of the valley of the river Ver. Painting:
author

*13 The Jewry Wall at Leicester. Like Wroxeter's Old Work (**colour plate 14**) it seems to be part of the baths' exercise hall, preserved in this case by being incorporated into a Saxon church*

14 The 'Old Work' at Wroxeter which formed part of the basilican-type exercise hall for the public baths. The gap indicates the former position of the doorway between the hall and the frigidarium. The wall is one of the largest surviving fragments of a Romano-British building.

15 *Remains of the* mansio *baths in the roadside settlement at Wall, Staffordshire (compare with* **78***)*

16 *The Balkerne (west) Gate at Colchester, view from within the city looking west. On the left is the entrance to the southern tower, to the right is the southern pedestrian thoroughfare. The main body of the gate lay immediately to the right.*

17 *The south gate at Silchester looking east. The remains of the city lie to the left, though nothing apart from the defences is visible now except for the extramural amphitheatre* (**70**)

18 *The remains of the south gate at Caerwent from within the city. Compare with* **83, 84**

19 Remains of the walls at Cirencester on the north-east side of the city. The stone wall seems to have been erected after c.200, with the bastions (foundations only remaining) being added more than a century later.

*20 The winged-corridor villa at Plaxtol, Kent, under excavation looking south-west. One of the projecting wing rooms is prominent in the foreground. It may have supported a tower, or simply been roofed over (see **90**)*

21 View of the villa and triconch hall complex at Littlecote as it might have appeared in the fourth century. Painting: author

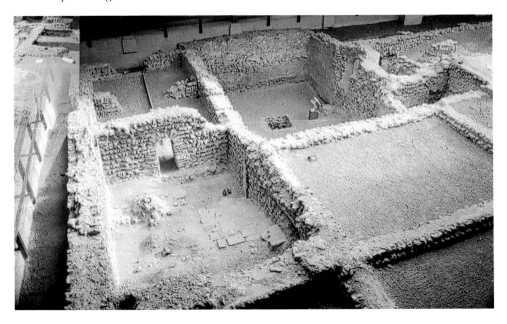

22 Remains of the villa at Lullingstone, Kent, as they survive today. The view is east across the northern part of the house. Note the tiled staircase (centre) leading to a blocked entrance to the 'Deep Room' (centre distance) which started life as a grain store and became a sealed chamber containing ritual items. The Christians' rooms were located in upstairs rooms above this wing

23 *The post-330 mosaic floor at Lullingstone laid in a new apsidal room inserted into the west side of the house. It depicts Europa being abducted by Jupiter, together with a Latin couplet, and a further panel showing the Four Seasons*

24 *Reconstructed view of the Bath Temple Precinct looking west towards the Temple of Sulis Minerva as it may have appeared in the fourth century. The vaulted cover building over the spring stands to the left (compare with* **124-6**). *Painting: author*

25 Reconstructed view of the fourth-century Romano-Celtic temple at Maiden Castle, built within the old Iron Age hillfort. Painting: author

*26 Reconstructed view of the octagonal Temple of Apollo at Nettleton as it may have appeared in its final form, prior to collapse during the fourth century (see also **134-5**). Painting: author*

*27 Reconstructed view of the hilltop temple at Lamyatt Beacon (see **136**). Painting: author*

*28 The remains of the temple of Antenociticus, just outside the fort of Benwell on Hadrian's Wall, looking south-east (see **146**). The temple, the only building associated with the fort to be visible today, lies in a modern housing estate*

*29 Stone abutment of the bridge at Chesters on Hadrian's Wall. Originally on a much smaller scale, the bridge was substantially enlarged in the early third century, incorporating earlier features. As at Willowford (**151-2**) a mill was built into the pier*

*30 Reconstructed view of the bridge at Willowford on Hadrian's Wall. The form of the superstructure, here shown as timber on stone piers, is hypothetical (see also **151-2**). Painting: author*

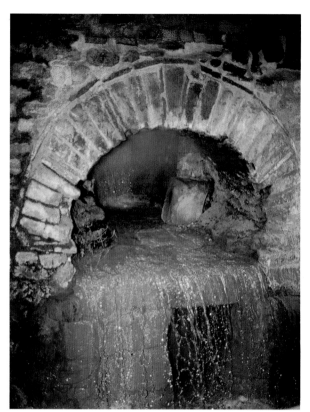

31 Drain for the sacred spring at Bath. The arch was a later modification to the drain which ran out below the capstone beneath, and was perhaps designed to relieve weight or to allow access to the sluices within.

32 The lighthouse, or pharos, at Dover. The upper section is medieval. Compare with **163**

67 Monumental building at Castor, near Peterborough. Little is known about this building but in terms of scale and appearance it is comparable with the stately homes of eighteenth and nineteenth century England. It stood on a hill-slope and looked west across the river Nene and east across the Fens. It is quite possible that it functioned as a residential headquarters for an imperial estate but this is pure speculation and it is equally possible that it was a private establishment. Extensive Roman settlement in the Fens which grew up after the area was drained has been noted but is rarely associated with villas, apart from a small concentration near the town at Water Newton

triumph of arcading and vaulting. These weight-relieving techniques made it possible to support the auditorium and provide a series of passageways through which crowds could be channelled. If a hillside was available then the theatre could be set into the slope.

Theatres and amphitheatres often survive in a very reasonable state of preservation partly because they have continued to serve as public meeting places and partly because of their very substantial construction. This was not always the case — an amphitheatre collapsed at Fidenae in Italy during the reign of Tiberius, killing 20,000 people (Suetonius — who was probably exaggerating — *Tiberius*, 40). A number of major sites around the Mediterranean can boast magnificent examples, such as the amphitheatres at Pompeii in Italy and El Djem in Tunisia, and the theatres at Ephesus (built into a hill) and Aspendus (free-standing) in Turkey.

Amphitheatres

Amphitheatres are known at a number of Romano-British sites, mostly towns. Commonly associated nowadays with the slaughter of animals and gladiators they were probably just as important as centres of public ritual ceremony where the whole community could witness the display. Romano-British amphitheatres surviving in recognizable form were built on earth embankments with stone revetments and timber seats. They were similar to the military *ludus* (**44-5**). At Dorchester in Dorset a Neolithic henge monument now known as Maumbury Rings was adapted (**69**). Henge monuments

68 Late building at Wroxeter. Careful excavation on the site of the baths has revealed the presence of a complex of timber buildings built on the ruined site during the fifth century. In most cases nothing more than the rubble platforms survived but these suggest that the buildings were carefully designed to emulate long-established 'Roman' styles. The centre-piece was a symmetrical winged structure with central entrance. Its identity is completely unknown but its size and central location suggest that it may have served either as an administrative centre for the sub-Roman town, or perhaps as the stronghold of a civic leader who might either have been a chief, or even a bishop. This has been interpreted as evidence for the survival of Roman ways but it is equally significant that the public baths were in ruins

were circular or oval mounds with an internal ditch. The Dorchester example was already around 2,000 years old when the Romans adapted it in the late first century. The central area was lowered and the earth used to raise the banks to around 9m (30ft). Timber was used to reinforce the banks. The site seems to have had a relatively short life and may have been disused by the late second century.

Silchester's amphitheatre also consisted of earth banks and timber revetments but was put up in the third quarter of the first century. Repairs during the second century did not change this basic design and it was only during the third century that stone revetments for the banks were incorporated when the arena was enlarged. Its design was probably fairly

69 Maumbury Rings, Dorchester, Dorset looking north. The site lies outside the Roman town walls and began life as a Neolithic 'henge' monument c.2000 BC. The Romans dug a deeper central area and used the spoil to raise the banks. Timber seating and revetments completed the conversion into an amphitheatre during the late first century

typical and included two entrances opposite one another, and two niches in the arena walls (**70**). These were almost certainly religious, perhaps containing altars or statues, perhaps to Nemesis (Fate) who had an obvious association with winners and losers.

The amphitheatre at Cirencester also lies outside the town and was also based on earth banks. It, too, was built in the late first century but was revetted in stone by the beginning of the second century. Unlike Dorchester's, which was so rapidly disused, this one seems to have remained in occupation until the fifth century. The recently discovered amphitheatre at London lies within the city walls. This can be explained by its proximity to the south-east corner of the fort in London built in the first half of the second century and incorporated into the early third-century walls. It therefore probably began life as a military *ludus* but at present very little of the building has been uncovered and very little can be said about its history. However, it seems to have begun life as a timber structure perhaps as early as *c*.70, being replaced in stone around 125-50.

Even small settlements could enjoy such facilities. Caistor St Edmunds, one of the smallest civitas capitals, seems to have had one, so far only identified from aerial photography south-west of the town. The mining community at Charterhouse in the Mendips was founded by 49 and at some point a modest amphitheatre (so small it may only have been used for bear-baiting or as a cock-pit) had been added to the associated town. Charterhouse is probably not unusual and many minor settlements may have had

101

70 *Entrance to the amphitheatre at Silchester. There were two recesses aligned on the short axis of the arena (centre background). They may have served as preparatory chambers for gladiators but it is more likely that they were vaulted and contained altars dedicated to Nemesis (Fate)*

amphitheatres, attracting visitors from the surrounding countryside. Elsewhere more economical examples have been found like the simple elliptical enclosure within the walls at Caerwent, though the identification here is uncertain — it is just as likely to have been a corral for a cattle or horse market.

All these examples suggest that the amphitheatre was a relatively early introduction into Roman Britain though subsequent histories could be very different. No doubt this reflected local tastes but unfortunately we have practically no specific evidence for the kind of entertainments which went on. That gladiatorial conquests were known is evident from the appearance of a series of matched pairs of cupids on mid-fourth-century mosaics at Bignor villa in West Sussex (**colour plate 2**). A much earlier gladiator's helmet has been found, but not even in association with a Roman settlement, let alone an amphitheatre. Curiously no evidence of any kind of gladiatorial or other gaming equipment has been found in association with an amphitheatre in Britain, even at Silchester's which has been completely cleared only in the last decade. It is worth recalling Vitruvius' comment that in first-century BC Italy it was customary to give gladiatorial shows in the forum (V.1.1) — obviously this has no direct connection with Britain but it does mean that we need not assume that a lack of an amphitheatre meant local people went without such displays.

Theatres
Even fewer theatres are known than amphitheatres. The best-known examples have been identified at Canterbury, Colchester, Gosbecks (Colchester) and Verulamium. We can be

almost certain that they existed at other major towns, particularly London, York, Cirencester and Gloucester, though it is worth bearing in mind that Silchester has yielded no trace of one at all, despite having been almost completely excavated. Recent detective work in London has isolated a probable site in the far south-western corner of the city where the medieval streets of Ludgate Square and St Andrew's Hill curve to the east, perhaps preserving the line of the auditorium; the rear wall of the theatre's stage would have been incorporated into the city wall. Only excavation will confirm the theory. The minor town of Brough-on-Humber had a theatre; we know because a local *aedile* (magistrate) called Marcus Ulpius Januarius commemorated his donation of a new stage to the theatre *c*.140-61 on an inscription (*RIB* 707). However, the theatre has not been found and it may very well be that it was built only of timber; this may explain the lack of evidence for theatres in Britain — they may have been largely temporary affairs, built of wood, and only erected when they were required. Theatrical masks have been found at a number of sites in Britain which have otherwise yielded no evidence for theatres, for example Catterick and Baldock.

Theatres were very far from being purely secular buildings. They were inextricably linked with religious activities because they were used for displays during religious festivals and the enactment of myth. The Verulamium theatre was built in association with a Romano-Celtic temple. The Gosbecks theatre formed part of the religious complex a few miles outside the walls of Colchester. Within the walls of Colchester another theatre lay adjacent to the precinct of the Temple of the Deified Claudius — indeed we know that a theatre (not necessarily the same one, or the same site) was in existence here by the Boudican Revolt of 60/61 because Tacitus mentions it (*Annals*, xiv.32). The theatre at Canterbury also probably lay next to a temple precinct (**72**). Correspondingly, it is a virtual certainty that the temple precinct at Bath would have been accompanied by a theatre, though we have no specific evidence for it yet. Nevertheless we should not forget that there was a rich tradition of secular, sometimes very bawdy, Latin plays which may have eventually become popular as Latin became more widely spoken in Roman Britain.

The Roman theatre was almost invariably a semi-circular auditorium facing a stage. A certain amount of activity took place in the *orchestra* (between the auditorium and the stage). In Britain we have only the traces of wall footings and none of these supply any particularly useful information about the superstructure as the plans show (**71-4**). The reconstruction of the theatre at Canterbury gives an idea of what the building may have looked like in the third century, but the drawing is completely hypothetical and is based only on the dimensions of the plan. The best-known theatre, at Verulamium, also the only one visible to any useful degree (**73-4**), seems to be something of an exception because it lies somewhere between an amphitheatre and a theatre, employing elements of each.

What little evidence we have suggests that very early theatres in Roman Britain were initially built out of solid banks and timber. This was the case at Canterbury where gravel banks supported wooden seats in the first period building, put up *c*.80-90. Only in a reconstruction during the second decade of the third century was the theatre rebuilt in stone (**73-4**). No comparable evidence for Colchester exists but the known stone remains probably belong to the second century, perhaps replacing the one which Tacitus mentions (**71**). The theatre at Verulamium has been excavated completely and this has revealed an

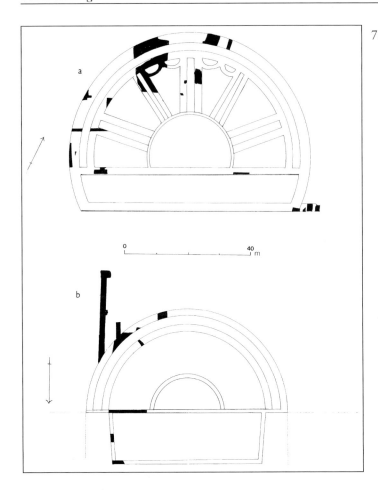

71 *Plans of the theatres at Canterbury (Period 2, c.210-20) and Colchester (second century?). It is apparent that while on one hand very little of the plans of either of these buildings has actually been located, on the other the distinctive form of the theatre makes restoration of the general outline relatively straightforward. The Colchester theatre was built into a north facing slope while the Canterbury theatre was free-standing on a level site*

interesting sequence of activity (**73**). The visible building was put up after *c*.155 on a site in the town centre which was almost certainly reserved for it because no traces of earlier buildings have been found beneath it; this does not mean that the site was unused and it may well be that theatrical activities took place using facilities which have left no trace. The new theatre was not semi-circular and resembled an amphitheatre in being based on an ellipse; however, the stage was inserted into one of the long sides. Although it was revetted in stone the auditorium was built out of earth banks. At the beginning of the fourth century it was substantially enlarged suggesting that considerable demand for its services still existed. We have no specific evidence for what these may have been apart from it being sited next to a temple.

Bath buildings

The process of bathing in Roman times is well-known and briefly discussed in chapter two. Substantial public bath buildings are known to have existed in Roman Britain but none survive to such an extent that we can confidently reconstruct their original

72 *Period 2 theatre at Canterbury, built c. 210-20 (axonometric reconstruction). Less well-known than the theatre at Verulamium, Canterbury's developed theatre seems to have been classical in form though apart from its probable dimensions little more has been discovered. The curious curved walls within the auditorium may have acted as buttresses to support the outer walls. The earlier theatre, built in the late first century, is known to lie beneath and resembled that at Verulamium in having an auditorium built of gravel banks held in place with a retaining wall. The stage is hardly known at all but it flanked a road, on the other side of which seems to have been a temple precinct. The two were probably used together for religious rituals and festivals*

appearance, even though the remains at Leicester and Wroxeter (**75-6**, **colour plates 13**, **14**) include some of the highest standing Roman walls in Britain. Recently more of the huge bath building complex on Huggin Hill in London has been uncovered (**5, 77**) and the recovery of tiles stamped P.P.BR.LON (for the procurator of the province of Britain at London) confirm that this establishment was a major public facility.

Roman baths were traditionally associated with large open exercise areas known as the *palaestra*. A particularly good example survives at the Stabian baths in Pompeii where separate bath suites for men and women were ranged around a colonnaded palaestra. This emphasizes the social nature of the bath building but obviously the design reflected not just a Mediterranean way of life but also a Mediterranean climate. Some of the early public bathhouses in Britain retained the open colonnaded palaestra, for example in the first-century versions built at Silchester and Wroxeter (later buried beneath the forum), though in both these cases the bath-suites and exercise areas were laid out in a linear sequence rather than the former being ranged around the latter. In the second century this idea, common to a number of baths in Gaul, was still in use but the palaestra was built as a covered hall, resembling a basilica, for example at Leicester (**75, colour plate 13**), Wroxeter (**76, colour plate 14**) and Caerwent. It has been suggested that the Wroxeter palaestra is so large that it may have been intended as the town's basilica but that for some reason plans were changed. However, as such similar buildings exist at Leicester and Caerwent this seems unlikely. The Huggin Hill baths in London have not been excavated

Period 1

extra seats

by Period 4

0   20 m

seats

73 *The best known in Britain, Verulamium's theatre was excavated many years ago (74).*
Nevertheless the broad pattern of development seems fairly clear. The site, north of the town's
administrative centre, seems to have been reserved from an early date. Although the theatre was
not put up until the mid-second century the space was apparently empty so the theatre's
construction must have been anticipated. The area set aside is immediately east of a large temple
precinct in Insula xvi. It can be assumed that the theatre was designed to play a role in religious
ceremonies.

In its original form (Period 1) the orchestra was almost circular, and was surrounded by stage
buildings, and earthen banks supporting wooden seats. The banks were revetted with stone walls.
By c.160-80 (Period 2) the theatre had been altered to accommodate extra wooden seats within
part of the orchestra, and an enlarged stage which further reduced the orchestra area. If the theatre
had previously been used in part for activities more appropriate to an amphitheatre (such as bear-
baiting) it can be assumed these pastimes had been removed elsewhere. Seat access was improved
and the stage itself was now rebuilt in Corinthian style.

During the third century (Period 3) the building was kept maintained and external staircases
were added. In the early fourth century (Period 4) the building was altered. The extra seats in the
orchestra were removed, though the retaining wall of the auditorium was moved eastwards to
provide extra seats on the ramps. A new perimeter wall was put up and connected to the old with
a vault. This allowed a new, higher tier of seats to be added to the auditorium. However before
the end of the fourth century the building had become redundant and was used as a public
rubbish tip; this may have been because the pagan activities associated with the building had
ceased

74 The theatre at Verulamium looking south towards the site of the basilica and forum (beneath the church). The stage buildings lie behind and to the left of the surviving column. The track at the left represents the line of Watling Street

in their entirety but the remains uncovered so far suggest that the layout may have been modelled on the more traditional design, even during substantial reconstruction work in the Hadrianic period (**77**). As the building was almost certainly designed as much for members of the provincial government as the public this is hardly surprising.

Bath buildings were a stereotyped form of Roman building with various rooms dedicated to well-known functions such as changing, and the sequence of warm, hot and cold rooms (**42-3**). Sense can usually be made of their remains but no Romano-British examples give any idea of their internal decorations. At Pompeii and Herculaneum in Italy the walls and vaults were decorated with stucco and the individual rooms had statues, wash-basins and benches of carved stone or bronze. We can be sure that this was the case in Roman Britain. The vaults themselves raise an interesting problem. The bathhouse at Beauport Park undoubtedly had vaults in two of its rooms because parts of them were found on the floors where they had fallen; the same occurred at the Great Bath at Bath (**11-12**). Vaults were very important because the warm damp atmosphere was very unsuitable for timber roofs. In small bathhouses and private houses this was not especially important because timber was plentiful. However, with substantial bath-buildings the problems involved in repairs become rather more complicated. It seems very likely that most of the major baths in Roman Britain would have been vaulted. However, this creates a further problem because the vault would then have been exposed to British weather. It is very probable that vaults were protected by walls and timber superstructures supporting tiled roofs. This has formed the basis for the reconstruction of the second-century baths at Wroxeter (**76**), modelled on reconstructions of baths in Rome and Asia Minor.

forum

20m

10

75 *Baths at Leicester (axonometric reconstruction; after Neal), c.140 and later. The complex was begun in the Hadrianic period c.125 when the exercise hall and adjacent rooms were erected. The three parallel rooms (all hot rooms) extending the range were put up in the next 15 years or so. Part of the palaestra's west wall survives to an impressive 9m (30ft) in height and is visible along with part of the baths today, known as the Jewry Wall. The buildings undoubtedly formed the town's main baths, lying adjacent to the forum and basilica*

Inns (*mansio/praetorium*)

Roman administration throughout and between provinces was dependent on the *cursus publicus*, literally 'public passage'. Throughout the Empire inns and staging posts provided accommodation and facilities for people travelling on state business. Apart from the incidental evidence of official lead seals which probably accompanied goods or papers connected with the government, we have no specific evidence for the *cursus publicus* in Roman Britain. Nevertheless in a number of towns a large courtyard building has been

76 Baths at Wroxeter (isometric reconstruction). The complex was a large one and has not been built on since Roman times, which has allowed extensive long-term excavations to take place. The baths were built in the second half of the second century, replacing an earlier project on an adjacent site which was itself demolished to make way for the civic basilica. The new baths included an exercise hall which so resembles a basilica that it has been suggested that it was originally designed to be just that. The changeover of site function may have been connected with problems over water supply.

The main sequence of baths was entered from the south side of the exercise hall through a door. The section of wall with gap for the door survives in situ and is known as the 'Old Work' (**colour plate 14**). This led the bath to the cold bath with its plunge baths at either end, and on to the warm and hot baths. An extension suite of baths ran westwards from the main sequence towards the short-lived outdoor swimming pool). This was used as a rubbish tip by the beginning of the third century perhaps because of the weather. By the fifth century the site was ruinous and had been built over with an enigmatic complex of timber structures (**68**)

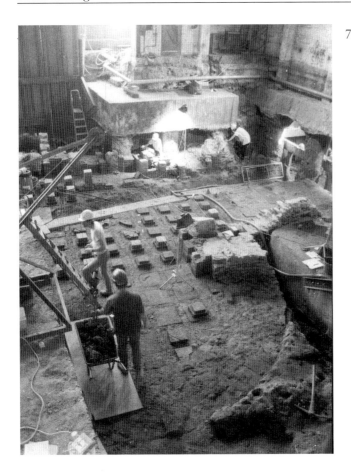

77 *Huggin Hill baths, London, under excavation in 1989. This is only a small part of what appears to have been a huge complex of public baths built close to the river bank during the Flavian reconstruction of the city. A number of procuratorial tiles (see **65**) have been found as well as painted wall-plaster and evidence of sophisticated drainage. Stacks of tiles for supporting the floor can be seen. The room shown was tri-apsidal in form, and the shape of the robbed curved wall of one of them can be seen in the foreground. The site has been re-buried under rammed sand and polythene. See **5** for a detailed view of the walls*

found and this has usually been interpreted as an inn connected with the *cursus*.

At Silchester a large courtyard building faces the end of a road which led to the forum. The complex included a substantial bathhouse and what appears to be a granary. Within the building rooms were arranged in groups of three and access seems to have been available from corridors on both sides of the north and south wings. It was probably built at a comparatively early date because it matches the orientation of the street grid which seems to have been established by the early second century. A similar building is known at Chelmsford though in rather less detail. Here the size of the building is even more obviously disproportionate to the area of the settlement. Two houses at Caerwent might be identified as a *mansio*. Both are larger than most of the other houses and both lie immediately within the town walls beside a main gate (the west and south). Obviously identification of these buildings is very tenuous and it remains quite possible that they are all simply the residences of affluent families. However, as we will see in chapter four, they are somewhat atypical of house development within towns.

The small settlement of Wall lies on Watling Street in Staffordshire. It was one of a number of minor towns on the major route from London to north Wales via Verulamium and Wroxeter. Although the site is known to have had a military origin its principal importance in subsequent years was probably as the location of a *mansio* with an elaborate

78 Mansio *baths at Wall (Letocetum), Staffordshire (see also colour plate 15) in their final phase.*
H = Hot rooms;
W = Warm room;
C = Cold room;
Ch = Changing room;
F = Furnace;
A = Aqueduct outflow

bathhouse. A bath-suite was erected here before the end of the first century but was demolished before ever being used. Subsequently a much more complicated replacement was erected in the second century which was effectively a small version of major civic public baths (**78, colour plate 15**). Excavations on the site suggest that the baths were connected with an adjacent courtyard building which has been interpreted as the *mansio* proper. Built in stone *c.*120 with painted wall-plaster and window glass it is unlikely to have been a private project, and along with its baths is probably the best preserved example of a type of building which would have been commonplace throughout Britain and the Empire.

Monumental arches

The monumental arch is one of the simplest but most expressive architectural statements of Roman civilization. The arch symbolizes the principal element of Roman architecture while its use to commemorate some event, usually a military success, embodies the basis of Roman expansion and power. The arches of Titus, Septimius Severus and Constantine the Great in Rome are amongst the city's finest monuments — as a group they are complemented by a host of equal and lesser examples known elsewhere in Italy and in other provinces.

At least six are known to have existed in Roman Britain but only one is known in

DIVO·TI·CLAVDIO·DRVSI·F
CAESARI · AVGVSTO · GERMANICO ·
PROVINCIA · BRITANNIA · F

79 *Monumental arch at Richborough. This building seems to have been one of the few truly impressive classical structures erected in Roman Britain. Sadly only its foundations have survived along with a number of fragments of the arch itself. The reconstruction here is therefore purely hypothetical but the original would have been of similar scale and appearance.*

Assumed to be the site of Aulus Plautius' landing in 43 Richborough would have been of obvious political significance. By c.85 or shortly after, with Agricola's activities in the north at their climax, a decision seems to have been taken to build an arch at the gateway to Britain. From this point Watling Street ran west to London and into the heart of Roman Britain. Arches were frequently used to celebrate military success and to embellish a major route.

This arch was quadrifons *(a four-way arch). Traces of its superstructure show that it was encased in marble and topped by monumental bronze statuary. By the mid-third century the arch was converted into a signal tower, and surrounded by ditches. Within another generation the whole site had been cleared to make way for the Saxon Shore fort* (**46**)

*80 The west gate (Balkerne Gate) of Colchester (see also **colour plate 16**). The gateway started life as a monumental free-standing twin portalled arch/gate on the main road to London, built c.75. Two Romano-Celtic temples built on either side of the approach road would have enhanced its appearance to a traveller. When the city walls were built in the early second century (?) the gate was enlarged with pedestrian passages and flanking gate towers and incorporated into the walls. In the fourth century the gate was made redundant by extending the ditch of the defences across the old London road, cutting off vehicular access*

architectural detail. Its original site is unknown but was somewhere in London. The sculptures which survive from it suggest that it was actually an entrance into a religious precinct (**148**). Of the other five, three stood in Verulamium and a fourth formed the first period of the Balkerne Gate at Colchester (**80, colour plate 16**). However, the fifth formed a dramatic gateway to the province of *Britannia* at Richborough. The Richborough arch was probably the most impressive at around 28m (90ft) in height but it was demolished in the late third century to make way for the Saxon Shore fort (**79**). It was probably built in the late first century but within two centuries it was being used as a signal tower before finally being cleared away. Now only the concrete base for the passageways through the arch survive but a few architectural fragments were found during excavation. Reconstruction is extremely difficult because these fragments are so small that a number of possibilities exist, though it is certain that it was a four-way arch, had marble veneer and a bronze statue group on top. The Verulamium examples were simpler and smaller single portal arches, perhaps about 12m (40ft) high. Two were built on Watling Street to mark the town's first-century limits around the time that the third-century walls were put up.

81 North gate of Lincoln. This is the only Roman gate in Britain to retain an arch from one of its main thoroughfares. It was built in the third century and rising ground levels have diminished its scale. Note how the pedestrian way drops to allow access through the foot traffic arch. The view is from within the city. The smaller blocks of stone in the higher courses are medieval work. There would probably have been a corresponding pair of arches on the left for wheeled and foot traffic going in the opposite direction

The other was built in the fourth century, also over Watling Street, between the theatre and macellum.

Defences

Like the forts of the Saxon Shore the walls of the towns of Roman Britain have survived in part because they continued to serve a purpose long after they were originally built. The walls either formed the defences of medieval successors or proved less easy targets for stone robbers. So at Silchester and Verulamium the city walls are the main visible survivals of the towns though they are for the most part only ragged, fragmentary cores.

Town defences consisted of walls, gates, ditches and ramparts. This simple format conceals the fact that Romano-British town defences remain a very awkward archaeological problem, made worse by a modern tendency to try and interpret them as a unified provincial or civic response to a single problem. It is as well to make it clear that

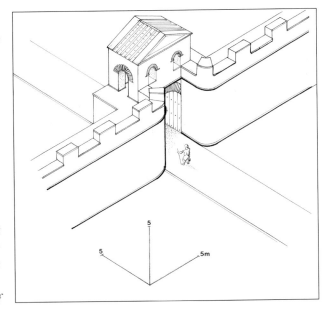

82 *North-east gate ('Duncan's Gate') at Colchester (isometric reconstruction based on the revised elevation by Hull). This was a single portal gateway built behind the line of the city wall (built in the early second century) which turns in to meet it. A large portion of the fallen superstructure remained in* situ *and showed that there was a guardroom with at least two windows above. Whether it extended right across, or just above the arch (as shown) is unknown as is the type of roof*

we have no inscriptional or literary evidence for the erection of any town defences, gate or wall, at any time. All we have is Tacitus' record of how Colchester fell easily to Boudica in 60 because it had not been provided with fortifications (*Annals*, xiv.31). Archaeology has confirmed that the defences of the former legionary fortress were filled in after the colony was established in *c*.47. When Vitruvius described city walls he did not perceive them as a response to an immediate threat, rather they are described as a routine part of establishing a town once the site had been chosen and communications established (V.5.1).

Unfortunately walls are not generally associated with much in the way of archaeological evidence except for material swept up in earth banks behind walls, and, naturally, this includes mixed-up rubbish of almost any earlier date that happened to be lying around. Tolerably reliable evidence can only be found where the walls, or gates, overlie some earlier building or feature, and where a component of the defences such as a gate-tower contains dateable evidence of occupation. The underlying feature will give a 'time after which' (*terminus post quem*) the defences were built complicated by the presence of earlier, residual, pottery; the occupation evidence will give a 'time before which' (*terminus ante quem*) the defences must have been built. Needless to say such evidence is rare, especially as underlying evidence is generally only available by demolishing part of the defences. Worse still is the fact that it is clear that gates and walls were not necessarily contemporary (*see* **80**).

Walls and ramparts

It does seem to have been the case that some first-century towns were defended by earth ramparts, for example at Chichester, Silchester, Verulamium and Winchester. Verulamium seems to have been founded by *c*.49 but its early earth defences were rapidly outgrown. The other towns may have all been settlements within the client kingdom of the Atrebates up to the late first century. These early examples, and also towns which grew up in former

*83 Elevation and plan of the south gate at Caerwent from within the town walls (after Ward but reconstructed) (see also **84**, and **colour plate 18**). This gate has survived in excellent condition largely because it was completely blocked up in antiquity (not shown here). As a result a number of the arch stones survive in situ. The detailed lower part of the drawing shows the section which is still visible today. The rest of the tower is hypothetical. The walls were at least as high as shown because the south wall of Caerwent stands in part to a height of 5.5m (17ft). The stone curtain seems to have been added to a pre-existing earth rampart by the late second century. A drain ran beneath the roadway*

forts and fortresses, like Lincoln and Gloucester, were the only settlements to have defences. There does not seem to have been any concerted policy to build them; instead Romano-British towns were able to spread naturally along the roads and rivers which gave them life.

Towards the end of the second century many of the major settlements were surrounded by an earth rampart and ditch; there are exceptions, for example Leicester, but here the ramparts may just not have been located yet. Subsequently, and this may have been much later, stone walls were added by cutting back the rampart and installing a stone revetment. This meant that the towns generally retained the size to which they had grown except in a few cases, like Caistor-by-Norwich where the walled area was smaller. It may well be that the Romano-British earthworks reflect a more leisurely precautionary approach to an unsettled northern frontier during the second half of the second century. As official permission was necessary for building town defences this suggests that the decision was a provincial one, rather than a series of individual schemes. But the later second century was not notably more unsettled than the early second century and we should not necessarily feel the need to connect an archaeological fact with what little historical information we have. It is equally conceivable that the building of town

84 Detail of the south gate at Caerwent from within the town walls as it appears today

'defences' (after all, we do not know that they were specifically defensive) was connected with civic prestige, or even the control of traffic for the purpose of levying local taxes.

Evidence from stone gates does not necessarily date stone defences because stone gates were often erected at around the same time as the earth defences, for example the 'London' and 'Chester' gates at Verulamium. But fortunately Verulamium is one of the very few places which has produced evidence for a 'time before which' the stone walls must have been built. The 'Silchester gate' was built in one with the stone walls, and one of its towers contained a coin hoard ending in 273; clearly the tower was in existence by 273 or within a few years after. A tower on the walls of London contained a coin-forger's equipment which included a mint condition coin of Caracalla struck *c*.213-17; while hoards are unlikely to be left for very long after the date of the latest coin without being added to, a coin forger may have deliberately used 'older coin' because of their metal content. So it could have been 10, 15 or more years old when lost. At any rate it is unlikely that London's walls were much later than *c*.225-30. Consequently it seems likely that if there was a general policy of adding stone walls, it took place during the first half of the third century or later. If we bear in mind Vitruvius' attitude towards city walls, mentioned above, it is equally plausible to interpret them as just the next project on the list once all

85 Caistor-by-Norwich, bastion in the west stretch of town wall now half lost in the wood which clings to the ramparts. The bastion stands to a height of 3m (10ft) and although robbed of all its facing stones shows the method of construction with flint nodules, cement and tile courses. Since this photograph was taken, the defences have been cleared of undergrowth and a public footpath marked out

the public buildings were up. This fits the broad time scale for the erection of the basilicas and forums; in fact if we take Vitruvius at face value Romano-British city walls were put up really rather late, and should have been built when the towns were laid out (V.5.1).

As far as the walls are concerned we have very little evidence for their original appearance. Stone-robbing has usually left us with rubble cores (**colour plate 17**) while medieval repairs have often long concealed Roman work. However, there are the remarkably well preserved remains at Caerwent (**83-4, colour plate 18**) and some fragments at Cirencester where the facing stones have survived (**colour plate 19**). Defences may have been brightened up with decorative patterns of brickwork, well-known on the continent, for example at Le Mans in France. The church of St Mary Northgate in Canterbury incorporates part of the Roman city wall into its north wall, including crenellations which may be of Roman date. If correct this suggests that the walls could be patrolled. Excavations on the Bishop's Palace site in Chichester showed that the stone wall had been built without foundations. Some of the lower sections of the London walls have been well-preserved behind later deposits and these show, for example at Tower Hill, that the wall, built of squared ragstone facing blocks, a rubble core and double or triple courses of bonding tiles, stood on a chamfered sandstone plinth.

A particularly interesting development of late date is the so-called riverside wall in London. The early third-century wall enclosed the city on the east, north and west. The

86 South wall of Caerwent looking east showing one of the six prominent semi-octagonal bastions. The bastions are not bonded to the wall and were therefore built later. There were more bastions on the north wall, but apparently none on the east and west walls

river Thames formed the southern defence but in the fourth century a new wall was added right along the river front. It included a great deal of re-used masonry, preserving a large quantity of sculptured stone from buildings we would otherwise have no knowledge of. It was up to 3m (10ft) and was built in part on timber piles which have made it possible to use radiocarbon and dendrochronology dating techniques which suggest that it post-dates 330. It was not necessarily built all at once because some parts were built carefully from new masonry. It does not appear to have had a rampart because it collapsed northwards, back onto the slope up from the river. It was probably part of the same phase of defensive work as the bastions (see below) commonly associated with Theodosius in 367.

Gates

Gates are more complicated because it is even more difficult to be certain of their original appearance and a large number of different types of plan have been recovered. Gates were not necessarily defensive — they could form impressive statements of civic pride. The incorporation of masonry gates into earth defences suggests this, for example the 'Balkerne Gate' at Colchester (**80, colour plate 16**) and the 'London' gate at Verulamium. Typically a major town gate had four passages: two large ones for wheeled traffic in the middle and two smaller on either side for foot traffic. Only the north gate at Lincoln retains an example of each still standing (**81**). These were flanked themselves by two 'towers' which could project in front of the passageways but this was not always the case. There may have been guardrooms above the passageways but even if so we do not know if these were as high as the towers. The Balkerne Gate at Colchester is particularly interesting because it seems to have begun life as a free-standing monumental gate in the manner of a triumphal arch with two portals, built *c*.75. Only in the second century were the foot passages and towers added when the gate was incorporated into the new city walls. Lesser gates, like the south gate at Silchester were single-portalled (**colour plate 17**).

Towns often had minor gates too and these were usually of 'single portal' design. Sometimes the walls turned in to meet the gate, for example at Duncan's Gate in Colchester (**82**), or they stood more or less flush with the wall, for example at the south gate in Caerwent (**83-4, colour plate 18**). Such minor gates could be added at quite late dates. The west gate of the lower town at Lincoln was cut through the city wall in the early fourth century as a straightforward archway; subsequently projecting rectangular towers were added which made use of redundant carved stonework from other buildings.

Bastions

In *c*.367 Count Theodosius began the reorganization of the defences of Roman Britain. This has been thought a likely explanation for the addition of bastions to town walls; the effect would have been to make them resemble the forts of the Saxon Shore (see chapter two) and it is reasonable to assume that they too were designed to support defensive artillery. Of course dating is simply not precise enough and there are no relevant inscriptions which are even rarer from this date than any other time. Bastions could be solid or hollow (**85**). They were built out of any available stone and projected from the existing walls in either semi-circular or polygonal form (**colour plate 19**). London's bastion 10 in Camomile Street was found to contain not just building blocks from former buildings but also tombs; bastion 2 in Trinity Place contained the blocks from the tomb of the first-century procurator Classicianus (*RIB* 12). This does tend to suggest an element of crisis and it is perhaps more legitimate to associate the bastions with a specific historical episode than the building of the walls. The bastions on the north and south walls at Caerwent (**86**) are particularly interesting because they survive to heights of up to 3m (10ft). They do not bond in with the existing walls, thus demonstrating that they were a later addition, and holes in the stonework show where the scaffolding was inserted during construction.

Other defensive works

The division between military and civil building is very fine when it comes to discussing any other defensive building. Signal towers have been discussed in chapter two but it is worth noting that civil defences may have been augmented by signal towers at some distance from the towns. Any decision to build them probably came at the same time as the decision to build the bastions. Only one is known for certain — at Shadwell, about 1.4km (0.9 miles) east of the Roman city wall, where the 8m (26ft) square stone tower, surrounded by a timber palisade, had a view downstream and of the city. It may have been one of a series but no others have yet been located. Dating is very uncertain but the tower may have been built as early as the late third century.

4 Houses

Introduction

The houses of Roman Britain were of many different types. Not only did these dwellings reflect the relative wealth of their owners, but they also reflected the cumulating or declining wealth of individuals and their families. Consequently, some houses were both substantial and extravagant while others were extremely modest. In between there is a very large number of houses which represent an almost infinite range of variations on a very few basic schemes. While most of the larger houses are of third- or fourth-century date and had their origins in simple buildings, houses at all levels of sophistication appear throughout the period. From a structural point of view they present a number of problems arising from the lack of any surviving examples and the fact that most excavated plans consist of nothing more sophisticated than variations on rows of square or rectangular rooms.

Problems of interpretation

We do not know for certain the name of a single owner of a specific house in Roman Britain so we cannot know if any house remained in the possession of a single family. Tantalizingly the Antonine Itinerary (an early third-century route book of the Empire) preserves the name *Villa Faustini*, a place somewhere between Caistor-by-Norwich and Colchester, but we do not know where the actual site lies. Presumably Faustinus was the owner or builder of a large villa estate. A building stone carved with the name *Firmini* from the house at Barnsley Park may conceivably represent the owner's name (i.e. *[Villa] Firmini* = 'the villa of Firminus') but is equally likely to indicate the name of the mason or builder (i.e. *[Officina] Firmini* = 'the workshop of Firminus').

We do not even know if any one particular house was owned by someone and let to another. We do not know if country houses were usually owned by town dwellers who employed bailiffs to manage the estate (if one existed). In cases where the houses were particularly big, or where there were at least two distinct residential blocks (for example Sparsholt), we are almost certainly dealing with the homes of two or more families who may have been related, or perhaps one employing the other. Such evidence as exists from other parts of the Empire (mostly graffiti from Pompeii and papyri from Egypt) suggests that letting parts of urban property to various different tenants was quite normal. These might be shops downstairs and accommodation upstairs. An alternative was to purchase a share in a fraction of a property, similar to the way in which several people might club together to buy a flat in a block today. Evidence from rural sites is even rarer. The first-century writer Columella, in describing the operation of country farm property, referred to the use of either tenant farmers or slave overseers to run a farm on behalf of the

70-100

late 2nd/early 3rd

c. 300+

h = 1st cent hut

s = Saxon post-holes

b = burials

87 Brixworth, Northamptonshire (isometric reconstruction). The plan (after Turland) shows the development from a first century round house, through the Roman period and finally to traces of Saxon settlement. The first rectangular house, built c.70-100, had painted walls, an unusual feature for so early a date. Despite the addition of a bath-suite in the fourth century this was apparently never used. The final plan is of a slightly haphazard house, an interesting mixture of pretensions and economy. A nearby out-building contained traces of bronze working in the late second century and most of the third. The building's modest scale suggests that the 'estate' was never an especially rich one even though it survived the period landowner (*On Agriculture*, 1, 6-9). It is clear from what he says that tenant farmers might actually live in a town and use their own slaves to operate the farm, though this was better avoided. Clearly he is describing a situation in which very wealthy landowners were dealing with several, dispersed, components of their huge estates. There may well have been some families in this position in Roman Britain but we will never know the extent to which the rural houses were occupied by tenants or landowners.

Only one legible 'monumental' inscription has been recovered which certainly refers to the actual structure. Found on the site of the Combe Down villa near Bath it records the restoration of a headquarters building (*principia*) by an imperial freedman called Naevius during the reign of Caracalla (212-17; *RIB* 179). It is therefore almost certain that the 'villa' was actually the headquarters of an imperial estate, and a long-established one at that. This means either that the land was inherited by the imperial family, or that it had been confiscated. Milestones, re-used as building material, have been found at Rockbourne in Hampshire and an inscription dedicated to Carinus, as Caesar (heir), in 282-3 at Clanville, also in Hampshire, may either be another re-used milestone or indicate imperial ownership (*RIB* 98). Apart from this we are left only with slogans or couplets on mosaics (and these are generally religious or literary in content) and occasional graffiti on metal vessels, pottery or building materials. We do not even know 'how much' a house was worth though a cryptic text preserved on a wooden tablet found in a well at the Chew Stoke villa seems to record the sale of land (*RIB* 2443.13).

So, all that we have to work from rarely consists of anything more than the foundations of walls, their footings and the rubbish that was left behind. From this an archaeologist has to establish approximately when the first house was built on the site, what it was used for, and if applicable, how it changed in succeeding years. It may be possible to make estimates of the numbers of people who may have lived there at any one time, and perhaps make an assessment of their relative standard of living. For houses involved in farming it may be possible to estimate the size of the estate but unless there are obvious natural boundaries or traces of man-made boundaries this is particularly difficult. The numbers of rooms may not always be very clear-cut because internal divisions, even in a stone-built house, may have been of lathe and plaster and these leave traces which are difficult to identify. Doorways and entrances are elusive in a house barely surviving above its foundations. Even establishing what individual rooms were used for is more difficult than it might seem because unless artefactual or other evidence of say, cooking, is found it will be quite difficult to be sure which room was the kitchen.

However, in the better-appointed houses, it is probably reasonable to assume that larger decorated rooms were the principal reception rooms such as the *triclinium* (dining room). It is also worth remembering that a single house building may have been only one component of a residence that actually consisted of several different buildings (such as barns, baths and stables). This was certainly the case with many rural villas but early archaeologists tended to chase walls, making it unlikely that extra buildings would be located. The large 'courtyards' at Stroud and Woodchester for example (**95, 111**) may really be very misleading. The plan of the Bancroft site may be much more representative (**100**). Even apparently separate establishments may have been connected (see Stanwick below).

88 *Plan of the house at Quinton, Northants (after Taylor). A late first-century rectangular stone building was found to overlie an early first-century circular timber house. It is clear that the roundhouse would have had to be demolished before the stone house was built. The later house remained in occupation until c.160-70*

Emergence of Romanized housing

It was not until the late first century that a number of pre-Roman sites began to show a change in living habits. This is hardly surprising; the invasion only took place in 43, and it took the Boudican Revolt in 60 to shake up the Roman administration into a more positive frame of mind. Tacitus tells us that Agricola exhorted the British to build *domos* (= homes; *Agricola*, 21.70) and this almost certainly represents policy well-established by this time (*c*.78-84). Such an approach was designed to encourage the British to perceive Roman rule as beneficial in an obviously material sense; at the same time the level of manufactured imports leapt, a fact testified right across south-eastern Britain but especially in the nascent towns like London and Verulamium. In archaeological terms the change on any particular site from a pre-Roman roundhouse to a rectangular stone structure with room divisions may seem abrupt. The change is often described as an 'early' one if the evidence points to a late first-century date. On the other hand this also represents the passing of a whole generation. We may know nothing of the ownership of any one house but a great deal can happen to the fortunes of a farmer in 30 years and the attitudes of an adult son who had grown up after the year 43 might have been quite radically different in terms of expectations of standard of living.

Most identified first-century houses are relatively simple and have been identified through analysis of the plan of a later, more elaborate, house. There is no convenient way

89 *Reconstruction of the winged-corridor house at Redlands Farm, Stanwick, Northants. The building suffered a partial collapse and one of the fallen gable ends was left where it fell, allowing an unusually confident reconstruction of the house's original height and appearance. The stone may have been rendered or whitewashed*

of discerning those belonging to a 'Romanized' household but it seems reasonable to begin with those which use approximately straight walls, roughly right-angled corners and two or more rooms.

This raises the general point of 'influence' and distribution of typologically distinct varieties of houses. When we are dealing with military or public buildings it is easier to perceive the dynamic of influence through official organizations. With private houses this is not so apparent. Certain types of houses, like the 'winged corridor' or the 'aisled', appear throughout lowland Britain and in the Romanized parts of northern Europe. It is a little too easy to read more into this than can really be justified. As we will see later the plans of most houses in Roman Britain were no more than elaborations on rows of rooms arranged in wings. There is comparatively little one can do with such an arrangement without involving techniques of vaulting or requiring extremely complicated roofing arrangements (see below). And of course we have very little idea of what the houses actually looked like — it is possible that two typologically similar plans were originally two completely different houses. The reconstructions of Littlecote (**91**) and Stroud (**95**) show

how different these can be. Even if house types were copied from one area to another we should remember that influence might range from casual observation to professional research and even individual inspiration.

Although they lie outside the brief of this book there are two very important points to be borne in mind when considering individual buildings. Firstly, recent archaeological techniques have begun to reveal hitherto unsuspected timber houses in towns. Fourth-century Wroxeter is one of the best examples and it raises the unavoidable conclusion that

90 (opposite) Winged-corridor house at Sedgebrook, Plaxtol, Kent — a typical example of a modest country house, probably associated with farming. The site looks west across the fertile valley of a tributary of the river Medway. Traces of a much more substantial house are known less then a mile to the south possibly forming the centre of an estate which included this house.

The house seems to have been built by the early second century though apart from the cellar, which contained several complete (but broken) late second-century samian vessels, the house was disappointingly devoid of datable finds. A handful of barbarous Carausian coins (287-93) found in the roof-fall and a single early fourth-century coin serve only to indicate that the house may have remained in occupation that long. The house seems to have been carefully cleared before being abandoned. It apparently fell down of its own accord and the entire site was covered with shattered roof tile. The illustration shows the house as it may have appeared in its final stage of development, looking south-west. The precise lay-out of the rooms make it hard to reconstruct the building with towers (see 91), therefore the opportunity has been taken to show a roof which is actually a great deal simpler

town plans, like Silchester's, are very misleading. In other words the density of urban housing, and therefore the population, may have been much higher than we can ever really know. The second is the density of rural settlement. The villa site at Stanwick in Northamptonshire has been the subject of recent close scrutiny. This has revealed a villa with many subsidiary buildings, including a bailiff's headquarters (?), contained within an extensive series of enclosures. This has been described by the excavator as a 'villa and its related "village"'. In other words, the population of this one estate may have been much bigger than a simple examination of the villa building and its immediate environs would ever have suggested. This has considerable implications for interpreting the Romano-British countryside as a whole.

The architecture of Romano-British houses

However complicated Romano-British houses became, the large majority of excavated plans are only elaborations of a very simple kind of linear structure: literally a line of rooms. The simple house at Brixworth (**87**) and the vastly more sophisticated house at Woodchester (**111**) are two versions of the same thing. Most houses began as a handful of rooms laid out in a row in a rectangular plan, for example Quinton (**88**). They generally had stone footings, though some early examples of apparently isolated bathhouses with a short period of occupation may have been associated with unlocated timber houses belonging to families who were never able to afford long-term development. Houses in the countryside and of certain first-century date are often found to have succeeded a roundhouse, possibly of pre-conquest date. Most of these houses underwent some sort of elaboration at some point in their histories. Generally this involved attaching a corridor to one side so that rooms could be accessed individually. The corridor usually had a chamber at either end, creating a symmetrical facade to the house, and is now known as the winged-corridor villa (**89, 90**), though what this actually meant in terms of appearance is not quite as clear-cut as orthodox reconstructions imply. Houses developed to this extent either stayed as they were or were subsequently enlarged by extending the wings, and eventually a fourth wing might enclose a courtyard. Then the original two wings might be extended further and a second courtyard created.

In architectural terms all that was happening was that the basic format was being extended, rather than being radically altered. Instead of rows of rooms being added adjacent to the existing structure, new rows were strung out at right angles. This was probably because of two quite straightforward factors, in addition to some of the points raised in chapter one about Romano-British architects. Firstly there was little pressure on space, or at least this appears to have been the case. We have no evidence for the kind of pressure on space that created the multi-storey apartment blocks in Ostia (the port of Rome). So a house could spread as space required. This even seems to have happened in a number of Romano-British towns. Secondly there was the question of roofing. The only means of spanning very wide rooms or buildings is to use exceptionally long timbers, or to use vaults. Vaults required colossal walls to absorb the lateral thrusts, even if the vault was built with hollow tiles (**10**). There is very little evidence for them in Roman Britain apart from bathhouses, both public and private. The only alternative was wood but, until the invention of the hammer-beamed roof at the end of the fourteenth century, any wooden roof could be no wider than the length of the longest timbers available. In an island probably still undergoing extensive deforestation, timber of the right size would have been available. But then there would have been the problems of re-roofing the existing structure to accommodate new rooms, and lighting internals rooms. In any case it is quite possible that the additional wings were used to house sons and their families, servants, or even tenants and a degree of separateness would have been desirable.

We have no idea of whether these houses had upper storeys. Sometimes it is claimed that excavated walls in specific cases are too thin to have supported an upper floor. But the walls may have been built with lower courses of stone only, the upper parts being made out of timber frameworks resembling medieval half-timbered houses. And it is quite possible that in any one case there was an upper storey but the stone supporting walls had not been built strongly enough, creating structural problems for which we would have no evidence.

On the other hand the stone walls in another house may have supported only a single storey but had been built more thickly than was strictly necessary (it is of course sensible to make a building capable of absorbing more stress than it is ever likely to have to endure). In other words it is impossible to say that any particular building had an upper storey or not unless there is incontrovertible evidence like the base of a staircase or collapsed superstructure. All that can generally be said is that buildings were usually enlarged by adding wings and this implies, but nothing more, that if space was needed it was gained by growing sideways rather than upwards. A curious building at Chalk, probably an out-building of an undiscovered villa, preserved traces of a wooden staircase but this ran down to a cellar. At Littlecote a stretch of wall running from one of the wing towers parallel to the corridor may be the remains of an external staircase (**91**). Within a building, stairwells may be represented by narrow rectangular rooms in the plan.

Many houses had at least one 'cellar' like the Chalk example. Here the room had niches for lighting from lamps and a ramp probably used for rolling barrels down into storage. At

91 Facade of the villa at Littlecote, looking west (c.360; based on a painting by L. Thompson), developed from a second-century winged-corridor house. Remodelling of the wings of the house involved thickening of walls and the plan is not particularly easy to interpret. However a wall running north from the south wing may have represented external stair access to the south wing. This and the thickened walls may mean that the wings were in tower form as shown here. The clerestory windows in the main block would have been essential to light the internal rooms. Recent work has extended knowledge of the surrounding area. The villa was approached through a masonry gatehouse built about 75m (250ft) to the east in c.300. A barn sited a few metres south of the midway point between the villa and the gatehouse was built c.260 but underwent substantial alterations. These included room divisions and a small bath suite so it may have been converted into some sort of residence

Lullingstone the so-called 'Deep Room' began life in the late first century probably as a similar storage area (**92, colour plate 22**). By the late second century a re-modelling of the house involved converting this chamber into a cult room containing a niche painted with water nymphs. Subsequently it became a repository for marble busts, probably belong to an earlier owner. Such rooms created problems of their own: at Plaxtol the cellar was prone to flooding and had to be equipped with a drain which when cleared helped the excavation of the site (**90, colour plate 20**).

As ever there are exceptions. The aisled houses, or at least those which appeared to be 'aisled' or 'basilican' in form, are the most important group. The building type appears elsewhere in Britain as the military *principia*, the public basilica, and the Mithraic temple and as part of the Fishbourne house, its earliest manifestation in a 'domestic' context. The type is known throughout Britain but curiously it usually appears as an outbuilding to the main house (and as such is assumed to have served a non-domestic purpose) for example at Llantwit Major (**94**). There are three areas though where examples which seem to have been a dwelling house are grouped: in Hampshire, the Fens and around the river Humber. In the houses concerned part of the aisled 'hall' appears to have been fitted with rooms, and in some cases equipped with a bath-suite. In many of these cases it is quite likely that

92 *The villa house at Lullingstone, Eynsford, Kent, as it may have appeared during the first and second centuries AD. The Lullingstone house is the* only *building of Roman date in Britain to contain certain evidence for Christian religious activity. However this belonged to the final phase. a = The house as built c.80-90. The site lies at the bottom of the western slope to the River Darenth which runs north to the Thames Estuary. The slope was cut back to provide a level terrace for the house above the flood plain. The late first-century house seems to have been a 'winged-corridor' type which included the 'deep room' (here shown cut away, and see* **colour plate 22***). At this date the 'deep room' seems to have acted as a grain store with access on a ramp from the entrance to the house, and a staircase to the west.*

b = The house in the second century. A bath suite has been attached to the south on levelled land gained by cutting further into the hillside — a well further south supplied the necessary water. Immediately to the west a thatched hut supported on tree trunks seems to have contained the kitchens — subsequently it became a tannery (during the third century while the rest of the house was apparently unoccupied). The northern side of the house was radically altered to adapt the 'deep room' as a cult chamber. A niche was cut into the wall to contain a painting of nymphs, and a deep pit sunk into the floor.

Occupation of the house proper is thought to have ceased by the beginning of the third century. However the later owners found possessions of their predecessors left behind. These included two marble portrait busts of second-century style and fine workmanship. They portray two aristocratic Roman men, probably relatives, and suggest that the second-century occupants were of high status. The combination of such a modest house and such remarkable objects implies that it may have been owned as an occasional residence by a wealthy person the resident family shared their roof with the farm animals. This is not unusual in other cultures right up to modern times — it is both convenient and secure. The Stroud house is one of the most curious, for despite its aisled interior it seems to have been built to look like a 'winged-corridor' villa, or one with wing towers (**95**). The aisled house at Meonstoke was extended at one end but the new wall collapsed, preserving a facade of decorative brickwork (**96**).

The remarkable villa at Lullingstone is also one of the most unusual in structural terms (**92**, **93, colour plates 22**, **23**) because alterations to the original winged-corridor version were very compressed and the end-product was a far from conventional plan. However, the site is severely restrictive. The first house on the site was at least as early as mid-first century but it occupied a narrow terrace between the river Darenth and a steep hillside. Some later expansion of the Roman house involved cutting back the hillside but it would have been quite impossible to extend the house in the conventional manner. Radical alterations in the fourth century changed its appearance but it actually grew very little in absolute size. Even the bath-suite fell into disuse long before the rest of the house. In the fourth century it contained a strange combination of pagan mosaic material alongside rooms apparently used as a Christian house church (**colour plate 23**). Lullingstone's site is highly unusual and hence it is a highly unusual house. Even so there may have been far more houses like Lullingstone but building into a hillside almost inevitably means that the ruins are eventually covered by material running off the hill, making the site almost unidentifiable. Lullingstone was only located because the excavator was looking for a building to explain a gap in an otherwise regular series of Roman structures in a single river valley. Houses built on flat open sites are more likely to be found, and those were the ones with room to grow.

Even if most known Romano-British houses were variations on elementary themes their owners sometimes incorporated very extravagant extensions. These were usually the bath-suites and their designs may, in a few cases, have dwarfed the main house. The villas at Lufton (**97**) and Holcombe are the best examples particularly at Lufton where the octagonal plunge bath seems outrageously ostentatious compared to the house. At Ashtead the bathhouse formed a separate structure altogether (**98**) which reminds us that rural houses in particular were usually only one component, albeit the main one, of a complex of buildings. Of course this would have depended on the kind of estate being operated. At Ashtead one of the sources of income seems to have been the manufacture of tiles, and a kiln is associated with the house. The house at Gatcombe seems to have been involved in exploiting local iron ores, and at Chew Stoke lead extraction seems to have taken place. At Bancroft (**99**, **100**) extensive stripping and excavations have revealed a number of outbuildings which also include a mausoleum (**166**). At Llantwit Major the house was one of several buildings bordering on an L-shaped courtyard (**94**). However, we have no knowledge of the size of any estates though it has been suggested that the capacity of granaries or natural boundaries may be helpful. Frere has quoted a possible figure of 400ha for Ditchley based on the granary size, and 800ha for Bignor. Research conducted around the house at Ditchley has shown that it is surrounded by stretches of dykes of Roman date mostly about 1 mile (1.6km) away. Some of the dykes have terminals and the space in between is still filled with woodland. Together these suggest that the villa estate was

93 *Lullingstone as it may have appeared during the late fourth century, before its final phase. During the third century only the old kitchens were in use as a tannery. By the close of the third century the house had been reoccupied and a number of structural alterations and additions were effected. Firstly the marble busts were placed in the deep room together with a number of pieces of evidence for cult activity. Access from within the house was sealed off (but see below). A granary was built between the house and the river with a long axis at right angles to that of the house. It was about 25m (80ft) long by 10m (32ft) wide and contained a raised floor to allow the grain to dry. About 300 a man and a woman, in their early twenties, were buried in lead coffins together with grave goods. A pit was dug on a terrace above the house and over it a mausoleum was constructed. The coffins were placed in a wooden chamber at the bottom of the pit and sealed. The circular shrine was dismantled.*

After c.330 the house itself was radically altered though careful comparison with the earlier plan shows these changes were largely confined within the old structure, reflecting the constrained site. The most obvious change was the reconstruction of the central range of rooms which included pushing out the west wall in order to build an apse. This room and the central room were decorated with mosaics clearly formed the focal part of the house. A room in the northern range was adapted for use as a kitchen (the old kitchen/tannery having long since fallen out of use) and it seems likely that the house was still only used as an occasional residence. It is worth noting that there was limited potential for sleeping accommodation — the south end of the main structure had, for example, become an open court.

About 370 the house entered its final phase. The baths were demolished and the mausoleum became derelict. The granary was also allowed to decay and was demolished. The chamber above the deep room seems to have become a Christian house chapel. Wall-plaster was recovered which depicts a number of individuals engaged in Christian worship. This impression is given credence by an access room which contained wall-plaster with the chi-rho symbol. The cult activities associated with the marble busts continued beneath — new pots, open for libations, were placed in a fresh clay floor. By the early fifth century the whole house had been burnt down and it was abandoned. The nature of the place must have remained in local lore because the ruinous mausoleum was eventually built over by a Saxon church, still standing in the eighteenth century

94 Llantwit Major villa (axonometric reconstruction). The site had a long history dating back possibly to the first century though the first stone house was not built until the second century. It is a particularly interesting site because of its remote situation in south Wales, far removed from most Romano-British country houses in a military area. Development was slow and the site may even have been abandoned in the third century. The drawing shows the whole site as it may have appeared in the fourth century when the L-shaped house had been augmented with a number of additional structures creating a semi-enclosed courtyard. The basilican-type building in the foreground may have been a residence for workers on the estate and belongs to the category of aisled buildings sometimes found on their own. The ditch was either a defensive precaution or, more likely, a simple way of controlling livestock. The impression is of an estate large enough to require a number of persons and needing to provide sufficient accommodation for them, animals and equipment

defined by dykes, woodland and Akeman Street, which runs from east to west about 2.5km (1.5 miles) to the south. A modern footpath runs from Akeman Street towards the site of the villa and almost certainly represents the survival of the original approach road to and through the Roman estate. The villa at Barnsley Park has been shown to be surrounded by a network of earthworks on a south-facing slope representing small enclosures which were probably fields and stockyards.

The fact that many houses underwent significant alterations and elaborations in their plans does not mean that rudimentary rectangular and roundhouses did not continue to be built or lived in throughout the period, and it would be quite wrong to imply otherwise. Indeed it may even be that they constituted the majority of Romano-British homes, shops and farms at any given period. One need only look at the plans of the settlements outside forts, for example Vindolanda, or villages like Catsgore in Somerset to see the kind of far less sophisticated building which continued in use. The Stanwick site in Northamptonshire has already been mentioned — here most of the dwellings are roundhouses in various enclosures. There may have been far more of the kind of ribbon development settlements like Hibaldstow on Ermine Street in Lincolnshire than we are currently aware of. Here a series of basic rectangular structures fronted the road, presumably offering basic services and accommodation to travellers. There are also a

95 *(opposite) Aisled villa and accompanying buildings at Stroud, near Petersfield. Little dating evidence is avaliable for this site because it was excavated around 1900. The main feature was the aisled house with wings which would have given an outward appearance similar to the winged-corridor villas. In its original form the building apparently had no internal rooms apart from the wings though the excavators may have overlooked timber partitions. At this stage it was accompanied only by the eastern building which may have been a barn or granary. Subsequently a number of internal divisions created separate rooms in the west end of the aisled house, some of which were heated (hatched walls on plan). A separate bath suite was built and faced the barn across a now enclosed courtyard. An octagonal structure of unknown purpose was built by the barn. This shows how a simple house could be remodelled to create a more sophisticated residence. It also shows an unusual blend of styles which are normally considered distinct. The Bancroft villa by contrast (**99**) was preceded by an aisled house which was demolished to make way for a more conventional winged-corridor house on a different orientation. It also had an octagonal building of unknown purpose close to the main house. It is quite possible that the empty looking courtyard actually contained a large number of smaller structures which were not identified by excavators*

number of 'native settlements' known, like Chysauster in Cornwall. At Chysauster a pre-Roman settlement of stone-built oval houses remained in use right up to the beginning of the fourth century. Other similar settlements are known in the vicinity of Hadrian's Wall, for example Milking Gap though these were generally suppressed when the frontier was consolidated. Interesting though these kind of settlements are, their lack of architectural sophistication makes them of little relevance here, apart from appreciating that for every Woodchester or even Bancroft there may have been hundreds of simple houses. At Winterton in Lincolnshire roundhouses were still in use in the second century (**101**).

Town houses

In the towns of first-century Roman Britain we have evidence for early living quarters. There are two main types: living quarters adapted from military buildings and those which were built from new. Roman towns were almost as susceptible to change as their modern counterparts and it is difficult to distinguish these early dwellings from later structures. However, the three earliest major towns of the province (Colchester, London and Verulamium) experienced considerable destruction during the Boudican Revolt in 60. Subsequent rebuilding in some cases buried, and protected, the pre-60 structures and supplied a *terminus ante quem*, i.e. the burnt buildings must precede 60 (assuming the fire damage has been correctly attributed).

At Colchester the legionary fortress, probably of the XX legion, was given over to the new colony by the late 40s. The new residents were veterans (some from elsewhere in the Empire) and their families. On the evidence of excavations at a number of sites within the old fortress, parts of the barrack blocks seem to have been adapted for use as houses, the remainder being demolished and the land used for farming. The external walls of the barracks were based on mortar and stone plinths which only had foundations of about

96 Gable end of the aisled house at Meonstoke, Hampshire. During the early fourth century the house was extended and a new east end was constructed. Light was allowed in through three round-headed lights but at a subsequent date these were blocked up. Later the whole new east end collapsed probably due to inadequate foundations and bonding but large sections were left where they fell. Excavations have recovered these allowing a reasonable reconstruction of its original appearance. The remains of the gable seem to have been quite steep, something which is difficult to reconcile with the considerable weight of roof tiles. The remains are now displayed at the British Museum

40mm (1.75 inches). The rest of the wall was made up mainly of sun-dried daub blocks; internal walls were made of timber frames filled with wattle and daub. They were not ideally suited to use as houses because barracks consisted largely of a series of independent rooms for groups of ordinary soldiers. However, each barrack had quarters for the centurion, consisting of a block subdivided into smaller rooms. In the main these were used with the independent rooms being demolished. These houses were simple structures with earth, or occasionally timber, floors. The walls were rendered with sandy clay, and in some cases plaster. Roof tiles are easily reusable and this might explain their absence. However, this would not have occurred during the Boudican sack so it is reasonable to assume that roofing was made out of thatch or shingles (wooden tiles).

Identifying early structures in London is naturally extremely difficult, but a certain amount of basic structural evidence has survived. Three timber buildings were put up *c*.55

97 The house at Lufton was a late foundation — occupation seems only to have commenced in the late third century at the very earliest, and very possibly somewhat later. It remained a modest establishment consisting of four rooms facing east with a connecting corridor.

This unprepossessing residence was however equipped with a large bath-suite to the north. Even this would excite little comment were it not for the astonishing octagonal frigidarium. *The octagon contained an ambulatory and central plunge bath. The bath walls probably supported a colonnade which may in turn have supported a central lantern. It was undoubtedly of some height because the huge lateral forces generated made it necessary to subsequently strengthen the whole structure with massive buttresses.*

The relative heights of the flanking rooms are less easy to establish but some reconstructions show these as higher than the octagon's ambulatory. This is very unlikely because the effect would have been to diminish the octagon which was obviously the centre-piece of the whole establishment

by a probable market place in Gracechurch Street. The best preserved consisted of a rectangular building fronted by a verandah; it seems likely that it was a series of shops with private quarters behind. It was much more simply built than the ex-barracks at Colchester. The walls were just timber frames filled with mud bricks or wattle and daub and were secured with wooden foundations. The site is similar to the better-known Insula xiv at Verulamium (**102**). Here a series of shops housing bronze-smiths seem to have been built as a single timber-framed construction. Again the shops were fronted by a verandah and behind them there seem to have been living quarters. If the interpretation of the structure is correct then we may be dealing with a single entrepreneur landlord putting up a scheme

98 Villa and baths at Ashtead villa. One of the very few Roman buildings known to the south-west of London, Ashtead seems to have been a centre of light industry rather than agriculture. Note how the bathhouse lies at a substantial distance from the main house. It may therefore have been for the use of workers. There was a kiln for the manufacture of tiles including a distinctive design of box flu-tiles which have been associated with the later part of the second century. Tiles made from the same dies have been found at Beddington villa near Croydon. However the site is comparatively remote and it is difficult to see how finished tiles could have been transported significant distances without an unacceptable level of loss

to capitalize on the demand for business premises by craftsmen who themselves wished to supply the demand for their products. The landlord may have been a private individual, or the government (through the army).

The connecting feature with all these early town buildings is that they were not built or lived in, apparently, by the indigenous population. They seem to bear more resemblance to the frontier towns of western North America in the nineteenth century. The parallel is not inappropriate — these towns sprang up to service the people who were making it their business to exploit new territory. Britain was probably regarded as a source of easy money, a complacent attitude proving costly, and there would have been little point in making serious investments in buildings. The buildings are not even really houses — on the whole they seem simply to form extensions of shops or craftsmens' workshops, generally belonging to the 'strip' form of construction. This contrasts with rural houses where there seems, in relative terms at any rate, to have been more incentive to improve housing.

out buildings

10

10

10

10 m

walled garden

99 Winged-corridor villa at Bancroft, Buckinghamshire (isometric reconstruction). The drawing shows the house as it appeared after c.340 when the bath-suite was rebuilt and a number of rooms had mosaics laid. In an earlier phase the house was an aisled structure on a different alignment. In the front there was an ornamental garden including an octagonal building of unknown purpose, perhaps a shrine, or simply a garden house. A number of out-buildings have been found (100) and these indicate an active and large agricultural estate. Some 300m (1000ft) to the north-west, a mausoleum was found, probably built for family members though it was subsequently robbed out

*100 Bancroft villa estate plan (after Williams), see **99***

101 *Roundhouse at Winterton, Lincolnshire (axonometric reconstruction; 'Building E'). Underlying the substantial villa house this round building appears to date to the second century between c.130-80 with two distinct phases. The roof seems to have been supported on four central posts. The house shows how even in the later second century domestic architecture in remote areas of Roman Britain was still quite elementary*

By the time of the Flavian reconstruction of the province in the 70s, Roman Britain was already well over a generation old — the sons of soldiers who participated in the invasion and subsequently retired in Britain would have been adults; the indigenous population in the south-east would have been made up largely of people who had experienced nothing but Roman occupation. Curiously though there seems to have been little incentive to invest time and money in urban living accommodation. At Verulamium the simple timber-framed structures endured though they were often improved with plastered walls and *opus signinum* floors. Here it seems to have taken the Antonine fire of *c.*155, which destroyed much of the town, to stimulate more robust house building (**103, 104**).

As wealth was accumulated and skills were developed so it became possible for the better-off town dweller to invest in more comfortable accommodation. A similar transition took place in Cirencester. Here too there were simple timber framed wattle and daub shop units but during the second century more elaborate stone-built houses appeared. A number of basic plans were used which can be identified in most of the towns in which it has been possible to excavate. Not surprisingly the basic strip form remained in use but the corridor type, already well-established in the countryside, became relatively common.

It would be wrong to assume that all these structures *developed* from simple corridor houses. Some may well have been built in this form right from the start. But classical houses were not entirely absent from Britain. The courts built into the various wings of the Flavian Fishbourne house belong to the Mediterranean tradition of internal gardens

102 *Shops at Verulamium, insula xiv (elevations of Watling Street frontage), selected periods. This remarkable site lies close to the centre of Verulamium, between the theatre and forum and faces north-east. Despite destruction in the Boudican Revolt of 60 and in the Antonine fire of c.155 the site seems to have been used almost continuously as a series of shops and workshops. The fact that periods of rebuilding seem to have involved the whole site suggests that it was in sole ownership throughout. The relative ground levels of a and b are marked on c, showing the build-up of occupation debris*

a = The timber shops in Period I, c.49-60

b = The timber shops in Period II D, c.150-155

c = The masonry shops in Period III, third-fourth centuries

103 House at Insula iv.10, Verulamium (isometric reconstruction). This townhouse was one of a number of masonry (or at least with masonry footings) houses put up after the fire of c.155. In the main range a central row of rooms was flanked on either side by a connecting corridor one of which fronted on to the road to the north-west. A single wing projected to the rear with an apsidal termination. By the fourth century the house had been connected by a corridor to another, larger, building which had a street front on the north-east side of the insula

surrounded by colonnades. By the middle of the second century in Caerwent one such house was put up (**105**): it consists of ranges of rooms built around a small central court. Similar houses are known at Gloucester. Both may have had military connections — they certainly resemble houses built for officers in legionary fortresses. Gloucester used to be such a fortress and Caerwent is close to the fortress at Caerleon.

The improvements and sophistication in town house plans went hand in hand with other, perhaps more significant, changes. It became relatively common to equip at least parts of a house with central heating systems, install timber floors supported on joists and to decorate main living rooms with mosaics. Both Verulamium and Cirencester have produced the most extensive evidence for these expensive investments. Not only do these mosaics indicate the growth of a craft industry but also the accumulated wealth which paid for them. However, at Verulamium very few of these new houses had their own bath-suites and none seem to have been connected to water or drainage facilities.

For obvious reasons town houses never expanded to the degree we find in a number of rural cases like Woodchester and Bignor. This was due both to space and probably because spare money was invested in houses outside the towns. Occasionally very large 'houses' are found within town walls and these are normally interpreted as the official inns for

104 Reconstructed section through town-house at Verulamium, Insula xxviii.1. The drawing should be compared with the published plan (Frere, 1983, facing p.245, fig. 98). The house was built in the third century and included an underground passage with apsidal shrine (?) though this appears to have remained unfinished and instead served as a cellar. The house and apse are visible on site today, near the theatre

users of the *cursus publicus*, though it has to be said on very limited evidence (see chapter 3). Only a single house at Verulamium enclosed a central courtyard with four wings; most of the others barely grew beyond the winged corridor stage and this was despite the fact that the town exhibits some of the earliest evidence for urban masonry houses. It seems that town houses were slightly more likely to be equipped with underground space for the same reasons. At Verulamium one house had a subterranean passage and apsidal shrine (**104**) and others had cellars. A cellar has also been found in Leicester and as at Verulamium there seems to have been provision for lighting these chambers with splayed windows at ground level. Very few town houses had their own bath-suites and it seems likely that their owners must have relied on public facilities. This was the case for most houses at Verulamium, even including the single large courtyard house in Insula iii.

Whether or not towns became less obviously congested within their walls during the third century and later is not clear. Town plans suggest that houses were fairly widely dispersed, perhaps two to an insula. This would have allowed them to combine reasonable garden space yet still operate shops from their street frontages. Such views are necessarily based on the plans of Verulamium and Silchester, the only towns known well enough in detail. It has been suggested that this reflects a social change in favour of the curial class (those eligible in wealth terms to sit on the town's senate, the *curia*) but equally it may represent the families who were commercially successful in earlier years buying up land and consolidating their wealth in better appointed houses. On the other hand the serious fire in Verulamium in *c.*155 caused widespread destruction and was possibly responsible not just

105 *Town-house at Caerwent, Insula iiiS (cut-away axonometric reconstruction). This house lay in the south-west area of the town. Note the central garden surrounded by a colonnaded ambulatory. The gutter around the garden caught rainwater, which ran through a drain to the latrine at the rear of the house*

for the greatly increased use of masonry for construction, but also the wider spacing of houses. However, archaeology is beginning to reveal much larger numbers of timber houses in towns, Wroxeter being the prime example, and it may be that in time we will have to entirely re-think ideas about Romano-British towns as fourth-century 'garden cities'.

Even so, there are comparatively few known examples of new houses of significant size in fourth-century Romano-British towns. The curious little house at Dorchester (**13, 106**) was built in the early fourth century and had mosaics in almost all its main rooms, glass windows, decorative columns and central heating. In Leicester shops were rebuilt in masonry in the early fourth century and in insula xiv at Verulamium the long-established row of shops continued to function (**102**). In London very few houses of later date are known at all but there is one particularly interesting site close to the north bank of the Thames in the south-east part of the city (**107**). Built in the third century, the building had an unusually placed bath-suite, too big for domestic use but was neither a grandiose facility (like Lufton's, **97**) nor big enough for public use. It may have been an inn, perhaps run by a single family, and evidently successful enough to remain in occupation right up to the end of the fourth century at the earliest.

The evidence from some towns suggests that town and country were becoming less sharply defined. In Cirencester a previously unoccupied part of the town (a narrow strip of land between the stream and the city wall; insula xii) was built over with two houses and several outbuildings (**108**). They differ in plan from most other houses appearing as rather compressed groups of rooms though their outward appearance may have resembled winged-corridor houses. Evidence of agricultural activity was found in one of them and

106 *Fourth-century townhouse at Colliton Park, Dorchester, Dorset looking west. There were two ranges of rooms opposite one another and therefore the plan of the building is a little unconventional. The house had a large number of mosaics for its size, every room in the north range having one. The building is almost unique in retaining a window opening though this was reconstructed from collapsed fragments (**13**). The south range seems to have been originally separate and may have been either a bath wing or possibly an industrial business, perhaps fulling or dyeing (one of the rooms is adapted to allow surface water to drain off)*

107 *(top, opposite) House(?) and baths at Lower Thames Street, London. One of the few residential buildings of late date known from London. The central feature is the bath building which seems to have occupied most of what would have otherwise been the courtyard of a winged house. The baths are known in detail but only the eastern half of the house's plan has been recovered — the symmetrical reconstruction shown here is hypothetical. The main room of the baths was the* frigidarium, *with the heated rooms represented by the smaller apsidal chambers and fed by a small furnace. The baths were served by a number of drains and were connected by a short corridor to the house which was built, strengthened by a retaining wall, into the hillside close to the north bank of the Thames during the third century. The house was quite well-equipped, having several heated rooms fed by a furnace in the end of the east wing. It also had painted wall-plaster. Although the baths are small compared to public facilities an alternative possibility is that the buildings served as a small family inn for merchants or sailors, for whom this would have been a convenient resting place both close to the river and the commercial and administrative centre of London*

the complex includes an aisled building in a context similar to those found in country houses. It seems likely that they were at least in part involved in farming though whether this means farming land inside or outside the walls is unknown. The Barton Farm house, found in the early nineteenth century just outside the city walls, may be another indication of a blurring of town and country houses in this period. In fact the town walls may represent a compression of the urban area and originally the house might have been 'within' the town. Some of the larger houses at Silchester have enclosed yards and outbuildings (for example Insula xix.2) and may have been farms, an idea supported by the lack of villas in the town's vicinity.

Other houses

Romano-British towns were not developed out of any comparable pre-Roman settlement. Settlements there were but these were not conurbations of permanent structures. In the countryside the situation was different. Farms already existed from sheer necessity and these were usually centred on some sort of house, albeit a simple one. As we saw earlier a number of sites have shown a radical transformation in the late first century from Belgic roundhouses to late first-century rectangular houses consisting of several rooms,

*108 Axonometric view of a house at Cirencester, insula xii.2. The house was built on a previously
untouched site within the town walls in the late fourth century. Excavations produced evidence
for metal-working and weaving, while the outbuildings suggest the house may also have served
as a town. Another house, of similar function and date, stood nearby*

sometimes fronted by a verandah which allowed independent access to each room.

How these changes took place is not so clear. It seems strange that a simple lifestyle, unencumbered by the sophistications of provincial classical society, could apparently have become unsatisfactory overnight. The new houses were much larger than the ones they covered and at the same time rubbish begins to include fine pottery wares and other accessories of Roman life. It is difficult to account for this financially because we have no knowledge of how much this sort of activity must have cost. If it cost 'more' to live this way then where did the money come from? It may have come from loans to the Britons we know from Dio to have been made by wealthy Romans. Recall of the cash in the year 60 helped provoke the Boudican Revolt (*Dio*, LXII.2). Another reason may have been that the introduction of a cash economy was beginning to filter throughout society. As money was received for produce so it could be saved and invested in a new house.

But this still fails to explain the motivation: people are notoriously resistant to change. Of course we have no way of knowing if the householders were the same people; it may be that in the cases where we can see a dramatic change in the archaeological record we are actually looking at new money and new people, though this may mean no more than a new generation rejecting the 'old ways'. All but the most conservative types must have seen that multi-roomed houses, sometimes with *opus signinum* floors, represented an objective improvement in their way of life. In a number of cases, for example at Lockleys, Ditchley and Quinton (**88**), the first stone house actually overlies the preceding house. This suggests a break in occupation unless the owners made temporary accommodation arrangements during construction. Perhaps the original site held a certain superstitious significance for the owners who were unwilling to move away, even a few yards.

But these houses were not the 'villas' people will now pay to visit. They did not have mosaics, painted walls and only in a few cases had bath-suites attached. They were really no more than elongated huts. At Gadebridge Park in Hertfordshire the late first-century buildings consisted of a timber house and an isolated three-roomed bath-suite. Some were slightly more elaborate: at Lullingstone the first stone building, built *c*.80-90, had a central range of rooms, a rear corridor, and a front verandah flanked by two 'wings' (**92**). Although built with at least stone footings the lack of associated tiles suggests it was thatched. Not every late first-century farm became Romanized in this way. At Frocester in Gloucestershire a long-established Iron Age farm, possibly centred on a rectangular house, little seems to have changed. Unlike many contemporary sites the better quality fine wares are conspicuous by their absence and only in the late third century were better quality stone buildings put up.

Found (or at least rediscovered) in the early 1960s the huge house at Fishbourne (**109**) has earned itself a considerable reputation both because of its size and its supposed association with a client king called Togidubnus, known to have had local connections (*RIB* 91). This it may have been but the idea is pure supposition and in any case distracts us from the real point: Fishbourne is one of a small number of exceptional and substantial first-century houses known to have existed in Roman Britain. They have nothing to do with the more mundane trends of developments in housing elsewhere because they were built with imported money and craftsmen at colossal expense.

By the late Neronian period a substantial stone house with baths and enclosed garden had been put up on the former military site at Fishbourne. The house was expensively decorated with monochrome mosaics, *opus sectile* floors, and a colonnaded verandah. By *c*.75 the site had been levelled to make way for a much more ambitious project based on four wings built around a garden. Although this bears superficial resemblance to corridor villa construction (**117**) a closer glance will show how it owes more to the classical tradition of internal courts surrounded by ranges, rather than rows, of rooms. It was built around a formal garden which was itself designed to flank the building's central axis of entrance hall ➤ garden ➤ 'audience chamber' with apse. Like its predecessor the building was fitted with monochrome mosaics, stucco work and architectural embellishments. Below the house towards the sea to the south a further, terraced, garden of more relaxed style led down to a mooring.

Fishbourne is the most remarkable of the large early houses to have been found but it was not the only one, though it may have been the richest. At Eccles in Kent a corridor house with 12 rooms had been put up by *c*.65; like Fishbourne it was built with mosaics in several rooms and sported an ornamental water basin. Nearby was a detached bathhouse which was decorated with painted wall-plaster. Eccles at this period is not remarkable by Fishbourne's standards but it is far closer to Fishbourne than almost all other contemporary houses in Britain. At Rivenhall in Essex rich Belgic occupation is testified by a number of costly items, for example a decorated bronze mirror. During the first century a double courtyard villa seems to have been built on the site (**110**). In this case it seems possible that a well-to-do Trinovantian family had found favour with the new Roman administration and had welcomed official encouragement to build a *domus*. On the whole these elaborate houses did not become common elsewhere for over a century. These wealthy first-century houses are found in south-east Britain and this gives us two possibilities: either they belonged to native aristocratic families who had decided to back the right side (and profited thereby), or they belonged to opportunists or members of the provincial government and army who decided to build themselves houses in the style they were accustomed to. However, in the absence of specific evidence we can only guess — Rivenhall might equally have been handed over to a wealthy Roman, or Gallo-Roman provincial in an effort to erase the memory of the former owners.

During the third and fourth centuries many Romano-British houses enjoyed their greatest periods of expansion. They included a number of the houses which enjoy a reputation in modern times for representing the highest standards of country house living in Roman Britain, for example Woodchester (**111**), North Leigh and Bignor (**117-18**). In general the great houses of the fourth century were elaborations on the corridor house, normally expanded to create four wings around a courtyard though this need neither be

109 (opposite) The so-called 'palace' at Fishbourne, near Chichester. Fishbourne was an early military site. Traces of military buildings, including a granary, have been found. Subsequently it became the site of the Neronian 'proto-palace' which, if it had remained the only house on the site, would still have been of great importance. Built in the 60s it had baths, a colonnaded garden, and rooms decorated with mosaics, marble and stucco — all were remarkable for the date in Britain where such luxuries remained hardly known until the mid-second century, and even then they were still rare.

*By c.75 the 'proto-palace' was demolished to make way for the palace proper which was put up in the years following. Although there are slight eccentricities in the plan it was oriented around an east-west axis. The main entrance lay in the centre of the east wing, and led through a formal garden to the west wing which was built on a higher level. Steps led up into an apsed building. Interpretation of this as an 'audience chamber' and the sheer scale of the whole house led to suggestions that it was built both as a residential and government centre. The owner is unknown though it is normally assumed that it was connected with the client king, Togidubnus, known to have been living and active in the area at this time. However, it is also possible that this was an early governor's palace (see **65**).*

Like the proto-palace it was lavishly decorated with mosaics in the black and white style of the first century, wall-plaster, marble and stucco-work. The residential quarters were in the north wing, though the main bath suite was at the south-east corner. It consisted of rooms ranged around enclosed courtyards — these also appear in the east wing. During the second century the north wing was radically altered and new baths were inserted in the west wing. Polychrome mosaics were added, as were hypocausts. The fate of the rest of the building is unknown but shortly after c.296 it was destroyed by fire. A period of stone-robbing followed and then it was abandoned, ironically just as the first Romano-British villas were beginning to equal its original scale and magnificence. Medieval ploughing took its toll and little now remains above the floor levels.

Further work has shown that more landscaping took place to the south, probably running down to a jetty. It is also certain that there would have been many 'out-buildings' to service all the various needs of the house

symmetrical or continuous. This has been seen as the product of wealth which was used to transform a farmyard into a more refined enclosed area. Brading on the Isle of Wight consisted of at least five distinct structures connected by walls. Woodchester seems to have had at least two courtyards and North Leigh was distinctly trapezoidal in shape. Unlike town houses bath-suites were normal, even in the slightly more modest houses like Bancroft (**99**) and Brixworth (**87**) though the latter was never apparently used. We can be sure that the richer estates would have had large numbers of outbuildings, which have not been identified. Aerial photographs of North Leigh show that there were a large number of buildings and compounds very close to the main house. Projecting rooms were added if pretensions and necessity required them, for example the rooms at Keynsham (**112**), which is otherwise a simple, if sprawling, house. The triconch hall at Littlecote, discussed in more detail in chapter 5, may actually be no more than a very extravagant detached summer dining room some yards north of the main house (**91**, **colour plate 21**).

110 *Rivenhall, Building 1 (after Rodwell). Late Iron Age residents in the vicinity were wealthy
enough to own decorated bronze mirrors which may have been deliberately buried as votive
deposits. Stone buildings of Roman type appear around the beginning of the second century
apparently forming a large complex arranged around a courtyard. At least two distinct houses, of
contemporary date, appear to have been put up one of which (the smaller) is shown restored
here. The plan is heavily restored from earlier excavations based on trenches. Speculation on
ownership is obviously completely hypothetical but it has been suggested that the combination of
early date and continuity may mean that the house was built by natives*

Some of these houses seem so elaborate, particularly in their provision of bath suites
that it has been suggested that they actually represent hostelries for visitors to a shrine.
Chedworth contained a small temple-like structure, which stood above and behind one
corner of the house. At this point the wings of the house both terminate with bath suites,
and the gap was filled with steps which led up to the 'temple' (**113a**). Another temple, now
destroyed, lay in the vicinity of the villa. Inscriptions and altars apparently representing
Lenus-Mars, a Romano-Celtic version of Mars as a healing god, suggest that if it was a
hostelry for a shrine, then Lenus-Mars was the subject of attention. But it was not at all
unusual for villas to feature temples and shrines on their estates, and their presence need
not force us to assume that the prime purpose of the villa was as anything other than a
residence and estate headquarters.

More difficult to understand is the very curious house at Great Witcombe (**114-15**).
This house seems to have been built right over a spring. The house, built in the form of

111a Woodchester villa (axonometric reconstruction). *The plan of most of this villa has been known ever since its excavation by Samuel Lysons in the 1790s, though there are considerable shortcomings in the available evidence.*

The villa lies on the western slopes of a valley running north. The stream feeds the River Frome, a tributary of the Severn. The vicinity is well-known for its numbers of Roman buildings, and the villa is about 16km (10m) from Gloucester and Cirencester. The villa complex faced south but it is evident from circumstantial evidence that far more remains to be identified — note for example the walls which continue off the plan. A surviving water conduit fed the building from the west.

The general appearance of the three courtyards and their surrounding buildings is so symmetrical that there would be good reason to believe that the villa was built more or less as one unit. But a certain amount of second century samian ware, coarse pottery and other material, along with limited excavations in the early 1970s now suggest that the complex represents a longer period. Clarke, the excavator, argues that the site began with the east-west strip of buildings on the north side of the central courtyard in the late first, early second century. At some point during the next 150 years the site was extended southwards around the centre courtyard and beyond to create the outer courtyard. Some additions to the north may date to this phase

111b Throughout its phases Woodchester seem to have been lavishly decorated, indicated for example by marble veneers and architectural fragments. Only during the first half of the fourth century, and in common with many other major houses of Roman Britain, did the villa reach its full extent. During this phase the northernmost room, containing the great Orpheus mosaic, was built. The photograph shows the characteristic circular parade of animals, though the central figure of Orpheus himself is lost.

At 15m square, this is the largest single room known from a villa in Britain. Its substantial walls suggest a considerable height and spaces for four columns in the mosaic indicate that a gallery may have existed. The Orpheus mosaic is one of a series of similar designs known from the Cirencester area. There is a possibility that at least some of the buildings containing these designs were used more as religious centres than domestic premises. However the rich have never been noted for a lack of ostentation and the size of this house and its facilities may simply indicate a desire to impress, using iconography that was in currently in fashion

an 'H' and with various additions, ended up as a very peculiar building which seems to have had bathing facilities which were quite disproportionate to the available accommodation space.

Gadebridge Park's growth and its associated swimming pool have led to the suggestion that it was operating as a business, perhaps one with a cultic curative significance, which funded a substantial house (**116**). While this might have applied to Holcombe and Lufton (**97**) too such extravagant buildings may have been purely ostentatious displays of wealth and need have no more esoteric reason for their existence; and of course in the ancient world there was far less one could do with spare money than there is now, apart from hoarding it or spending it on property.

These later villas are those popularly associated with mosaics, wall-paintings and a

112 *Keynsham villa, room W (cut-away axonometric reconstruction). The villa is essentially a simple, if sprawling, example of a courtyard villa with wings on three sides. However at the south-west corner a curious hexagonal room with three further chambers protruded from the main block. On the opposite side the entrance to the room was flanked by two niches. The floor was covered with a geometric mosaic. A larger room of similar design was attached to the north-west corner. Their purpose is unknown and they may simply represent an owner's desire to own impressive dining rooms. This room in particular might be compared to the enigmatic triconch hall at Littlecote which may be no more than an even more extravagant version of the same thing (**144**)*

113a Chedworth villa, north-west section (isometric reconstruction, based on a perspective drawing by S. Gibson). Chedworth villa lies in a secluded wooded valley near Cirencester. Built originally in the late second century the villa consisted of two houses and a separate bath-suite. Further rebuilding took place in the third century, but only in the fourth century were all the elements combined into a single structure. The result was two parallel east-west ranges connected by a central covered verandah. Another range of rooms, parallel to the verandah, connected with the south range. However it was not built up to the north range and terminated in a bath-suite. The north range also terminated in an even more elaborate bath-suite and this is the section shown here. Through the gap led a path and steps up to a small shrine with an octagonal pool. The garden 'shrine', which marks the source of natural water for the site, and a nearby temple (now destroyed) has led to a suggestion that the villa was actually a guest house and cult centre for the healing god Lenus Mars. A few small altars have been found on the site and one room contained a large number of coins. These could either be payments to farm estate staff, fees from pilgrims who wished to use the facilities or even votive gifts. Even if there was a cultic element to the site this need not have precluded normal domestic or agricultural activities. Temples are known to have been features of other villa estates, like the Temple of Ceres at one of Pliny the Younger's homes. It was a matter of pride to Pliny who paid for repairs and maintenance

113b (opposite) Chedworth. The soft Cotswold stone lends itself to carving. This section of balustrade from Chedworth is just a tiny fragment of the carved decoration which will have embellished the villa house generally luxurious level of facilities. The general subject is covered in chapter 1 but it is worth noting that even the greatest houses, like Bignor (**117**, **colour plate 2**) had mosaics in only a small number of rooms. More modest houses might have only a single mosaic, if they had one at all. So the idea that such decorations were commonplace is completely false. The houses with them tend to be among the more architecturally interesting ones which is why more have been dealt with here.

Not all villas ended up as such extravagant houses. The modest house at Brixworth undoubtedly underwent alterations and extensions, but it was little bigger than its original size (**87**). The constraints on the site at Lullingstone have already been mentioned. The winged-corridor villa at Frocester was only built in the late third century. By the late fourth century little had altered apart from the addition of a bath-suite. The sprawling house at Rockbourne was never particularly lavish — it had few mosaics and a modest bath-suite (**119**) and the impression is more of a working farm than a luxurious country residence.

The distribution of houses

The villas of Roman Britain are found mostly in the lowland zone because being principally associated with exploiting land they were bound to reflect the distribution of superior agricultural areas. There were rural settlements in the north of course but presumably the poorer land was less likely to yield the kind of surplus which would fund the building of a better house. Such northern settlements were also less likely to have the advantages of being close to a town, though these are of course as much a consequence of rural settlement as a cause. There are a very few, for example at Maiden Castle outside the

114 *Great Witcombe villa (isometric reconstruction). It was built around the middle of the third century but substantial additions were made within a generation. The site is on a steep hillside riddled with streams. These have made it difficult to imagine why anyone should wish to build a house in a place where the risk of walls being undermined is so great, despite the beauty of the location evident still today.*

The springs may have formed the attraction — this is another site for which a cult connection has been suggested. However there is even less evidence here than at Chedworth for such a purpose and the whim of an eccentric to reside in such a place is no less valid a reason for the house which had to be propped up with buttresses to resist the effects of the water. The house had a substantial bath-suite, represented by the rooms in the foreground

modern city of Durham, and the large estate at Llantwit Major in south Wales (**94**).

Despite this general view villas are distributed unevenly in the south with pockets of concentration and other areas where they are virtually absent. The forests of the Weald of Sussex and Kent are particularly noticeable. The houses at Ashtead and Bignor are amongst comparatively few, contrasting with the dense concentration of houses in the Darenth and Medway valleys in north Kent. Further north the Fenland had been

*115 Part of the south wing at Great Witcombe. Lying next to the bath-suite this room had a central font and three niches in the wall. It may have functioned as a domestic shrine, perhaps dedicated to water nymphs. The 'deep room' at Lullingstone had a painting of nymphs in a niche (**colour plate 22**)*

extensively drained during the Roman period and although there was a steady growth of village-type settlements from the early second century on, none of the individual farms appear to have developed into substantial houses. This factor, the reclamation works and the remarkable buildings at Stonea (**66**) and Castor (**67**) all suggest that the whole area was an imperial estate run for the benefit of the state. Under such conditions farmers, who were probably tenants, would have had no opportunity to accumulate wealth in property. A similar situation probably prevailed in Salisbury Plain where small, native-type farmsteads of clustered roundhouses exist but no villas.

The largest concentrations of villas were in the Mendips and Cotswolds. Along the river Windrush in Oxfordshire and Gloucestershire, for example, there are a large number of villas and settlements separated by only 2-3 miles (3-5km) at most, with more to the north clustered around the general path taken by Akeman Street, for example Stonesfield. Other clusters exist around Cirencester, Bath, Water Newton, Verulamium and Leicester. There are very few examples of villas which are immediately in the vicinity of town walls, though there is usually one, and this suggests that most of the land around towns was owned and farmed by the townspeople. Where such a house does exist, like Gorhambury to the west of Verulamium it may represent the privileged estate of a particularly important person in the town.

116 The villa at Gadebridge Park looking north (periods 5-6, c.300-50; based on drawings by Neal). Gadebridge Park developed from a late first-century wooden house with detached bathhouse into a very substantial variation on the winged-corridor type in the fourth century. The late house was set into a slope and may have had towers at either end of the main range. However, the bath-suite had become so elaborate, incorporating a swimming pool that the excavator has suggested this was the primary feature of the settlement, perhaps operating as a commercial spa. There is no evidence that there was a religious element to this. The whole house was demolished by c.350 but occupation centred on an out-building continued in the rest of the Roman period with cattle stockades (?) built over the site of the former main house

The late fourth and fifth centuries

The period of Roman Britain's decline lasted from the late fourth century until well into the fifth, a period of at least three generations or more. During that time occupation of Roman-type houses seems to have ceased. Settlement of many towns and almost all villas is no longer detectable through conventional artefactual evidence. Traditionally this was associated with the province being overrun periodically by bands of raiders from northern Britain, northern Germany and Denmark, and Ireland, particularly during the 'barbarian conspiracy' of 367. The significance of such references was much exaggerated — St Patrick's account of his life implies that villa owners were continuing to run their estates at least up to c.430, even if they had to suffer the privations caused by intermittent raids. Altogether the evidence was generally interpreted as a violent threat permanently

117 *The villa at Bignor in its final fourth-century form. The villa began life as a single-corridor villa, progressing to a winged-corridor lay-out during the second and centuries. In the fourth century the wings were extended to incorporate a barn, and bath-suite (**118**). The resulting courtyard was enclosed with another wing, while further small extensions added more architectural features, equipped with lavish high-quality mosaic floors (**colour plate 2**)*

disrupting the socio-economic structure on which both towns and villas depended as well as eventually resulting in the physical destruction of houses.

There is a certain amount of evidence for the violent destruction of some houses. For example the villa at Brislington in Avon seems to have been destroyed by the late fourth century. Traces of fire are not conclusive on their own but the fact that the remains of four or five people and a dozen cattle were thrown down the well does suggest that the destruction was caused by a third party. At Keynsham, also in Avon, fire destruction at some time during the fourth century was associated with a wall collapsing and burying an individual whose remains were not recovered. It is extremely difficult to attribute these events, which are only examples amongst many, to specific incidents; they may be just symptomatic of a protracted period of instability. But the period concerned is quite a long

118 The cold plunge bath at Bignor, room 55a, in the south-east corner of the complex. The bath-suite belonged to the fourth-century expansion of the villa. The baths themselves underwent considerable alterations. The photograph shows the hills of the South Downs to the south which not only provided a natural boundary for the villa estate but were also crossed by Stane Street running from London to Chichester

one — plenty of time for isolated and unrelated incidents to take place. There are all sorts of possible situations potentially leading to localized damage: farm-workers responding to years of supervision by a cantankerous foreman, a dropped oil-lamp or even over-heated hay in a tinder-dry wooden barn. Just because we do not have specific evidence of such incidents does not mean that we have an obligation to associate the destruction of a house (or anywhere else for that matter) with the historical references that we do possess. Who, after all, would have guessed that London burned down in 1666 because someone forgot to put a fire out in a bakery if it was not a recorded fact?

But many houses show decline of a more innocuous kind and it may be more appropriate to look at how the fires or structural decay were *not* followed by repair or reconstruction — this is a much more important perspective. At Keynsham the fire was followed by re-occupation but of a much more low-key nature: a rough hearth platform was laid over the fire debris and a mosaic in a corridor. But this is unusual, more often such damage was simply followed by abandonment. The techniques of construction seem neither to have been available or desired. Lullingstone burnt down in the fifth century and was just never rebuilt, despite the presence of a house church which one might have

119 North wing of the villa at Rockbourne showing the octagonal plunge bath attached to the frigidarium. This bath-suite was added c.300 to a house which began life in the second century replacing a first-century predecessor and a late Iron Age circular house. It was gradually extended to surround a courtyard with three wings though these were not continuous. Despite its size the building does not seem to have been particularly luxurious and this may reflect its relatively isolated position on the edge of the New Forest. Nevertheless, it had carved stone finials on its roof and amongst the finds was a carved stone table

thought would create a kind of vested local community interest in repairing, or at least replacing the building. Instead the site was abandoned, possibly passing into local lore, and eventually a Saxon church was built over the adjacent 'Temple-Mausoleum'. At Gadebridge Park the substantial fourth-century house was demolished by the mid-fourth century and enclosures marked by post-holes were built across the site. A single small two-roomed outbuilding originally put up around 300 remained in use possibly into the fifth century. This is an interesting case of what seems to be sub-Roman activity during the Roman period but it may be that the estate had become part of another, unidentified, villa estate. Some villa estates have produced evidence of fifth-century and later occupation in the form of grass-tempered pottery, for example Frocester and Barnsley in Gloucestershire. However, this kind of material is normally associated with fields around the old houses, rather than the structures themselves. In any case it is fairly self-evident that the population would have had to feed themselves anyway so it should come as no great surprise that fields were still used in some shape or form, even if the houses were not.

In the towns decay may have been held off longer — some houses in Verulamium were occupied well into the fifth century. One particularly well-known example in Insula xxvii was built in or after 370, subsequent alterations included the laying of mosaics, which eventually wore out, one being cut for the installation of a corn-drying oven. Eventually (the time scale is unknown) the house was demolished and built over with a masonry hall, which was itself demolished and a water pipe laid across the site. At Cirencester one of the houses in Insula xii mentioned above, built only by the late fourth century, functioned long enough for structural alterations to take place including laying a hypocaust and a new mosaic over another mosaic. This kind of evidence and the presence of a substantial timber public (?) building at Wroxeter (**68**) suggests organized community living, probably in houses, at least into the early fifth century and possibly running on for several decades after the formal end of the province.

Ultimately all these arguments depend on isolated excavations, many conducted in a period when techniques were not developed enough to identify occupation in periods when artefacts had become rare. The only common thread, which ties all the evidence together, is that by the late fifth century all traces of occupation of Romano-British type houses had ceased and certainly no new ones were being built. Now, obviously there was a population and it was living somewhere: evidence of this period has been found in early Anglo-Saxon villages like Mucking in Essex or the re-occupation of some hillforts like South Cadbury. Some villa estates, like Orton Hall Farm, near Peterborough, remained in occupation, albeit of a distinctly less Romanized nature (**167**). But the villas and town houses of Roman Britain belonged to a redundant, if more sophisticated, architectural form: there is practically no evidence of structural continuity into the late fifth century and beyond for domestic buildings of Roman date in Britain.

5 Sacred sites

Introduction

Religious or ritual activity is a fundamental need of all human societies but it is never quite so clear where religion begins or ends. We live in a more secular age so it can sometimes be difficult to fully appreciate how much cult and culture are the same thing. On the other hand it can be very easy to use religion as a convenient repository or descriptive term for any artefact or building whose purpose is not otherwise immediately obvious, and archaeologists are often accused of doing this.

But with Roman Britain we are on slightly firmer ground than we are with the anonymity of prehistory or post-Roman times. Inscribed altars and votive gifts make some buildings and associated structures obviously religious in intent. In other cases, especially classical-style temples, the architecture alone makes the intention clear. The range of Romano-British buildings which can be associated with cults is very broad and some are amongst the most interesting of all the structures covered in this book.

Inscriptions recording temples or shrines form the largest category of those which mention buildings. Unfortunately, none gives us any indication of the architectural forms involved and can almost never be associated with actual remains. However, they are useful reminders that religious buildings not only existed in towns and in the countryside, but were also found in and around forts. A stone from Old Penrith, for example, mentions the restoration of an *aedes* (shrine), dedicated to the Matres Tramarinae and the imperial house of Severus Alexander, which helps date the work to 222-35 (*RIB* 919). A number of other forts in the northern frontier area record temple restorations around this time, such as Netherby (*RIB* 979), and Ribchester (*RIB* 587).

Temple types

Most temples were associated with precincts and outbuildings though excavations, particularly earlier ones, do not always include these. In fact the plan of a temple in isolation is almost certainly misleading — they should normally be seen as components of a religious zone. In towns like Verulamium, or special places like Gosbecks near Colchester, this extended to including theatres closely associated with religious rituals. Temples themselves were not generally devised as buildings for the public performance of ritual. Instead, they were private and enclosed. Public ritual was generally performed outside around an altar. There are exceptions and the most obvious examples of these are temples associated with exclusive eastern mystery cults, especially Mithraism. These are almost invariably isolated and self-contained structures.

120 The so-called 'Triangular Temple' at Verulamium (axonometric reconstruction), built in the early second century. Watling Street, running north from London, entered Verulamium at an angle to the established street grid, creating an intersection where the temple was built.

The cella was surrounded by an ambulatory extended to flank the colonnaded open court in front of the building where public ritual activities took place. The external wall was painted red. The cella was flanked by two rooms both of which contained water tanks; they may have acted as additional cellas. In front of the porch entrance to the enclosure was a chalk foundation which may have supported an altar. The only serious anomaly with other temples is the way in which the temple lies so far back in the enclosure; however, bearing in mind the peculiarities of the location, this is almost certainly a practical solution to a practical problem.

Excavation revealed a number of pits containing animal bones including an ox-skull behind an altar. Many miniature pots were also found and several bases may have supported altars and/or statues of the gods or goddesses. There was no specific evidence for the deity, or deities, worshipped here but it has been suggested that the water tanks (for ritual purification), and carbonized pine cones, indicate an oriental cult. This may have been the cult of Cybele and Atys, or even Bacchus with whom pinecones were also associated, but this is purely speculative. Nevertheless there seems to have been a guild of dendrophori *('branch-bearers' attached to the Cybele cult) in the town (RIB 2503.114).*

The peculiar nature of this building makes it difficult to reconstruct and there are a number of different ways of doing this. This version is based on the conventional Romano-Celtic temple, roofed accordingly

121 Temple precinct at Springhead, Kent (isometric reconstruction), an important stopping point on a journey to London. The spring almost certainly had pre-Roman religious significance. The two Romano-Celtic temples visible here are known as Temples III and II respectively (left to right). They succeeded an earlier temple, Temple I, which lay to the south-west of Temple II. The presence of projecting wings has been taken to indicate that the ambulatory walls were solid. That there were windows in the cellas is suggested by the fact that an iron window grill was recovered from Temple II. The precinct boundary is known but the siting of the altars shown is hypothetical

The types of precincts and associated buildings are very varied and they reflect the type of cult and its location. Where a temple was located within a town like Verulamium the precinct, or *temenos*, was usually marked out with some sort of wall, perhaps colonnaded. This could be very modest in extent, for example the 'Triangular Temple' (**120**), or even be large enough to accommodate more than one temple, as at Springhead (**121**) and Caistor St Edmunds. Such precincts focused attention on the main altar. At Colchester's Temple of Claudius the altar seems to have been a substantial example, in keeping with the outright classicism of the temple itself (**122**). In rural areas temples might be associated with a scatter of buildings — the roadside Shrine of Apollo at Nettleton is a particularly good example (**135, colour plate 26**). In these cases it is not quite so clear where the precinct began and ended, though the neat symmetrical layout at Harlow shows that careful planning was possible even where there were no urban buildings to impose a

TI·CLAVDIO·CAES·AVG·GERM·IM·P·XVIII·PONT·MAX·TR·P·IX·COS·IV·PROV·BRITAN·L·D·D·D·

constraint (**127**). Some sites may have served for occasional fairs, attracting traders and customers alike from a wide area. At Lamyatt Beacon in Somerset the temple was sited on the narrow crest of a steep hill, and apart from a single outbuilding there seems to have been little more (**136, colour plate 27**).

Classical temples

There are very few certain examples of classical temples in Roman Britain. In general those which are known seem to have been founded in the first century, apart from the recent discovery at York, but underwent considerable alterations in succeeding periods. Only the celebrated Temple of Sulis-Minerva at Bath is known in any architectural detail even though very little of the actual building has been explored.

Impressive though it must have been, the Bath temple would have seemed tiny compared to the arrogant magnificence of the Temple of Claudius at Colchester (**122-3, colour plate 24**). This temple's existence is mentioned by Tacitus in his account of the Revolt of Boudica so we know that it must have been in existence by 60 though it may very well have still been under construction. Had it survived, even in a ruinous state, to early modern times this temple would bear comparison with some of the more famous ruins in France, Italy and North Africa. However, it does not and we are left with the circumstantial evidence of its vaults now forming the substructure of the eleventh-century Norman castle.

122 (opposite) Facade of the Temple of Claudius at Colchester, Essex, about the mid-first century looking north. The core of its podium survives beneath the eleventh-century castle keep and was identified by Wheeler and Laver in 1920 who showed that the vaults were structurally separate from the castle walls. There are four rectangular vaults built in pairs whose relative proportions suggest those of a classical temple's cella and pronaos.

It is clear that we cannot now be certain of the exact dimensions of the Roman temple. The podium survives to nearly 3.5m (11ft) above the Roman ground level and was probably about 32 x 24m (105 x 79ft). It seems likely that the temple was surrounded by 36 Corinthian columns, eight at each end, though there was a second row at the pronaos.

In front of the temple there was an altar, as was customary. It stood on a podium which was approximately 10m (33ft) wide and was surrounded by the pedestal bases of statues. Traces of the precinct have been identified; combined with the street plan of Roman Colchester they indicate that it was about 150 x 120m (492 x 393ft).

The reconstruction here is based on standard proportions and decorations of classical temples though no exact detail is known. There may have been a series of sculptures within the pediment, probably illustrating the conquest of Britain. Fragments of marble and limestone veneers found on the site suggest that the building was impressively decorated.

Tacitus says the temple was dedicated to the divine Claudius. Claudius died in 54, just six years before the Boudican Revolt when the temple was destroyed. It seems unlikely that the temple could have been built in six years and so it is more probable that the first temple was begun well before 54 and subsequently re-dedicated. The inscription shown here, again hypothetical, lists Claudius' titles for the year 49-50 and represents the building as it may have appeared some time in the 50s. It would have been re-built after 60. It has been suggested recently that in the late Roman period the temple was demolished. Traces of reconstruction bear comparison with government audience halls known at Trier and in fact many of the more exotic stones on the site seem to belong solely to this later, post-temple, phase

The Temple of Claudius seems to have stood in a monumental precinct befitting its status as the home of the imperial cult of Claudius, conqueror of Britain (**123**). It was an outright political statement and there is little likelihood that it was sited on a place of pre-Roman religious importance. The site at Gosbecks to the south of the settlement probably marks this — it grew to have both a Romano-Celtic temple and a theatre. The temple at Bath is of particular interest because of its association with the sacred spring of Sulis, and the substantial baths complex. This gave the town its name, *Aquae Sulis* — ancient temples were generally sited somewhere for a specific purpose, usually because the site had a traditional status as the home of a god, perhaps a minor local one. It was Roman policy to tolerate, synthesize and absorb local cults. Thus a Celtic sacred grove, tree, pool or spring was often transformed into a place where a god could boast more than just a name. The temple and its altar became the focus of ritual. Other buildings may have housed priests, or pilgrims. The god became the subject of carved reliefs and statues.

At Bath this took a particularly dramatic form. The nature of the hot spring and the huge quantities of healing water produced meant that engineering works were needed to control and channel the supply. The spring itself was given a stone-built pool creating a

*123 Temple precinct at Colchester, Essex. This shows the classical style temple within a colonnaded precinct (see **122** for the temple facade). Note the large scale of the altar which is based on excavated evidence. Much of the rest of this reconstruction is hypothetical but the theatre is shown in its correct position adjacent to the precinct*

head of water to supply the baths. The commercial possibilities were huge and whatever the religious nature of the site there is absolutely no doubt those who controlled the spring and the baths must have stood to make a very great deal of money. From an architectural point of view the peculiar nature of the site produced a curiously quaint and cluttered temple precinct.

Despite being several metres below modern street level, Bath has been the subject of numerous excavations since the nineteenth century and the site is now known in tantalizing detail. Cunliffe's recent excavations have made sense of the large and complicated site and it is now possible to appreciate some of the history of the site as well as actually walk through the temple precinct itself (**124-6, colour plate 24**).

Other classical temples are known to have existed elsewhere, for example at London adjacent to the Flavian forum, and at Wroxeter. Fragments of a Corinthian capital and column, once 6-9m (20-30ft) high, from the temple precinct point to another. None is known in detail. However, it is virtually certain that more existed especially at London and in the other major cities such as Cirencester. Hadrian visited Britain early in his reign and may have been involved with the construction of London's second period basilica and forum. Whether he was or not it is likely that some sort of temple would have been

124 *Temple of Sulis-Minerva at Bath. This perspective view shows the temple as it may have*
appeared shortly after construction in the late first century. The facade of the temple is known
from collapsed fragments but apart from its basic dimensions the appearance of the rest of the
building is unknown. The statues on top of the pediment are hypothetical, but likely, accessories.
This type with a pediment supported by four columns is known as 'tetrastyle'. As the diameters
of the base (about 9m; 29ft) and the columns (about 0.8m; 2.6ft) are known it can be shown
that this example is built in the 'sistyle' version (where the gap between the columns is equal to
twice the diameter of a column). The height of the columns is not so certain, and in fact there is
a certain amount of variation in surviving temples. Vitruvius said that the ideal for a tetrastyle
temple with sistyle divisions is a height nine and a half times the diameter — the conventional
reconstruction (see Cunliffe, 1984, fig. 14) shows this. However the product is a building
which appears a little high for its width so this reconstruction shows columns equal to about
eight times the diameter (as with the Temple of Fortuna Virilis in Rome). Either may be
correct, or something in between. A single surviving capital from one of the columns shows that
they were carved in Composite style (adapting elements from the Corinthian and Ionic orders).
By c.200 the precinct was substantially altered: a number of sculptured facades and structural
additions were made around the precinct. The podium of the temple was enlarged to create a
raised area around the building which enclosed a new set of steps. These steps, heavily worn by
the steps of pilgrims, are the only part of the temple visible in situ. *Two small 'chapels' were*
incorporated into the new podium on either side of the steps. Their form is uncertain (but see
125 *and* **colour plate 24***)*

125 *Temple precinct at Bath in the fourth century (axonometric reconstruction; based on views by S. Gibson but adapted). Much shown here is hypothetical (see **colour plate 24**).*

The precinct is dominated by the covered sacred spring. The roof is shown broken away in order to reveal the spring itself within. In the south wall three windows (two of which have survived complete) allowed pilgrims to hurl their offerings to the goddess of the waters. A number of statues may have stood around in the water. The vaulted cover building was put up in the late second century, or early third century (the huge buttresses were put up later). Parts of it were found in the spring where it had collapsed in post-Roman times. Prior to that the spring was probably open to the sky though Roman engineers in the late first century had enclosed it to form a walled pool. This created the necessary head of water to supply the baths.

In the middle of the precinct itself the base of the altar has been found in situ. *The modern visitor to the site is currently able to enter the precinct at the west, just between the temple and the western buttress. The steps of the temple are visible in a recess in walls which support modern levels above. The raised walkway then runs along the precinct between the altar and the porch.*

*The temple itself is shown with pilasters around the cella, an alternative to **124***

126 *Temple precinct at Bath looking south. The view is taken from a line running continuously
with the north side of the temple cella. The main feature is the north wall of the building
covering the sacred spring. The spring was enclosed and covered somewhere around the late
second century. Access to the precinct was through the little door just visible in the centre beneath
the Sol porch.*

*The vault of the spring cover building created lateral forces to great for the massive walls of the
cover building to bear. By the early fourth century the north-east corner had given way. Three
massive buttresses were added on the north wall, and one on the west. The central northern
buttress was constructed as a porch to the spring, with entrances on the west, east and north. It
seems to have been decorated with a pair of water nymphs holding up a bust of the sun god,
Sol, though the surviving pieces are very fragmentary. The buttresses on either side were
probably plain, but the north-west one may have incorporated an arch. However, as so little
remained, it is quite possible that the buttresses may have been part of a much more complicated
facade, perhaps including a vaulted portico. The reconstruction shows those components which
are certain (though not necessarily their exact form). It seems to have been balanced by a facade
depicting the moon-goddess, Luna, on the northern side of the precinct (not shown).*

*Between these facades stood the main altar — the focal point of public ritual. Two of the corner
slabs, decorated with Jupiter and Hercules, and Bacchus and an unknown female deity, have been
located on the site. A third depicting Apollo and an unknown god was removed in the middle ages
and built into the church at Compton Dando about eight miles away. The plinth of the altar was
found in situ. Immediately to the west of the altar stood a statue base dedicated to the goddess
Sulis ('DEAE SULI') by the* haruspex *(interpreter of entrails), Lucius Marcus Memor.*

*The precinct was entered by an arch to the east, indicated here by a dotted line. In the
background on the left can be seen the vault of the Great Bath, and behind the temple to the
south can be seen the portico surrounding the temple*

dedicated as a commemorative gesture. If so it may have been a circular classical temple, known as a *tholos*, which would have suited Hadrian's penchant for Greek styles. Remains of the entablature from such a building have been found at Bath but its site is unknown. A temple to Diana is known to have existed at the legionary fortress of Caerleon because an ansate tablet commemorates its restoration around the middle of the third century. The dedication was by the legion's legate, Titus Flavius Postumius Varus, who was eventually promoted to be prefect of Rome (*RIB* 316). All this suggests that it was probably classical in form but it remains unlocated.

The structural remains of several buildings at Corbridge have been interpreted as temples. Some of these were almost certainly classical in form. The exciting remains of a classical style temple were discovered in York in 1989 and were associated with extensive remains of cult activity including votive coins scattered around the base of a statue plinth outside the temple, and a number of ritual pits containing animal remains within the temple. The building seems to have been put up by the 180s but was wrecked by fire within a generation. It was subsequently reconstructed and a monumental gateway was added to the precinct.

Romano-Celtic temples

Much more common than classical temples in Roman Britain were the so-called Romano-Celtic temples. These temples are found in Gaul as well and they form a distinctive regional form of religious architecture. None seem to have been political foundations but many, except those found within towns, seem attributable to a pre-Roman cult and sacred place.

The excavated plans of these buildings are usually very simple amounting to no more than two concentric squares. 'Romano-Celtic temple' was coined by Mortimer Wheeler in a study of the temple at Harlow (**127**). He was interested in a series of temples with square or rectangular plans containing an inner chamber and a concentric outer one. The inner is normally interpreted as the sanctuary (*cella*), and the outer as an ambulatory or series of rooms. Wheeler noted that there were other temples which followed a similar pattern but which had circular or polygonal plans. It seems quite reasonable to consider them all together because they probably belong to the same general type of building. Even so buildings with very similar plans are found in different contexts and the modern enthusiasm for classifying according to the available information has led to the assumption that all such plans must belong to the same kind of building. The so-called 'Temple-Mausoleum' at Lullingstone (**93**) is one of the better-known examples though it is apparent from the site report that there was no evidence to support either the idea that it was a religious shrine, or that it looked like what we assume a Romano-Celtic temple looked like.

Romano-Celtic temples are mainly distributed in central and northern France and Britain. This suggests in itself that they may belong to a much earlier tradition because much of the material of Roman date from these sites has a very distinctive regional flavour. A very important discovery was made at Heathrow (on the site of the airport) of a late Iron

127 *Temple (of Minerva?) at Harlow in its final phase. The Harlow site seems to have been sacred
in the pre-Roman period as the Bronze Age burials and large numbers of late Iron Age coins
found here testify. Recent re-excavation has revealed an Iron Age round house within the temple
precinct. The site itself occupies the brow of a small low hill which rises only about 6m above
the flood plain of the River Stort — it may have been regarded as a sacred wood, perhaps
centred on a particular tree.*

*In the late first century the cella and ambulatory were put up, surrounded by a cobbled area.
Later the rectangular area around the temple was enclosed with a timber palisade, probably
with a dividing wall which ran in front of the temple.*

*By the early third century the timber palisades were replaced in stone and rooms were added to
the temple building to bring it up to the dividing wall. The open area seems to have had
buildings added to the east and west walls (the division into rooms is hypothetical), and an
imposing entrance added to the south wall. An altar base was found just outside the entrance to
the temple. By the fourth century the site seems to have fallen into disuse.*

*The recent re-excavation of the site produced a large limestone head of Minerva which may
have been the cult statue, and a carving of a warrior god. Earlier excavations produced a
fragment of an altar reading …INI A… expandable as NUMINI . AVGVSTORUM, 'the
spirits of the emperors'. While this is perfectly normal for the Roman period it can hardly
account for the site's original religious importance, which must remain a mystery*

128 Circular temple and temenos at Hayling Island (isometric reconstruction), built c.55-60 over an Iron Age shrine retaining the circular plan. The Iron Age shrine seems to have been built of timber, wattle and daub and was surrounded by a fenced courtyard.

The new temple was probably built of dressed local limestone and rendered internally and externally with painted wall-plaster. It had a porch though the entrance into the courtyard has not been confirmed. The temple entrance may have faced a large niche in the courtyard. The early date of the temple and the presence in the vicinity of the contemporary 'palace' at Fishbourne suggests that the project was undertaken either by the Roman authorities or by local tribal aristocrats who were already influenced by Gallo-Roman tastes. The temple is unusual for Britain though similar examples are known in Gaul.

The temple's later history is rather obscure though the porch was enlarged. Coin and pottery evidence, combined with traces of burning suggest that the temple was no longer in use by the early third century though sporadic finds of later date indicate that it was still visited. In post-Roman times the site seems to have been re-occupied by Saxon peoples. During this time and later stonework from the temple was almost entirely robbed out

Age (or possible early Romano-British) building of similar plan, but built in timber. A similar example is also known from South Cadbury in Somerset. A circular Romano-British temple built over an Iron Age penannular ditched structure at Frilford in Berkshire emphasizes the point of continuity though neither the Heathrow nor South Cadbury examples were built over in this way. At Hayling Island an Iron Age wooden circular temple was succeeded by a very early Roman stone temple built on the same plan immediately above (**128**). At Wanborough in Surrey a circular temple of late first-century date was found close to a later, conventional, square Romano-Celtic temple dated to the mid-second century. Even so, traces of earlier activity were found under the circular temple, which suggests that the site had been venerated from at least the beginning of the Roman period and possibly before.

129 Late Romano-Celtic temple at Maiden Castle, Dorset (axonometric reconstruction). Built in the late fourth century on the north side of the Iron Age hill-fort, this temple is one of the best-preserved in Britain. There were probably a number of deities worshipped here because the small finds indicate several different gods, for example Taurus Trigaranus (a tribal bull-god), Minerva and Diana. In addition to the structures shown here an oval hut was identified nearby. Built of dry-stone walling the hut contained a large number of coins, pottery, a steelyard weight, a bronze statue base and a fragment of a marble statue of Diana. It is tempting to interpret this as the place where the enterprising establishment made its sales to pilgrims of various suitable souvenirs and votive gifts

The plan of a Romano-Celtic temple is usually very simple, for example at Maiden Castle (**129, colour plate 25**), though the more ambitious projects like Nettleton had more complicated plans (**134-5, colour plate 26**). On the whole Romano-British examples are very poorly preserved but fortunately evidence from the continent is available to help reconstruct them. These include a coin reverse (though this is rather dubious), a carved relief and the remarkably well-preserved remains of the so-called 'Temple of Janus' at Autun, near Dijon in France (**130**). The cella at Autun still stands high enough to show that it was at least 13m (43ft) high, had three windows in each side above the ambulatory and was built with decorative brickwork, though it was probably plastered

177

130 (opposite) Romano-Celtic temples — evidence from other sources (after Lewis)

a = Reverse of a denarius *struck at Rome by Octavian (afterwards Augustus) between c.30-29 BC depicting the facade of a building (*Roman Imperial Coinage 266*). It may represent a Romano-Celtic temple despite the apparent lack of a roof for the ambulatory. However, the coin is identified as elsewhere as depicting the Curia Julia (the Senate house) in Rome which is much more likely. The building, restored survives intact and the resemblance is considerable.*

b = Restored elevation of the Temple of Janus at Autun (about 45 miles/70km south-west of Dijon in France). Much of the cella survives and beam-holes exist to show where the ambulatory pentice roof was fitted.

c = Relief from Titelberg which may also depict a Romano-Celtic temple. Doubt has been expressed over what seems to be a lack of an ambulatory at the front but equally it could represent a temple with entrance-flanking annexes known in plan at a number of Romano-British sites (for example, **136***)*

over originally. Recesses in the cella wall about halfway up show the height of the ambulatory roof and that it was pitched. The circular temple of Vesunna at Périgueux survives in a similar state. A few examples show that this Romano-Celtic external ambulatory with a lean-to roof could even be applied to classical temples, for example at the Temple of Lenus-Mars in the Altbachtal sanctuary of 70 temples at Trier. Together these pieces of evidence help to create an impression of a general type (**130**). There were exceptions, as there always are, for example the Hayling Island temple which seems to have lacked an ambulatory (**128**) and the temple at Uley where there was an ambulatory around three sides only (**132**). The late temple at Lydney Park resembles the Romano-Celtic type in certain respects but it also has some similarity to basilican forms as well as a few quite individual features which set it apart from other temples (**133**).

While Romano-Celtic temples conformed to a similar pattern they most probably differed in detail. For example the ambulatory may have had a lean-to roof supported by

131 Reconstruction of a Romano-Celtic temple possible details of how roofing was constructed

columns sitting on an external dwarf wall, or it may have been solid — the latter would have been more secure. Sometimes the presence of columns or their remains may help but the absence of columns may not be indicative either way. In fact, Romano-Celtic temple sites have yielded very little in the way of carved stonework. Nettleton is probably the most helpful site in this respect where a number of dwarf columns and various other fittings were found. At other sites traces, if at all, tend to be fragmentary, for example at Pagans Hill where small pieces of columns were found in a nearby well — obviously one cannot even be certain that these came from the temple. The problem is that this kind of material would have been particularly attractive to stone robbers or church builders in later periods, so we have no real idea of the original distribution of such material.

The cella was probably taller than the ambulatory and was usually roofed (on the evidence of collapsed tiles). In chapter 1 we saw how Romano-British architecture tended to be rather haphazard and how the result was a tendency to overbuild in some places and underbuild in others. Nettleton is an excellent example: it would be very easy to comment on the lack of external buttressing to support a central octagonal tower and reject this as a possibility (**134-5**). However, there was probably a tower, and precisely because of the lack of provision for the stresses involved it eventually fell down after a history of problems with inadequate internal walls (one only need look at the baths at Lufton villa, **97**, to see the kind of provision that might be necessary). In any case, as we have no idea of the timber content of upper parts of walls, we have no idea of the weight involved in any one instance.

132 Temple (of Mercury?) at Uley. This is another site which seems to have been used for religious purposes in the late Iron Age. It remained in occupation but by the fourth century the cult became centred on a new stone temple of unconventional plan. The ambulatory surrounds only three sides and a separate porch appears to have formed the entrance. A pit in the cella produced several hundred coins. This may have contained water or even a sacred tree in which case the cella may have been unroofed. However, with no provision for drainage, it is hard to see how this would not have swiftly become a bog as rainwater accumulated. More than 200 curses have been found on the site and along with a carved head of Mercury and two altars depicting him make it certain that he was the object of devotion here. Despite the partial collapse of the temple c.380 it remained in use and one subsequent structure built on the site resembles an early church

The sheer simplicity of Romano-Celtic temples makes it impossible to date them according to their ground plans, and there seems to be no chronological pattern behind the various modifications, originally designed or added. The basic design seems to have been used almost throughout the period and often it is very difficult even to be certain where the entrance was — there was no specific orientation, though many seem to face east. The walls were almost invariably covered with painted wall-plaster though none survives over a large enough area to draw up any kind of schemes of decoration. Flooring varied enormously from gravel, old roof-tiles and cement to, very occasionally, mosaics.

A number of 'cosmetic' variations to the plan are known. One of the most frequently encountered is the addition of wing rooms to one side of the temple, usually flanking the temple entrance, for example at Springhead and Lamyatt Beacon (**121, 136, colour plate 27**). In these cases such rooms would seem to preclude the possibility of a colonnaded ambulatory. Lamyatt Beacon also featured a semi-subterranean room attached to the south wall of indeterminate purpose. At Caerwent, Temple I had an apse at the rear of the cella and a portico at its entrance (**137**). Temple II at Springhead, instead of having a cella with solid walls, seems to have had one with eight piers. At Wood Lane End in Hertfordshire a particularly enigmatic site has been identified which seems to have involved a number of different types of building centred on a monumental structure resembling a Romano-Celtic temple (**139**).

We even have little evidence of the gods worshipped at any particular site and where we do have some idea it is clear that almost any god or any number of gods might have been the subject of devotion. Lamyatt Beacon produced a number of statuettes of classical gods: Uley seems to have been dedicated to Mercury, Harlow to Minerva (and possibly the *numen Augusti*), Nettleton to Apollo and Cunomaglos (a Celtic hound prince) — these are all assumptions based upon representations of deities and a few very rare inscriptions. Only one site appears to have been named for its temple — the fort at Bewcastle, north-west of Hadrian's Wall, which was probably called *Fanum Cocidii* according to the Ravenna List. This means 'the shrine of Cocidius' (Cocidius was a Celtic warrior god often associated with Mars). However, the temple building has not been found, though votive items from the site confirm the presence of a cult of Cocidius (*RIB* 985-9).

Romano-Celtic temples have excited much debate precisely because it is so difficult to classify them in any kind of really convincing way. Lewis, who wrote the standard work for Romano-British temples of this kind, identified three broad possible variants: the tower cella with ambulatory (the orthodox reconstruction), the continuous roofed-type (a single roof covers cella and ambulatory), and the open cella type. The fact is that we only have contemporary evidence for the first type and virtually none for the other two or his various sub-classifications divided up according to various combinations of solid and colonnaded walls. This is simply because almost all known examples do not stand above ground height, and no ancient descriptions exist.

So we are left with many excavated examples, which on the whole have very similar plans, though differing in detail, and seem to belong to all kinds of different cults at different places and at different times. The truth is that from a general point of view very little else can be said and it only remains to examine sites more closely to trace their individual histories. English medieval parish churches offer a parallel because they all belong to a similar type with similar function, yet each is unique in detail and patterns of repair, alterations and rebuilding. The scattered evidence available suggests that Romano-Celtic temples were similar in this respect. Having recognized this as a general probability there is no need to substitute for the lack of exact information a series of classifications which cannot really be supported by surviving structural evidence from a single site and which gives an illusion of knowing more than we really do.

Temples associated with eastern religions

Roman civilization and society was very catholic in its attitude towards cults of any sort so long as they did not conflict with state cults. This is not always an easy attitude for us to appreciate because it is so different from the Christian tradition of intolerance developed during the Middle Ages. Throughout the Roman period there was a penchant amongst certain groups of people for religions which had grown up in the eastern part of the Empire or beyond. These spread across the Empire and included the worship of Cybele and Atys, Egyptian gods such as Isis and Osiris, Mithras and Christ. We traditionally separate Christianity and explore it as a different phenomenon but it shared with Mithraism a promise of salvation and a life to come. But Christianity was initially just a troublesome cult whose more enthusiastic disciples refused to even pretend to worship official gods and emperors. For many others Christ may have seemed a useful deity, worshipped literally as the mood took them along with any other god who seemed a convenient solution to the problem at hand.

133 (opposite) Temple of Nodens, Lydney Park, Gloucestershire, period 1 (as built). The site of this shrine and its associated buildings were excavated in the 1920s by Wheeler. Since then there has been a reassessment of the temple's date but the site remains one of the better documented religious centres of Roman Britain.

The site of the shrine is an Iron Age promontory hill-fort on the western slopes of the Severn Valley. Until the late third/early fourth century the site was used for the extraction of iron ore. Then there was a dramatic change and the site became an important centre of a healing cult (period 1), at a time when rural pagan cults seem to have enjoyed a revival in Britain. Antiquarian records of a mosaic in the temple and a number of inscribed votive goods make it plain that the god concerned was called Nodens, associated with water, hunting and healing. His origins are obscure and it seems odd that, if he had local connections, his cult had been ignored at least since late prehistoric times. He was associated with Mars.

The temple's plan is unique but seems to have been derived from the Romano-Celtic and basilican forms. At the rear of the cella were three rooms where the cult statues or altars may have stood. In the first period the walls of the cella were supported on piers but unfortunately the builders and architect were unaware of a natural fault in the limestone which chanced to be beneath one of the piers. This 'swallow hole' gave way by c. 365-75 and the pier above collapsed bringing down much of the temple's superstructure. The temple was rebuilt and this time the piers were incorporated into solid walls (period 2).

The cella mosaic no longer exists but an antiquarian drawing exists to show that it consisted of a scene of sea monsters, geometric motifs and a dedicatory inscription recording an interpreter of dreams (RIB 2448.3). His presence may explain the bays around the ambulatory where pilgrims could sleep in the presence of the god, and awake to have their dreams explained. Other finds suggest a healing component, represented by a figure of a dog. Dogs were, for example, believed to have powers in licking wounds.

Whether the temple had a clerestory or not is uncertain but had it not had one the cella would have had no source of light. It has also been pointed out that if the building had been roofed in a single span then the collapse of the swallow hole would have caused little damage.

It seems certain that the various buildings in the temple enclosure were intended to house pilgrims to the shrine. The largest is comparable to a courtyard house and lies next to a substantial bathhouse

Christianity

There is a reasonable amount of evidence in the form of ritual equipment and inscriptions for the worship of a number of eastern gods in Roman Britain. A scratched reference on a flagon and an inscription make it certain there was a temple to Isis in London though the building has not yet been located. There is no certain evidence of a Christian church of Roman date but structural remains at Icklingham, Lincoln, Richborough, Colchester and Silchester are considered as possible candidates. The most likely places are shrines built around the tombs of martyrs within a cemetery. The abbey of St Albans is almost certainly the final product of a line of untraceable buildings on the site of St Alban's tomb outside the town of Verulamium. A church-like building at Icklingham was surrounded by an inhumation cemetery, and the settlement as a whole has produced some of the most

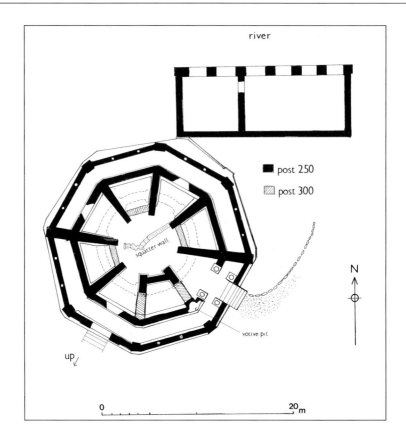

Figure labels: river; post 250; post 300; squatter wall; votive pit; up; N; 0 20 m

important evidence for Christianity in Roman Britain in the form of lead baptismal(?) tanks. But the only building which has exhibited what must be incontrovertible evidence for the actual practice of Christianity is the villa at Lullingstone in the late fourth century (**colour plate 23**). This takes the form of wall-paintings in one wing of the villa house and seems to have involved no specific architectural planning and design (**93**). The mosaic from Hinton St Mary in Dorset may be evidence of another house church. However, a mosaic from Frampton, also in Dorset and possibly by the same mosaicist (but now lost), combined a number of mythological scenes with a Christogram showing how difficult it is to interpret these floors. In any case, interpretation of a building's function from mosaic iconography is a rather dubious and very unsure practice.

Even so we can be fairly sure that churches existed in Roman Britain. By the beginning of the fourth century an episcopal framework existed in the province because three British bishops (from York, London and Lincoln or Colchester), a priest and a deacon attended the Council of Arles in 314. They must have had churches in their respective sees. Gildas, who wrote in the mid-sixth century, refers to the rebuilding of churches which had been destroyed (*renovant ecclesias*, *De Excidio*, 12 and 24). Bede's eighth-century description of Augustine's mission to Canterbury in 597 includes a number of references to the repair and recommissioning of Roman churches in and around the town (*Historia Ecclesiastica*, i, 26 and 33). Interesting though these examples are they are very hard to match with evidence on the ground. The extra-mural churches at Canterbury, for example St

134 (opposite) Plan of the octagonal Shrine of Apollo at Nettleton, Wiltshire (after Wedlake). The site lies in a narrow valley which runs west to east crossed by the Fosse Way running north-south which was built c.47. Pre-Roman occupation, probably of a religious nature, seems to have attracted Roman attention and on the higher ground to the south an early Roman ditched military (?) enclosure was built at the same time as the road.

By the Flavian period a small circular shrine had been erected on the slope running to the south bank of the stream about 100m west of the Fosse Way (Period 1). Its plan is indicated here by a dotted line within the later temple. Over the succeeding years the shrine was surrounded by various buildings which were probably designed to house the priests of the cult and serve the various needs of visitors; as the road was a major arterial route, running between Cirencester and Bath, there would probably have been many potential visitors.

By c.230 the shrine was surrounded by an octagonal podium (Period 2) but by c.250 it had been burnt down. It was replaced with a much more ambitious structure (135). The old octagonal podium was expanded, with a slight eccentricity to abut a nearby building (Building VII — possibly a schola *for an inner circle of devotees of the cult). The new temple (Period 3) consisted of a central octagonal cult chamber with a vaulted roof and eight, arched, doorways to eight flared side chambers (walls in black). One of these chambers acted as an entrance passage to the central area; some of the chambers seem to have had windows to the ambulatory. By c.300+ there seems to have been concern about the building's safety and the two radial piers were replaced with walls. Other alterations involved strengthening walls and closing off four of the side chambers (hatched walls).*

Curiously after c.330 the nature of the site, which had become quite a cluster of buildings, seems to have altered from one of great religious veneration to a centre of light industry. Buildings were converted for the use of metal-workers. During this period the temple itself seems to have suffered partial collapse but by c.360 a haphazard arrangement of building debris in the central chamber was used to create a dividing wall (dotted wall — plan). It seems that renewed pagan activity took place here until the remains of the temple's vaults finally came down (Period 5). The upstanding walls on the south side were used to form the basis of a late fourth-century farmstead. Occupation on the site as a whole seems to have ceased in the early fifth century; a number of skeletons lying where they fell and bearing cut marks suggests that a skirmish took place around this time

Martin's, are built partly out of Roman material though cannot be associated with artefactual evidence of Roman occupation. At Stone-by-Faversham a late Roman mausoleum seems to have been used later as part of a Saxon church and it is possible that part of St Martin's is a Roman mausoleum rather than a church. Only St Pancras at Canterbury seems possibly to have had a church-like form during the Roman period though local tradition held that before 597 it was a pagan building.

The Silchester 'church' has been described as such ever since it was discovered but the truth is that there is no positive evidence for this description apart from its form (**140**). It does indeed resemble a church or a *martyrium* (a chapel commemorating the site where a martyr died) and traces of a small structure outside its entrance have been interpreted as a baptistery. But we have to remember that the church shape belongs to a long-established

*135 Reconstruction of the temple of Apollo at Nettleton. The plan at Nettleton is extremely similar to the church of San Vitale at Ravenna in north-eastern Italy which is still intact (see **134**). Like Nettleton, San Vitale is based on concentric octagons but without the external ambulatory. It too has radial walls and these radial chambers have pitched roofs which rest against the walls of the central octagonal tower. San Vitale was finished by the middle of the sixth century and so was not directly contemporary. Unlike San Vitale, Nettleton lacked substantial buttresses which would explain why the former is still standing and the latter fell down. Given the other similarities the structures probably resembled one another — it is quite possible that at Nettleton we have an early experiment in a building type which was later improved on elsewhere in the Empire.*

At this period there were only six radial walls, the other two being piers. Around the whole there seems to have been a roofed ambulatory with open walls, the roof being supported on piers at the angle points. Subsequently the two open radial walls were blocked up and four of the concentric chambers were blocked

type of Roman building, which includes the basilicas and pagan temples (particularly mithraea, see below). Consequently it is rather unwise to extrapolate backwards.

Much the most convincing church site so far discovered lies outside the south-west corner of the town walls of Colchester in Butt Road. Here an extensive cemetery used throughout the Roman period has been known since the nineteenth century. Graves dating to the fourth century are orientated east-west, something normally associated with Christian burials (though the occasional appearance of grave goods and coins suggests that some pagan practices were maintained). Recent excavations have uncovered several hundred graves and a rectangular building 7.4m (24ft) wide by 24.8m (81ft) long with a simple apse at the east end. Post-holes within indicate that the east half of the 'church' had been separated by a screen and contained a nave with two side aisles (**140**). Coinage in and around the building suggested a period of use between *c*.320 and the early fifth century. There were no finds of wall-plaster or inscribed artefacts to confirm its identification as a Christian building. But here the combined circumstantial evidence of structural form and the cemetery means that it is reasonable to suggest that this was a cemetery chapel.

Mithraism

The temples of Mithras, or *Mithraea*, are known at London, near the forts at Carrawburgh (**141-3**), Rudchester and Housesteads on Hadrian's Wall, and also at Caernarvon in north Wales. Another one must have existed at Caerleon because an inscribed column found there refers to the god but no building has yet been located (*RIB* 322). This reflects the popularity of a cult which was exclusive to men and which was associated with themes of a righteous killing, endurance, virility and salvation of believers. Even the London example seems to have had military associations — one small relief was dedicated by an ex-soldier (*RIB* 3). The temples of Mithras show how mystery cults were completely different from mainstream classical and native religions. In most of the latter cases there was usually an element of 'place' — the site itself was of primary importance, and the temple came second. For Mithraism, and Christianity, this was not the case. The ritual itself and the temples were the principal factors. They were sacred because that was where the rituals took place. These depended on the active participation of the devotees and required intimate enclosed surroundings. The basilican design with an apsidal end was ideally suited and therefore they could be built wherever was convenient. For Mithraism running water was needed for purification. So the London mithraeum was beside the Walbrook stream and the Carrawburgh mithraeum was on a slope below the fort by a stream. In both cases the temples were liable to flooding which caused some structural problems, particularly at London.

The theology of Mithraism is complex. In its simplest form Mithras emerged from the ground and engaged in a conflict, which was essentially one of good versus evil presented as a brave and virtuous act of ritual killing. Mithras pursued and killed a bull created at the beginning of time. In doing so he released the creative essence of all life, which was contained in the bull's blood. Mithraea were normally built without windows to represent the cave in which Mithras sacrificed the bull. A possible mithraeum was excavated at Burham in Kent in 1894. Unlike the other examples it was built underground in a hillside and was reached through a winding passage, like a real cave. However, no Mithraic cult items were recovered and only its form suggests what it once may have been. The focal point of the mithraeum was the carved depiction of the bull's death. All Romano-British examples were damaged in antiquity, probably deliberately (the creation aspect was regarded with particular distaste by the early Christian church). Occasionally such attacks were foreseen — in London followers of Mithras carefully buried some of the votive statues and gifts which were stored in the temple. During excavation it produced a large haul of rich statuary and other items used in the ritual.

187

As a mystery cult, atmosphere was of the highest importance. A suitable mood was enhanced with lighting. At Carrawburgh, lamplight shone through holes in an altar and at London it is clear from scorching on statues that these had had flames held close to them. This was all part of the attraction of a mystery religion priding itself on exclusivity and endurance. At one point in the history of the Carrawburgh mithraeum an initiation pit was incorporated into the narthex where the would-be faithful could lie, covered with flag-stones, for however long was considered proof of their suitability (**142, 143**). No doubt other uncomfortable and bizarre experiences were incorporated into the agenda of the initiation ceremony but by the final phase the pit seems to have fallen out of use. Perhaps lying under the floor had become *passé* and more ingenious variants on self-flagellation had been devised — whatever these were they are not represented in the architecture; on the other hand a cult which excluded women could only grow by attracting followers from outside so standards may have been lowered to attract newcomers.

136 (opposite) Romano-Celtic Temple at Lamyatt Beacon, Somerset. The illustration shows a reconstructed elevation with section and plan. The temple was built in the late third century and remained in use up to the early fifth century. Subsequently the ridge became the site of a small post-Roman cemetery. The temple lay astride a narrow ridge on the 219m contour about 5km (3m) east of the Fosse Way. It has been suggested that a line of parish boundaries from the Fosse Way towards the temple site may represent the original access road.

The plan is fairly typical for this type of temple but includes two annexes on the east which probably flanked an entrance. To the south was a sunken room but this had suffered particularly badly, both from robbing and earlier excavations. The temple itself had also been heavily robbed but enough survived to indicate that the cella was buttressed by internal walls in the ambulatory. It therefore seems reasonable to assume that the cella walls stood higher than the ambulatory. The structure had stone walls, though the annexes were probably timber-framed internally. The roof was covered with hexagonal limestone tiles.

The site has produced a large number of votive objects, mostly buried in pits in and around the temple, including fragments of stone statuary and small bronze figurines of Jupiter, Mars, Mercury, Minerva, and a Genius. Mars seems to have been the most important and other circumstantial evidence implies that his worship here may have been conflated with a horned British deity, perhaps Cernunnos.

There was a small building just to the north of the temple proper. It may have been of later date, especially if it was associated with the small cemetery. Radio-carbon dates from some of the human remains indicate a period from the late sixth to eighth centuries. There is no specific evidence either to indicate a pagan or Christian association though there are obvious parallels with small 'oratories' in Ireland and south-west Scotland

Other cults

No other temples have been found which can be positively identified with other eastern cults. That they existed is certain. A well-known flagon from Southwark carries a scratched graffito mentioning 'the temple of Isis at London'. The flagon is a late first-century form and interestingly an inscribed altar of mid-third-century date, also from London, records the rebuilding of a temple of Isis (not necessarily the same one) by the governor Marcus Martiannius Pulcher (*RIB* 2503.127, and see *Companion*, 167 and figure 65). Of course we have no idea at all what such a temple would have looked like though its location, and a possible first-century date for its construction, suggest it may have been classical in appearance.

Other temples

Other buildings may have had a ritual function, but escape easy categorization. The Littlecote triconch hall is probably the most remarkable (**144, colour plate 21**). Discovered in the eighteenth century and re-excavated in modern times the site is known to consist of a dwelling house and a separate barn-like building. The latter was adapted and enlarged over the years and by the middle of the fourth century a triconch hall bearing a

137 Temple at Caerwent in Insula ix (axonometric reconstruction). The temple was built in the late third century or later across the street from the forum, but on a slightly different alignment. It replaced earlier stone and timber buildings. The precinct was entered through a forehall. During the fourth century rooms were built on to the north side of the forehall and these have been interpreted as quarters for the priest(s) and as small shops which sold votive gifts and religious souvenirs. Unusually for a Romano-Celtic temple the cella had an apse on the north side

mosaic depicting figures and attributes associated with Apollo and Orpheus had been built into it.

A triconch hall consists of a conventional rectangular chamber with three apses at one end arranged like the apse and transepts of a church. Much has been made of the building's shape. It has been described as a unique example of a type later represented by some of the churches built in the Eastern Roman Empire during the fifth century and later, for example the cathedral at El Ashmunein (ancient *Hermopolis* in Egypt, built *c.*430-

138 The surviving remains of the temple at Caerwent looking north. See **137**

40. There is also a certain amount of resemblance to the tomb of Galla Placidia (d. 450), daughter of the emperor Theodosius I, at Ravenna in northern Italy, but this building, which stands intact, has square 'apses' instead of polygonal ones.

The sheer separation in time and place means that it would be ridiculous to try and link the buildings in terms of architectural tradition, though a broad similarity in terms of superstructure is a possibility. However, the Littlecote hall's form is not quite as unusual as it appears: the earlier *frigidarium* of the Huggin Hill baths is now known to have been similar (**77**). Although the apses of the latter are circular and not polygonal this is really only a cosmetic difference — the structure may have been very similar.

Part of the problem in understanding the Littlecote building is that its purpose is really quite obscure. It was attached to a bath-suite but the mosaic has led to the suggestion that the building was a temple used by an Orphic cult. Orpheus was a mortal associate of Apollo who had been granted by him special powers over animals and inanimate objects with a magic lyre. He rescued his wife Eurydice from the Underworld and after he was killed his head and lyre floated out to sea, still playing. The cult was concerned with the concept of punishing the soul before it could be purified. This, combined with the idea that the soul had an independent existence, obviously has similarities to Christianity and it has been suggested that the mosaic and the building's church-like form are discreet references to Christianity. However, it is not certain that the mosaic depicts Orpheus at all and all this speculation may be rather an unjustified elaboration of not very much.

139 *'Sanctuary' at Wood Lane End, Hemel Hempstead, Hertfordshire. This structure and a*
number of associated buildings 5km (3m) west of Verulamium have now been identified as a
religious sanctuary. The central structure, Building 1, probably resembled a Romano-Celtic
temple but with a classical pediment-type facade. The massive walls of the cella with reinforced
corners suggest a considerable height. The vault within the cella may either have been a tomb or
a repository for valuables — no evidence survived. In front stood Building 6, constructed on the
same axis. Behind stood a basilican structure, Building 4, and a number of other structures,
including a small bathhouse, formed part of the complex. It may have been the private centre of
a guild of worshippers who met in Building 6. Such dating evidence as exists suggests a main
period of activity in the second century but by the third century the whole site had been
completely demolished. The excavator noted the contemporary abandonment of the nearby
Gorhambury villa and suggests this may be connected with the re-organization of land
ownership around Verulamium

140 Churches? (isometric reconstructions)

a = Extra-mural church at Butt Road, Colchester. Built c. 320 and remaining in use into the early fifth century. The building was surrounded by several hundred graves oriented east-west in Christian style and the itself conforms to church convention with the apse to the east.

b = 'church' at Silchester by the forum. Although conventionally described as a church since its discovery in 1892 this curious little structure, while church-like in form, has produced no evidence at all for Christian activity. Although it has an apse, nave, aisles and a narthex this also makes it similar to temples of known pagan dedication in Rome (like mithraea). It also faces west which creates certain problems because churches usually, but not always, face east. A brick base near the entrance of the building has been interpreted as the site of a font, possibly standing within a baptistery of which no certain trace remained. A recent reinterpretation of the site has convincingly explained that this apparently external feature was contained within a hitherto-unrecognized extension to the narthex. This would help the belief that it was a church but the total absence of any evidence like burials, or Christian material, to corroborate the idea leaves this building unexplained

141 *Plans of the* mithraeum *at Carrawburgh on Hadrian's Wall (after Richmond and Gillam).*
*See also **142-3**.The temple was built on the slope below the south-west corner of the fort near*
the stream in the second century (a). At this date it was a simple, modest rectangular structure.
Subsequent alterations extended the nave and included a rectangular apse. An ordeal pit was
incorporated near the entrance. In its final fourth century phase the apse was compressed and the
statues of Cautes and Cautopates, associates of Mithras, were moved further up the nave. The
internal structural components were made of wood and these included the pillars to support the
roof; these were well-preserved by the waterlogged conditions on the site. The ordeal pit was no
longer in use. Finally it was deliberately damaged, perhaps by iconoclasts, who seem to have
paid special attention to destroying the principal relief depicting the Mithraic myth. The site can
be visited today and is probably the most instructive religious site in Roman Britain after Bath

stream

well

altar to Nymphs & Genius

5m

142 *The* mithraeum *and shrine of the Nymphs at Carrawburgh. This drawing shows the temple as it may have appeared in the fourth century. Note the altars within and the reredos sculpture of the sacred act of killing the bull. The Shrine of the Nymphs lay immediately outside the entrance. Compare with* **143**

The Littlecote building lies very close to a villa (**91**) and may be just an elaborate summer dining room, *triclinium*, built by a wealthy man who happened to think the mosaic design was an attractive one and perhaps one which reflected his own interests in iconography, culture and philosophy. The mosaics at Bignor include a variety of mythological scenes, such as Ganymede being gathered up by Jupiter. Clearly a major decorative feature, it is unlikely to have had any greater significance. Likewise, the Keynsham, Lufton and Holcombe villas all show the kind of extravagant structural extensions some Romano-British were prepared to install. Dining rooms of very similar plan are known as integral features of some villas in the Mediterranean area, for example

143 *The* mithraeum *at Carrawburgh as it appears today. The altars and posts are modern reproductions, the original altars being now stored at the Museum of Antiquities, Newcastle. The fort lies to the right. The shrine of the Nymphs lay in the foreground (now buried) and 'Coventina's Well' (a sacred spring) lay in the distance (right). See **141-2***

144 *(opposite) Triconch hall at Littlecote, Wiltshire, originally discovered in 1727 when the remarkable Orpheus mosaic was revealed. Its site was subsequently lost and only found again in 1977.*

The site lies astride the main Roman road between Silchester to Mildenhall. Nearby the River Kennet flows east to join the Thames. Roman occupation dates from the late first century in the form of a round house, followed by an open-sided timber barn at the beginning of the second century. Subsequently this was replaced with a flint-aisled barn on an overlapping site a few yards to the east c.180. The new barn was associated with a contemporary winged-corridor villa about 30m to the south-west. In between the villa and barn was a simpler building, perhaps used to house estate workers. At the beginning of the fourth century a small set of baths were installed at the western end of the barn.

Some time after 357 the baths were enlarged and the south-eastern corner was removed to make way for the enigmatic triconch hall. The mosaic which was laid has excited much academic debate. The old barn's walls seem to have been reduced to create an open, but enclosed area. The triconch hall probably had a square tower supported by four piers with arches. Three arches led to the apses, the fourth to the nave. Access seems to have been from the baths to the north. Considering the symmetry of the structure it is strange that it was 'tacked on' in such an asymmetrical way; none of the existing walls were exploited and even more curiously it was actually built across the road. Even if the road was disused it is surprising that the architect was prepared to risk subsidence into the old north ditch of the thoroughfare, which indeed seems to have affected one of the apses

0   5 m

Piazza Armerina in Sicily, though here a triconch hall was physically connected to the rest of the house.

Of course there is the problem that at Littlecote the villa house was quite separate but all three ideas are quite valid. As ever we do not know and the subject remains open. It always seems a little unwise to place undue emphasis on a feature of a building which was underfoot and possibly even under furniture — and of course we have no idea what was on the walls either; these may have had paintings portraying something else entirely.

Less sophisticated and unfortunately now entirely destroyed was the beehive temple known as 'Arthur's O'on' just north of the Antonine Wall at Carron (**145**). Its identification as a temple is rather more certain even if the evidence is circumstantial. It seems that the building was one of a number in the northern frontier zone dedicated to Victory and presumably built by the army.

Even simpler is the quaint little temple or shrine dedicated to an obscure god called Antenociticus at Benwell on Hadrian's Wall (**146, colour plate 28**). Its identity is without doubt because it contained the head from the cult statue and two altars with dedications from the unit. However, it is so small and so irregularly built that it bears all the hallmarks of a kind of homemade temple and it is difficult to believe that it was even built by a soldier. Nevertheless its structural form and apse at one end are just the kind of clues that might have led to its identification as a church in the absence of other evidence and it serves as a salutary warning.

Some prehistoric monuments like Neolithic long barrows and Bronze Age stone circles attracted Romano-British attention, though they would have had little idea of their

145 Circular 'beehive' temple at Carron, two miles north of Falkirk, Scotland (also known as Arthur's O'on/Oven). The tragedy of this remarkable building is that it survived until 1743 when it was demolished. Fortunately antiquarian drawings survive, as does a replica built in 1763.

'Arthur's O'on' was built of dressed stone in beehive form and had an arched entrance and a window above. The diameter was about 9m (30ft) with a similar height. It may have had an oculus (an open space) at the top but this is unlikely for a number of reasons. Firstly the oculus was designed to let light in: at this latitude (56° north) it would have been unsuitable because at midday on midsummer's day the sun will shine down at an angle of approximately 67° 30' — the figure is calculated by subtracting the tilt of the earth on that day (23° 30') from 56°; this gives us the figure to take away from the vertical of 90°. As it happens this is roughly the angle required for the sun to shine through the window known to have existed on to the centre of the floor on midsummer's day. During the rest of the year the sun would shine further and further back on the floor and gradually up the rear wall. This is all based on the assumption that the window was south-facing. Secondly, the relatively heavy rain in the area might have made a central oculus hopelessly impractical.

It is not certain that the building was a temple but it is difficult to imagine an alternative function and there is the circumstantial evidence of a relief from Rose Hill, Gilsland, Cumbria. This relief, part of which is shown here (a), depicts a similar building on a rocky knoll next to which is a flying Victory. Early reports of Arthur's O'on mention carved Victories and Eagles on the walls within, so it may have been a temple to Victory which would have been appropriate for the location. There was almost certainly a statue within because a pedestal existed and a fragment of bronze statue was also found. It is restored here but the scale of the figure and its posture is purely speculative.

The facts that the temple was so close to the fort at Falkirk on the Antonine Wall, and the quality of its masonry, make it virtually certain that the army was responsible for its construction. The II legion Augusta is known to have built the wall along with detachments of the VI and XX. Any of these could have been the builders but this does not affect a likely construction date of post c.140. The temple would probably have fallen out of use by the late second century, along with the abandonment of the Wall

true age or purpose. They were probably regarded with a mixture of curiosity and awe, and for many communities local lore would have provided an explanation for their importance. Near the villa at Stanwick, Northamptonshire, a Bronze Age round barrow was surrounded by a polygonal *temenos* wall during the first century. A modest, but decorated, entrance led into an enclosure where an ambulatory allowed visitors to walk around the barrow. Several hundred coins were found around the ambulatory, and the barrow itself was surrounded by deposits of oyster shells. Together these suggest votive gifts and ritual meals. There is no evidence that the cult was connected with a god, but it may be that the community was continuing to venerate the tomb of an ancestor on into the Romano-British period. This is an interesting but tantalizing glimpse of local Celtic myths and legends based on the half-truths of a folk history almost completely lost to us.

*146 Temple of Antenociticus at Benwell on Hadrian's Wall (see also **colour plate 28**). This curious little temple with its apse and irregular walls was identified outside the east wall of the fort at Benwell in 1862. Three altars record its dedication to Antenociticus/Anociticus (RIB 1327-9). One can be dated to 177-80. The cult statue's head survives. Little comment can be made about the structure apart from the fact that its quaint eccentricity suggests a very home-made type of shrine. It is also worth noting that had the altars and statue not been found this is the type of building which might have been described as an 'early church'. As this is palpably not the case here it serves as a warning*

Rural shrines

Romans were particularly fond of setting up shrines in a rural context where local gods associated with hunting or water might be worshipped in an attractive setting. We do not know very much about these shrines because their simplicity means few survive in recognizable form. At Carrawburgh a small shrine to local nymphs and genius was established outside the mithraeum and seems to have consisted of a semi-circular seat and an altar (**142**). Two shrines, one circular and one rectangular, on Bowes Moor in County Durham, were dedicated to a local god associated with hunting called Vinotonus. An altar found here was dedicated by the commander of the nearby fort at Bowes (*RIB* 733). It may well be that these little shrines were dotted all over Britain but only those in remote northern areas have half a chance of surviving in identifiable form.

147 Capital, from Cirencester, probably forming part of a Jupiter column. Such columns were free-standing and would have stood in a prominent public place, like the forum. The surviving capital has four figures associated with Bacchus, who was Jupiter's son: Bacchus himself, Silenus, a female maenad or priestess, and Lycurgus, King of Thrace shown here. There would have been a statue of Jupiter on top of the capital while at the base an inscribed block would have recorded the dedication. Such a base has survived from Cirencester but is probably from a different column (RIB 103)

Civic religious monuments

It was normal for the state, the town government and local people to erect 'religious' monuments within a town. One of the commonest forms was the so-called Jupiter column, *columna* (**147**). Cirencester has produced remains of two (*RIB* 103) and part of another has been found at Great Chesterford. Their form is known from more complete examples found elsewhere in the north-west provinces. They consisted of freestanding columns resting on bases which recorded the dedication to *Jupiter Optimus Maximus*. The capital was usually decorated with deities or personifications connected with Jupiter and supported a statue of the god himself.

Remains of a monumental arch, *arcum*, decorated with carvings of various gods have been found in London (**148**). It is unlikely to represent a triumphal arch like that at Richborough and has been interpreted as a possible entrance to a temple precinct. Inscriptions record several others. At Ancaster, Trenico dedicated an *arcum* to the otherwise-unknown god Viridius, probably marking the entrance to a shrine or small temple precinct. At York, Lucius Viducius Placidus dedicated an *arcum et ianum* ('arch and entrance-way') to several deities including a Genius and the spirits of the emperors (for both these and another, see *Companion*, 113-14).

The London arch was erected probably in the late second or early third century but by the fourth it had been demolished to provide stone for the new riverside wall. This fate probably befell many pagan monuments in the late Roman period elsewhere in Britain (**14**). The same riverside wall contained other religious carvings probably from temples or shrines nearby in the city, including a screen depicting four mother goddesses and two altars. They may all have formed part of a complex of religious buildings not far west of the so-called governor's palace (**65**) and the baths at Huggin Hill (**77**).

148 *(opposite) Arch from London. The sites of a number of arches are known from Roman Britain — at Verulamium (two) and at Richborough (79) but practically nothing of their decoration or design is known, though they were almost certainly triumphal arches.*

Ironically, some of the decoration from the London arch has survived but its original site is unknown. Sculptured stones were recovered from the late fourth century defensive wall built along the riverbank. A number of older monuments were re-used in this wall but the arch stones all come from the Blackfriars area in the west of the city.

The illustration is based on work by the late Tom Blagg. The upper panel seems to have depicted the gods of the week (Saturn, Sol, Luna, Mars, Mercury, Jupiter and Venus - these names survive better in French than English). The four seasons may have been represented by busts in roundels on either side of the arch (as in many mosaics). On the pillars there seem to have been full length figures, including Minerva and Hercules. At one end a panel showing a wind god appeared above a winding scroll. The whole structure seems to have been about 8m (26ft) high.

If there was an inscription it was on the other side and is unknown. It has been suggested that the arch was actually an entrance way to a temple precinct - evidence of other substantial religious sculpture from the same part of the riverside wall suggests there may have been such an area nearby (these include a stone screen depicting a number of gods). Several others are recorded on inscriptions from elsewhere (see Companion 113-14*), at Ancaster, Nettleham and York.*

The date of the arch can only be estimated on stylistic grounds. These have been used by Blagg to attribute the arch's erection somewhere between the middle of the second century and the end of the Severan period in the early third century. However this is always difficult and it is not unknown for later sculptured material of the third century to emulate earlier work so the possible date range could be much larger

6 Other buildings

Transport (roads, bridges and quays)

The conquest and exploitation of Britain depended on adequate communications. The Roman army was pre-eminent at organizing this in the ancient world and by the second century most of the conquered part of Britain seems to have been criss-crossed by a network of roads. Much of the modern road system has its origin in Roman road-building (**149**). However, we know far less about the exploitation of waterways even though simple economic considerations mean that transport by water must have been not only cheaper than road transport, but sometimes the only feasible way of moving bulky goods. There must then have been a great deal of building work involving the artificial raising of river levels to make them navigable in their higher reaches, and the drainage of low-lying areas to create canals, though the use of narrow low draught barges would have made even quite small streams usable. Extensive drainage works took place in the Fens and the Somerset levels and some ditches of Roman date have been identified such as the Car Dyke in Cambridgeshire and Lincolnshire (though this particular example was not navigable). In general though very little tangible evidence for engineering works has been located though a certain amount of controversy surrounds the so-called bridge at Piercebridge, which may be a dam.

Roads

Road-building is the skill most popularly associated with Roman civilization. Communication between Roman forts and settlements was essential for the operations of government and trade. Clues lie not just in routes connecting settlements of known Roman date, but also the presence of an *agger* (a raised road surface), wide berms and side ditches (**149**). The latter in particular have usually been obscured by the passage of time and modern wide trunk roads can completely obscure all other traces. However, most major routes between towns have been identified largely because these settlements have endured to the present day and the roads have remained in use ever since the Roman period.

The main roads were almost certainly laid out during the military conquest of Britain in the first century. This even included the principal routes into Scotland, associated with the campaigns of Agricola (*c.*78-84). Most of the roads continued in use as the towns and commerce of the civilian province developed. Remains of milestones indicate that repairs of roads continued throughout the period into the fourth century, for example the milestone from Rockbourne villa (re-used as building stone) which mentions the emperor Trajan Decius (249-251), and another from near Carlisle which was erected under Carausius (286-293) but subsequently inverted and re-carved with the titles of

149 Dere Street between Risingham and Hadrian's Wall, looking north. It is a commonplace to state that Roman roads are straight; this is only partly true and it is more accurate to say that Roman roads were normally built in a series of straight stretches. Although a modern road now runs along this section of Dere Street two features can be seen which help identify it as a Roman road: the wide berms between the modern road and the field walls, and the height of the curved road surface relative to the adjacent fields

Constantine I, as Caesar, for the year 306-7 (*RIB* 2291). Another, of the same date and dedication, survives from the other end of the province at St Hilary in Cornwall (*RIB* 2233). A glance at the Ordnance Survey map of Roman Britain shows how little evidence we have for roads and Romanized settlements in the far south-west beyond Exeter, yet the St Hilary milestone shows that maintained roads existed in remote areas.

Our knowledge of minor routes is consequently rather poor so we really have no idea of their extent. A good example is the Darenth Valley in Kent. Here a number of houses of Roman date separated by only a few miles lie close to the river. There would have been some sort of track running north between them to join Watling Street (the main route between Canterbury and London). However, any such track has yet to be found. The majority of all villas lie at some distance from any known road, even though general distribution is biased to the main 'trunk' routes, which suggests that access to those roads was of some importance. In a few cases the houses lie very close to the main road — Stonesfield villa in Oxfordshire lies only a few yards north of Akeman Street running between Alchester and Cirencester. The site of the villa is a commanding one looking down across the road (the agger of which is still visible at this point). At nearby Ditchley a footpath seems to preserve the original track from Akeman Street up to the villa.

Dating roads is particularly difficult because it is unlikely that evidence will be recovered which provides a reliable *terminus post quem*. More useful is the kind of evidence from towns which shows that urban layouts took into account a pre-existing road. At Silchester the town baths seem to have been built according to a late first-century street

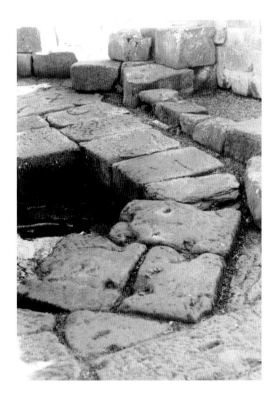

150 Bridge abutment at Chesters on Hadrian's Wall (detail). Here the Hadrianic pier can be seen incorporated into the enlarged Severan bridge abutment. The original structure was probably made of wood and supported on seven piers, similar to that at Willowford (colour plate 29). The Severan version was made of stone and supported on three far larger piers

grid; subsequent reorganization resulted in a reorientation of the grid and the bathhouse lost its portico which was now covered by a re-directed road. At Verulamium Watling Street entered from the south making for the mid-first-century fort and thereafter was clumsily accommodated into the street grid of the developing town. This created a triangle junction marking the site of the 'Triangular Temple' (**120**). But of course it may be that a Roman road was simply replacing an earlier Celtic track, which may have already been in use for generations at the time of the Roman Conquest.

Major Roman roads were designed to cope with the heavy wheeled and hoofed traffic of the day. A sound foundation was essential and this usually began with large stones embedded in the subsoil. Where the site was poorly drained or low-lying more support could be gained by ramming in piles. The road network south of the Thames at London was particularly dependent on this because during the period Southwark was made up of a number of low-lying areas separated by marshy areas, quite unlike its modern state. Above the foundations a series of layers of rammed gravel made up the surfacing though this could be augmented with stone if it was available. In Sussex iron slag from local iron works was used because it rusted into a solid surface. Drainage was vital if the road was to be able to cope with the elements and traffic, and this was why the raised agger was used with side ditches to carry the water off the berms. The whole effect is rather hard to appreciate in Britain today apart from few exceptional sites such as Ackling Dyke in Dorset. Much more impressive are the roads in North Africa, Tunisia in particular, where modern road surfaces form no more than a thin central veneer on an otherwise unaltered Roman road.

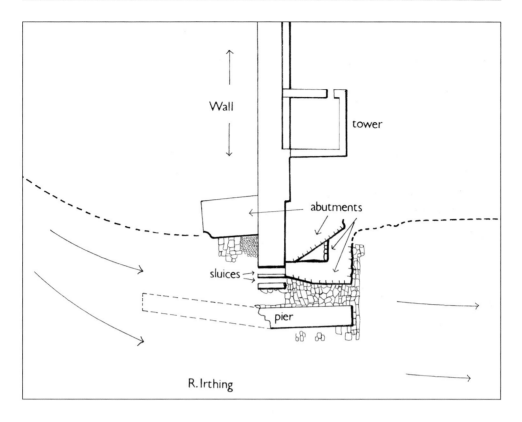

*151 Plan of the bridge abutment at Willowford on Hadrian's Wall. The river has moved west since Roman times and the site is now some yards from the present bank. It appears that the abutment supported a mill fed by water directed by the pier. A pair of sluices helped control the flow (see **152**). As the river gradually moved west so new abutments were constructed*

The heaviest wear came from wheeled traffic due to the direct effect of loads transmitted directly to the road surface through the wheels, unrelieved by suspension. Roads in long-term use had to be regularly resurfaced. At the legionary fortress of Inchtuthil wagon ruts were especially concentrated in the vicinity of the workshop and granaries (**18, 35, 39**), which is not surprising. The streets had never been resurfaced because the site was abandoned after only about three years of occupation. The road running west (the Fosse Way) from Cirencester by the town amphitheatre towards Bath was found to be heavily-rutted.

Roman roads were both recorded and mapped for official use. Some of these records have survived and they supply useful information about routes used and the ancient names of the settlements that lay along them. The Antonine Itinerary was drawn up in the early third century and the Ravenna Cosmography was assembled in the seventh century from earlier records. The Antonine Itinerary is particularly useful because it lists the distances between settlements. While these sources name many of the settlements they do not name the roads — titles such as 'Stane Street' or 'Watling Street' belong to the Saxon

*152 The abutment at Willowford looking south showing the north face of Hadrian's Wall with two sluices and a channel for the mill race to right (see **151**)*

period and later. Some of the settlements have yet to be located like *Villa Faustini* which lay between Colchester and Caistor-by-Norwich while others such as Asthall in Oxfordshire are omitted from the list.

The history of roads in Britain after the period of Roman occupation is as hard to trace as the history of almost anything else in the so-called 'Dark Ages'. However, for the most part the major Roman roads of Britain seem to have been retained as routes and of all the building works of Roman Britain they show the greatest continuity to modern times. Up until the eighteenth century this would have been in the form of ill-kept tracks and lanes. The construction of turnpike roads and subsequently modern metalled roads has preserved the routes though often with breaks in continuity. The reasons are probably to do with simple convenience and because of land ownership throughout the whole period which meant that field boundaries took into account the roads and often the wide berms too — it is quite common to find a modern road running through countryside with what appears to be an unusually wide space between the metalling and the adjacent fields. Although this does not always mean that the road is Roman, or pre-Roman in origin, it can often be a clue.

Bridges

In a small island criss-crossed by rivers and streams it may well be that most bridges were simple timber affairs needing regular maintenance and replacement. Many such crossings

153 Monumental remains at Piercebridge. This controversial site to the south-east of the fort, and across the River Tees, was discovered in 1972. It was identified as the remains of the Roman bridge, constructed as an artificial riverbed with piers. This is hard to reconcile with another Roman bridge a few yards to the west which actually lies on the main Roman road from the south. Moreover, this site now lies some yards to the south of the river and it is necessary to account for the fact that the river would have had to move north and then cut a deep channel to find its present course, whereas it has not moved at the point of the other bridge. A much more interesting, if unproven, explanation is given by R. Selkirk who has argued that the stone blocks formed part of a dam, created to raise water levels in the interests of freight transportation. This has the advantage of explaining the other bridge, the road, and avoiding having to explain why at this point the river's rate of erosion should have exceeded that further west. However no other traces of any possible dam have been located. Unfortunately, while Selkirk's case is published the excavators' case is available only in summary form and it is therefore difficult to form a conclusion

may have been fords, for example at Iden Green in Kent where flagstones placed across the stream bedding provided a firm footing for wheeled and hoofed traffic alike.

At other sites the evidence is hard to interpret. At Asthall in Oxfordshire Akeman Street appears to make a small diversion in order to approach the River Windrush at right angles. The *agger* running from the north is obvious today. It ends abruptly a few yards short of the river, presumably at a point representing the Roman riverbank. A few feet further south a number of stones, carefully placed to form a rectangle may be a small pier for a wooden bridge. A rare case of survival was found at Aldwinkle near Thrapston in Northamptonshire where a gravel quarry revealed the remains of a Roman timber bridge, which had once crossed the river Nene. The unusual state of preservation showed that the timber piles were up to 0.5m (1.5ft) in thickness and had been strengthened with iron sheaths. Even the bridge across the Thames in London seems, on current evidence, to have been built of a timber superstructure supported on timber piers in the shallower water near the banks, and piles across the middle (**154**).

154 Port buildings by the bridge in London, c.100. Recent excavations on a number of sites around the bridgehead in London have revealed traces of a complex and thriving port with many warehouses, containing remains of an extensive series of imported goods. The riverbank was embanked with a series of revetments which created quaysides. Behind the quays rectangular warehouses were built. They contained a number of rooms which may have served as entrances and shops with storerooms on an upper storey. Each building probably had a single owner with a number of merchant tenants. In later years the quays were moved further into the river to create more dockside space. This process continued right on into medieval times so the Roman riverfront now lies some way inland, though waterlogged conditions have preserved large stretches of the quays. The site must have been the prime commercial location for the province at the time. A well-known reference in Tacitus (Annals xiv.33) states it was an important port by 60

The only comprehensive evidence for masonry bridges exists on the northern frontier. The best known is the Chesters bridge which was built under Hadrian to carry the Wall across the Tyne, apparently just preceding actual construction of the curtain. At this date it was carried on eight piers (possibly with a wooden superstructure) but a later rebuilding remodelled the structure completely so that it was carried on only three larger piers (**150, colour plate 29**). The remains of stone masonry in the vicinity have been taken as evidence that the bridge was built entirely of stone, rather than having a wooden superstructure supported by stone piers as was the case with the bridge over the Danube depicted on Trajan's Column. Another bridge further west took the frontier across the

Irthing at Willowford, just east of the fort at Birdoswald. In its first period the bridge probably resembled the one at Chesters but here a later rebuilding, complicated by the river's rapid erosion westwards, seems to have involved a timber superstructure (**151-2, colour plate 30**). Both bridges incorporated mills into their eastern abutments. Other bridges undoubtedly existed in the Wall system — the Roman name for Newcastle-upon-Tyne, *Pons Aelius*, is proof of one and altars found in the river Tyne in the general area probably come from it. They were dedicated to Neptune and Ocianus respectively by the VI legion (*RIB* 1319/20).

The most controversial site is at Piercebridge (**153**). The site of the Roman bridge across the river Wear has long been known. It lay on the path of the main road (Dere Street), which ran to the east of the fort; its final traces were only swept away in early modern times. However, a monumental structure has been discovered about 100 yards to the south-east, and some yards south of the present course of the river. It consists of a rectangular area of flagstones on top of which lie tumbled piles of large blocks. These were identified as the remains of bridge piers, the flagstones a paving to restrict river-scouring. There are a number of problems here. Firstly the second 'bridge' is not on the road alignment; secondly why should the settlement need two bridges so close to one another?; thirdly the second 'bridge' is in such a position that one is required to believe that the river has moved some yards north horizontally and then rather abruptly downwards here, yet has not moved at all on the site of the other bridge. The recovery of rubbish and votive deposits from the whole period on the site of the other bridge makes it unlikely that one bridge replaced the other. An extremely interesting interpretation of the remains as part of a dam and its associated overspill has been suggested. This would have formed part of a system of dams and locks which would have made higher reaches of rivers navigable. If correct, though there is very little in the way of confirmatory evidence, the implications for interpreting and understanding Roman freight transportation within the province are considerable.

Wharfs and quays

As an island province Roman Britain was dependent on waterborne trade, though in the ancient and medieval world transport by any other means was so inefficient that almost everywhere would have relied on shipping of some sort. The evidence for trade with the rest of the Empire has been known ever since the sources of fine pottery wares in Germany and Gaul were identified along with the sources of amphorae around the Mediterranean. The sources and nature of perishable goods which did not require ceramic containers are unknown.

All these items had to be shipped in, and Britain's products shipped out. The most intensive period of trading was during the late first and early second century. By the third and fourth centuries there was much more of a tendency to manufacture goods within the province. Shipping in goods required not just quays on which to unload goods but warehouses for storage. Not surprisingly most of Roman Britain's major ports have remained as ports and there has been little opportunity to examine remains of the Roman period except as a result of the colossal redevelopment which has taken place in the City of London in recent years. Archaeological examination of waterlogged sites, especially the

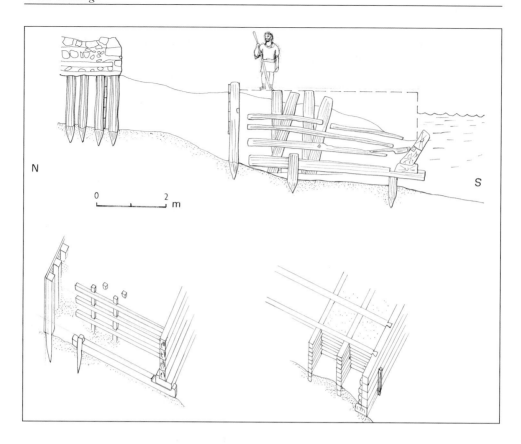

155 Riverside wharfs in London (after Miller et al). The upper view is a section through part of the third-century wharfs excavated at New Fresh Wharf in London. The foundations and piles on the left represent the footings of the riverside wall, erected in the late Roman period. The quay to the right (phase 4) was built with a front wall of oak beams held back by braces strengthened with piles. The space between the timbers was filled with dumped soil and rubbish. At the rear (between the quay and the riverside wall stood a further revetment, possibly involved with the construction of the phase 4 quay). At the lower left is an axonometric view of the same quay. At the lower right is an axonometric view of the second-century quay on the Customs House site to the east, built out of a box frame

St Magnus House (New Fresh Wharf) and the Customs House sites, have revealed the massive timber wharfs and revetments which were built along the north bank of the Thames in association with warehouses (**154**). The technique of dendrochronology (tree-ring dating) has made it possible to associate these wharfs with a long period of building and rebuilding running from the late first century well into the third century. Techniques differ from site to site but broadly speaking the actual quayside consisted of a number of horizontal timbers laced into timbers which ran back into the natural riverbank to the rear, thus bracing the riverfront itself. The spaces between the bracing timbers were filled with rubbish, flint, stone and tile rubble to create a level wharf surface (**155**). In time, land was reclaimed by advancing the riverfront. This was achieved by building a new quayside and filling in the space with rubble. This does not seem to have taken place after the early third century though there is continued evidence for use of the wharfs up to the late fourth century.

A number of buildings were associated directly with the wharfs. For the most part they have been identified as warehouses though their precise function in terms of storage (whether long-term or short-term, pre- or post-voyage) and dispersal is obviously unknown. Fairly typical seem to have been rectangular buildings subdivided into separate rooms all opening onto the wharf. In this respect they resemble a row of shops like those known at Ostia or Pompeii in Italy, which of course they may actually have been. In later years some of these warehouses seem to have remodelled with the individual components being redeveloped independently. This may suggest a move from single ownership, renting to merchant tenants, to individual ownership of units. On the south bank of the Thames excavations have revealed an exceptionally well-preserved timber building, possibly a warehouse (**156**).

More circumstantial evidence exists in the form of a huge dump of burnt samian ware found on the Regis House site. It was associated with burnt building rubble and it seems likely that the warehouse, which must have been nearby, burnt down and subsequently the debris was swept away and dumped into the quayside. Other material from the general area indicates storage of considerable quantities of pottery goods, for example samian from Billingsgate Lorry Park which was largely unused and may represent warehouse sweepings of damaged goods dumped in the river. Of course we have little idea of perishable goods apart from amphorae. One from the Thames contained olives while others bear inscriptions referring to contents such as wine, oil or fish sauce (for example *RIB* 2492.23, 28). All these would have required some sort of storage.

Water

Exploiting water as an energy source and bringing it into settlements by artificial means seem to have been new ideas for Britain. However, the widespread availability of water meant that aqueducts and other examples of hydraulic engineering never had to be quite as elaborate as elsewhere in the Empire, though we may simply lack the evidence.

Aqueducts, drains and sewers

Aqueducts are popularly believed to consist of a water channel suspended on stone arches carried from a natural source to a settlement. Their remains in Spain, France, Italy and North Africa are amongst the most impressive of all Roman feats of engineering skill. However, they were usually only built in this form to carry water across steep valleys or wide plains. In Britain's undulating terrain it was possible to exploit natural contours to carry the water down through channels cut in the ground. Also it was rarely necessary to bring water any great distance so aqueducts would never have been as important as they were further south, though the demands of major military and public baths may have made them essential for the fortresses and larger towns.

156 (opposite) Timber warehouse from Southwark, London (after Dillon). Southwark is known to have been the site of an extensive suburb of Roman London, covering at least 30 acres. It grew up around the southern end of the bridge which crossed the Thames to the provincial capital. In ancient times the area was low-lying marshland with a number of islands separated by streams. In 1987/8 a remarkable timber building was found sealed in silts on the edge of one of the islands.

The land was originally reclaimed with timber piles in the late first century and at some point in the early second century a rectangular pit about 0.8m deep was dug. Into this pit the building was erected directly onto the ground surface. It was based on sill-beams which supported the walls and joists which supported the inernal floorboards. It was 4.75m (16ft) wide and at least 11m (36ft) long (the building's full length did not survive). It was probably roofed with timber shingles. Access to the building was down a wooden ramp, part of which survived. The semi-subterranean nature of the building and the ramp suggest it was a warehouse designed to create a cool environment, suitable for storing food and drink. It was eventually buried by waterborne silts carrying late second- and early third-century pottery so it may be that a flood caused its demise, but also its preservation. The building was lifted for conservation and eventual permanent display. Such a rare survival is an important reminder that Roman Britain must have had far more timber buildings than is commonly recognized

Several towns were supplied at least in part by aqueducts. At Dorchester (Dorset) contours in surrounding hills were used to carry water in a leet around 1m (3ft) deep over a distance of about 19km (12 miles) into the town. A similar arrangement at the fort of Greatchesters on Hadrian's Wall carried water for 10km (6 miles) into the fort. The circuitous route was made necessary by the lie of the land and the source of water is actually only about 3.5km (2.25 miles) away. At Lincoln a rare case of piped water under pressure brought water uphill into the town. At Pompeii a special building at one of the highest points in the town contained tanks to provide a head of water — a large platform in the northern part of Lincoln may have provided the foundation for a similar structure. At street corners in Pompeii the water seems to have been stored within suspended tanks on brick towers in order to create a head of water. Within settlements water was channelled through pipes which made it possible to supply individual houses and water fountains. Lincoln had an ornamental octagonal tank, the inn's courtyard at Catterick contained an ornamental water fountain with a run-off conduit, and another can still be seen in Corbridge adjacent to the east granary (**37**). It was embellished with a carved pediment and statues though in later years the stone walls of the trough seem to have become excessively worn down by knife sharpening.

These isolated examples may well be representative of the province as a whole though we cannot be certain. A few inscriptions show that others existed at forts. Aqueducts were installed at Chesters between 177-84 (*RIB* 1463), and South Shields between 221-2 (*RIB* 1060). Between 198-209 under Septimius Severus, the *aquaeductium* at Caernarvon was repaired (*RIB* 430).

There is even less evidence for rural house and minor settlements being supplied in this way — they probably used wells (lined with timber if necessary), for example at

Lullingstone. However, the house at Woodchester does seem to have been supplied with water by an underground stone conduit. The conduit survives and apparently still carries water, recently actually supplying modern houses. It runs towards the Roman house from a stream some 550m (about 1800ft) and while its exact date is uncertain the circumstantial evidence points to it being ancient.

Getting rid of water was almost as much of a problem though it all formed part of a single system. At Housesteads the latrine was flushed by water which simply ran off out through a hole in the fort walls (**40**) into a septic tank or soakaway requiring no specific building works. However, within towns there was more of a problem because obviously each house would have had its own waste whereas a fort's occupants could all use a single central facility. York has yielded the best evidence for sewers. The main sewer, an elaborately built tunnel with a vaulted roof, was fed by side tunnels, which carried waste from buildings on either side (**157**). Lincoln and Verulamium were similarly equipped, at least in part, but there is very little evidence for comparable facilities elsewhere. A number have been identified at Verulamium, built of masonry or timber and usually in association with streets. The settlement lies on an east-facing slope and this may have assisted the civic authorities in arranging such a system. At Silchester the baths had their own drains and there does not seem to have been any form of sewer network, perhaps because the site's

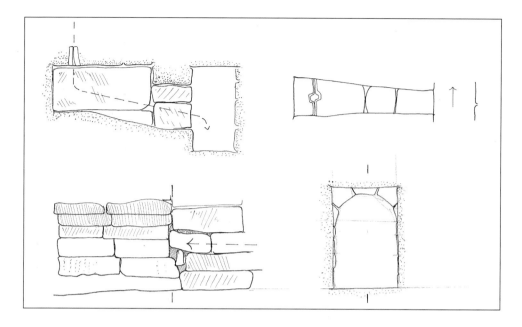

157 Sewer in Church Street, York, in the south-east section of the legionary fortress (after Whitwell).

a = Section through side passage 4 showing how water enters from above and runs out into the main channel (length of section, about 3m)

b = Side passage 4 from above

c = Elevation of the main channel; in the middle vaulting gives way to a flat roof; height about 1.5m (5ft), or just enough for a small man to walk through with some discomfort

d = Cross-section of the main channel showing the end of the vault as it meets a flat-roofed section

general flatness would have made creating a gradient complicated. At Bath a huge drain helped clear out the reservoir of the sacred spring; when the spring was covered over an arch was built over the drain capstone (**colour plate 31**).

Mills

In a world lacking mechanization the force created by moving water could be of great importance because apart from using animals it was the only means of supplying sustained power. The only certain evidence we have of its exploitation is the existence of watermills. They are known from a number of sites, both military and civil, for example: watermills associated with Hadrian's Wall at Willowford, Haltwhistle Burn and Chesters, Ickham in Kent (two), Nettleton in Wiltshire and Great Chesterford in Essex.

A channel and fragments of millstones is evidence for a mill. The mill-race (or head race) was usually an artificial channel, which diverted part of a flowing river alongside the mill building so that it could turn the waterwheel, though one Roman writer (Palladius) suggested that the outflow from public baths could be used (*Opus agriculturae*, I.41).

216

Sometimes the head race was splayed so that the flow was concentrated as much as possible at the point where the waterwheel was sited. It then flowed out on the other side through the tail race to rejoin the main flow. The easiest way of arranging all this was to make a cutting across a bend in a river, for example at Haltwhistle Burn (**158**). Alternatively the same effect could be created by building a channel into a bridge abutment, for example at Chesters or Willowford (**151-2**).

The waterwheel would have been made of wood because this was the only feasible way of manufacturing a wheel with paddles. The paddles were forced to move by the water and so the wheel turned. The rotating horizontal axis was connected to the vertical axis of the upper and lower millstones through a differential or lantern gear. The millstones or their iron spindles, and the bearing stones which housed the shafts, are the most likely sort of artefactual evidence for identifying a building as a mill, though of course a building may have housed a waterwheel in order to perform a completely different task such as moving cutting tools for wood or stone, or even hammers for metal-working (see below).

The Hadrian's Wall mills probably helped supply the garrison with food. All three are near forts: Chesters, Greatchesters (Haltwhistle Burn) and Birdoswald (Willowford). Evidence of metal-working at Ickham, remains of what may have been a water-powered hammer and military equipment, have been interpreted as possible evidence of a late Roman military establishment engaged in manufacturing armaments with the help of a watermill. The site was close to several Saxon Shore forts (Reculver, Richborough, Dover and Lympne). However, sites like Great Chesterford or Nettleton may be purely private establishments serving a local community simply as part of the local infrastructure of food supply. Such sites may have remained in use for long after the Roman period and some may have remained in use right through the medieval period though it would be very hard to establish a Roman origin for them.

Furnaces, kilns and ovens

Not strictly buildings, furnaces, kilns and ovens could be quite elaborate structures, which required considerable skill to make them serve their desired purpose. They would normally have been associated with some sort of settlement though it is very rare in Britain for the actual workshops to be located. At Caistor St Edmund near Norwich, excavations revealed the remains of what seems to have been a glass-maker's workshop close to the forum (**159**). Pottery production, of course, was far more widespread. While the kilns themselves are quite often found it is rarer for a potter's workshop to be discovered as well. An example is known from Stibbington, near Peterborough where a number of kilns are associated with a workshop containing a potter's flywheel (**160**).

Kilns
The purpose of a kiln is to contain heat in order to fire pottery. This required an effective structure, which both retained the heat but kept the direct heat away from the pottery. There were many different types. However, most kilns, apart from surface clamps, which were really just bonfires, had three parts: the stokehole, the furnace chamber and the

158 *Haltwhistle Burn watermill. The site is close to milecastle 42 and Greatchesters fort on Hadrian's Wall and was identified as a watermill by F. Gerald Simpson who discovered the site in 1907-8. The stream takes an extreme bend here and a channel was cut across it with a weir to concentrate the flow of water into the mill. Remains of millstones and use of the north-west wall of the building to form part of the channel suggest that the mill was of the under-shot wheel type, i.e. the water pushes the wheel from underneath, driving a mechanism within.*

a = Reconstructed view based on a photograph by the excavator

b = Reconstruction of the internal mechanism (after Spain)

c = Plan of the site (after Simpson)

159 Glass workshop at Caistor St Edmund, Venta Icenorum, Norfolk. Originally built c.200-
20, the site seems to have been modified c.300 by adapting two adjacent houses and building
furnaces, hearths and enclosure walls. Glass was then manufactured here for around 50 years

oven (**161**). The furnace chamber was usually made by simply digging a suitably-sized and shaped pit in the ground. An adjacent pit allowed access to the chamber through the stokehole and flue. The roof of the furnace chamber had to support the load of pottery and also allow the heat through. This was either done with a permanent clay floor pierced with vent holes or by making up the floor each time with fired clay rods, which radiated from a central pillar to the walls. The load of pottery was installed and only then was the oven actually roofed over, usually with clay or turfs in dome form. If the load was to be 'oxidized' a vent hole was left at the top. If it was to be 'reduced' the dome was completely sealed. Such kilns could be used over and over again but were generally abandoned when a firing when drastically wrong.

Ovens

These are best known from military sites where they are usually found close to the ramparts. Each century would have had its own oven which resembled a kiln but instead of a supply of direct heat being maintained the oven was raised to the temperature required by placing fuel within; this was raked out, the food loaded and the oven shut fast for the desired time. Consequently they are even simpler but are usually freestanding rather than partially buried (**162**).

160 Potter's workshop at Stibbington, Peterborough (restored axonometric view). The structure is simple enough and contained chests for clay. The building yielded remains of a stone flywheel which the potter turned with his feet to rotate the throwing wheel. In the foreground is a clay pit and to the right a well. They supplied two of the three basic requirements for pottery making. Fuel for the kiln sited at upper left would have come from nearby woodland

Lighthouses

Like modern lighthouses the ancient *pharos* served the straightforward purposes of informing and warning mariners. Only two are known for certain in Roman Britain and both overlooked the harbour at Dover, obviously being designed to guide shipping between them, though whether they were built at the same time is unknown. They may have been associated with the Dover forts belonging to the *Classis Britannica* in the second century, or possibly the later Saxon Shore fort built towards the end of the third century. Either way it seems they were military buildings. The western lighthouse is known only from its foundations whereas the eastern one still stands to an impressive height though this is in part due to medieval addition (**163, colour plate 32**). The eastern lighthouse is a simple octagonal tower, which rose in a number of stages. Interestingly a tile from London is thought to bear a diagram of a *pharos* though this cannot be certain (**2**).

161 *Cross-section of a coarse ware kiln (after Woods). There are many types of these kilns known but their simple structures all reflect an essentially similar technique. The kiln, usually circular, was made by digging a depression in the ground with an extension for the fire. The chamber itself was generally built out of dried bricks. The load was supported on a higher level, in this case by a clay pedestal and radial spars. In this way heat could circulate evenly from below. The kiln was filled and then capped with a 'vault' of turf or brick. If the pots were to be 'reduced' (starved of air during firing to achieve a black or grey ware) then the cover would be made airtight. If the pots were to be 'oxidized', the opposite to reduction, then a vent was left. The type is broadly typical of the first century and was already in use in Britain in Belgic areas before the Roman occupation*

Tombs

During the first and second centuries most of the Romano-British were cremated and their remains buried in simple containers like earthenware pots or glass jars. The graves were marked with headstones or wooden markers and sometimes were equipped with libation pipes. In the third century and afterwards inhumation became more the norm, but apart from using coffins burial practice seems to have remained unaltered except that as Christianity spread so the habit of burying the dead with grave-goods seems to have diminished. Burials were either isolated, in groups or in cemeteries depending on the nature of the settlement.

However, for the well-to-do, or those who aspired to posthumous prominence, such modest graves were considered insufficient. Their cremated or inhumed remains were interred in tombs, a number of which have been identified in Britain, or beneath earthen barrows. A couple of inscriptions give us an idea of what they were called. The tombstone of Amatius Ingenuus from Old Carlisle mentions his *tumulus* (*RIB* 906) and a dedication

162 Oven at the legionary fortress of Inchtuthil for barrack 53, c.84-7. The oven lay in the intervallum, *the zone between the buildings of the fortress and its ramparts, for shelter and to avoid other buildings. Unlike a kiln, an oven contained a solid floor and its contents were directly exposed to the heat. The superstructure of a military oven was usually clay but few traces of clay were identified; the oven may therefore have had a stone dome. It was probably used for baking bread and is broadly similar to better-known urban bread ovens found at Pompeii in Italy. Above: plan of the oven (after Richmond); below: reconstruction of the oven*

slab from the tomb at Watercrook of P. Aelius Bassus, a veteran of the XX legion, and others, calls it a *sepulcrum* (*RIB* 754).

Tombs were sometimes quite elaborate structures. They took two forms: a stone revetted tumulus or barrow, or a freestanding walk-in chamber generally with a subterranean burial immediately below. Tombs usually lay outside the area of settlement, for example those which stood beside Dere Street as it ran south from the fort of High Rochester (**164**), but tombs associated with villas sometimes lay quite close to the house itself, for example at Lullingstone (**92**) and Keston (**165**). Such buildings were built in a number of different forms, none particularly complex, but most seem to have fallen into decay during the Roman period and in a few cases were clearly deliberately demolished or their contents robbed out. Evidence from the continent, for example at Pompeii, shows

163 Lighthouse, pharos, at Dover Castle, restored elevation. One of a pair which overlooked the harbour, this building at 13m (43ft) is the tallest surviving Romano-British building. It is octagonal externally though the internal chambers are square. It was built in a number of stepped stages and its original height is obviously unknown, though 25m (80ft) is probably a reasonable guess. The tower was built of ashlar-faced rubble with the usual tile courses. At the top a fire beacon would have shone at night. Here the beacon chamber is shown roofed but equally it may have been open. The other lighthouse has not survived beyond traces of foundations. The date of the buildings is not certain but it is likely that they can be associated with the second-century forts of the Classis Britannica *below*

164 Tomb beside Dere Street at High Rochester, Northumberland. To the south of the fort are substantial traces of the cemetery associated with the fort. Most are small mounds covering cremations but a number of more elaborate stone-built tombs seem to have lined the main road, one of which is still visible. Only two lower courses of stone survive but the tomb may have been as much as 4-5m (13-16ft) in height. One of the surviving stones is carved with the head of an animal. The two figures on the right are standing on Dere Street which runs north from the right past and behind the tomb. The clump of trees in the left centre marks the site of the fort platform a little under half a mile away

that tombs were important meeting places for a family where the members would gather to commemorate their dead ancestors, sometimes within the chamber itself if it was designed for access.

The limited evidence that we have certainly suggests that tombs were built for people of wealth and status, for example soldiers of high rank. The High Rochester tombs would fall into this category but were modest structures compared to the substantial tomb known to have existed west of Corbridge. The Corbridge tomb was about 10m square (32 x 34ft) and was surrounded by a substantial precinct wall which was embellished with at least two carved figures of lions eating prey to symbolize death. It lay in a cemetery beside the Stanegate road.

Other tombs are largely associated with villas and this implies a certain amount of disposable wealth, which could cover the additional cost of what would have been as much of a luxury as it is now. It has been suggested that rural tombs may have acted as cult centres. The 'Temple-Mausoleum' at Lullingstone was called thus by the excavator because of its presumed resemblance to a Romano-Celtic temple in plan. The principal difference was the sealed chamber, which lay beneath the central room containing the inhumed burials of a young man and woman with their grave goods. It seems to have been built around the end of the third century. Nothing whatsoever is known of the identity of these individuals but it is notable that they are the only burials associated with the house (apart from infant burials) despite its very long period of use (*see* **92-3**). Others of course

165 Tombs associated with the villa at Keston, near Bromley. Discovered early in the nineteenth century the buttressed circular tomb was originally plastered and painted red. Next to this is a simpler rectangular tomb which contained an inhumation in a stone coffin. A third burial was discovered comparatively recently between two of the main tomb's buttresses, and consisted of a lead casket containing a cremation sealed in a tile chamber. Other graves were found in the vicinity and it is probably safe to assume that most villas had such cemeteries though they are not very often located because they can lie several hundred metres away

may lay further away but this particular structure was clearly designed to overlook the house, which lay only a few metres away down the hillside.

The Lullingstone building has been restored in Romano-Celtic temple form but it is clear from the excavator's account that no trace of roofing in the ambulatory was found. This is a very important point because it shows how easy it is to assume that a very simple plan represents the same type of building. Consequently the site is now quoted as a parallel for others with a circular argument arising when it is suggested that an assumed religious site like Wood Lane End was centred on a temple-mausoleum — because of its 'resemblance' to Lullingstone in having a vault, even though no evidence of burials was found at the former. The plans may be similar but there is no reason to assume that the superstructures, and by extension the functions, of the two buildings were the same. The central room at Lullingstone was vaulted with tufa blocks and decorated with painted plaster. It may be more accurate to restore the building as a single-chambered tomb within a walled area, and not as a 'temple' at all. Interestingly it was apparent from the sequence of construction that the burial chamber had been built and sealed prior to the erection of the tomb.

By the end of the fourth century the building had fallen into decay and the burials were partially robbed. However, a Saxon church was built directly over the building at an unknown date and it is tempting to suggest that local lore identified the place as one worthy of veneration. But this may actually have been from confusion with the house-

166 Mausoleum at Bancroft (isometric reconstruction). The plan resembles that of a typical Romano-Celtic temple but here the vaulted central chamber has been restored as a separate structure in the manner of surviving tombs at Pompeii, Ostia and Rome, with a surrounding wall. Unfortunately the building, put up in the fourth century, had been thoroughly robbed out by the early fifth century. However, evidence survived to suggest that the mausoleum had contained painted wall plaster (also known from other mausolea in Britain, for example at Poundbury cemetery near Dorchester, Dorset), a tessellated floor and a staircase for access to the coffins in the vault

church which existed within the main house during the late fourth century. Certainly no votive goods survived to suggest that the 'Temple-Mausoleum' had been anything other than a grave.

A very similar building has been identified more recently at Bancroft though it lies much further away from the main house (**166**). Like the Lullingstone example its plan consists of two concentric squares and the central square contained a subterranean chamber. However, in this case the building had been completely robbed out at a late date, to the extent that a ramp had been constructed to make removal of the spoil easier. A tomb found at Welwyn supports the idea that such buildings need not have resembled Romano-Celtic temples. Here the square tomb was surrounded by a concentric ditch, rather than a concentric wall; the ditch itself contained three burials. Concentric walls for tombs may therefore have been boundary walls rather than ambulatories.

The tombs at Keston in Kent were of the simpler stone-revetted tumulus kind but these had their own structural problems. The larger of the pair is circular and around 10m (30ft) in diameter. The earth core created lateral stresses as it settled and to combat this a number of buttresses supported the outside wall. It was probably capped with an earth cone. A similar, but much larger, example is known at West Mersea in Essex. Here the 20m (65ft) wide rotunda was retained with a masonry wall strengthened by 12 buttresses. The tumulus was further strengthened with six walls radiating from a central hexagonal chamber. But smaller tombs could be very much simpler — the circular tomb at High Rochester and another from Pulborough in Sussex were not big enough to require buttresses, and the smaller tomb at Keston is a simple rectangular chamber.

7 The ruin of Roman Britain

If we have little detailed history of the buildings in Britain during the Roman period we know even less about what happened to them afterwards. Only rarely do excavations yield some evidence for occupation after the Roman period. Frocester Court in Gloucestershire is a place where, thanks to patient and careful excavation, the Roman villa has been shown to have remained in use well into the fifth century but with a structure that was increasingly derelict. Around the year 360 the house was enlarged and enhanced. Coin evidence points to occupation into the early 400s, until a fire wrecked the villa house. Even so, the site seems to have remained in use, with some of the occupants removing themselves to a detached timber house just outside the villa compound. Others appear to have made use of the ruinous villa by converting the front corridor into a roofed hall for human and animal habitation. Likewise, at Orton Hall Farm in Cambridgeshire, new residents seem to have made use of the land but deliberately avoided the buildings of the ruinous villa complex (**167**). At Normanton, near Grantham in Lincolnshire, an Anglo-Saxon cemetery has now been unexpectedly found to lie in and around a substantial, and as-yet-unexplored, Roman villa complex.

But, apart from the observations of antiquarians in the sixteenth century and later, there are a few references to the buildings of Roman Britain dating from the fifth century onwards. The sixth-century chronicler Gildas referred to the practice of pagan rites amongst 'deserted city walls'. In the early eighth century the monk Bede commented that cities, forts, bridges and metalled roads remained as testimony of the Roman occupation. Later he even observed that Hadrian's Wall (which he thought was built in the fourth century) remained clearly visible in his day and was up to 12ft (3.6m) high, and 8ft (2.4m) thick. Bede also records that in 685 St Cuthbert visited Carlisle where he was taken on a tour of the Roman city walls, and a working aqueduct and fountain. Much further south an anonymous eighth-century poet seems to have wandered amongst the ruins of the bath complex at Bath (**168**). He was fascinated by the monumental scale of the collapsed vaults and attributed them to giants. Rather later William of Malmesbury, who wrote in the twelfth century, referred to an arched building, which was still standing in Carlisle and bore an inscription to Mars and Victory.

Probably the most vivid account of Roman remains is that of Gerald of Wales. He wrote towards the end of the twelfth century and recorded his *Journey through Wales*, including a description of remains at Caerleon. The passage is worth quoting in full.

Many traces of its former splendour can still be seen; immense palaces, originally ornamented with gilded roofs, in imitation of Roman magnificence . . . . and embellished with splendid buildings; a tower of prodigious size, remarkable hot

167 Plan of the villa at Orton Hall Farm, Peterborough (after Mackreth). The hatched areas show settlement identified as Saxon scattered in and around the ruinous Roman structures

baths, remains of temples and theatres, all enclosed within fine walls, parts of which remain standing. You will find on all sides, both inside and outside the circuit of the walls, underground buildings and passages, aqueducts; and what I think worthy of note, stoves contrived with wonderful art to transmit the heat insensibly through narrow tubes passing up the side walls.

Gerald's words form the most tantalizing surviving glimpse of the ruins of Roman Britain (**1**). Many other Romano-British buildings must have survived in a recognizable state well into the Middle Ages. The first serious antiquarians were John Leland (1506-53) and William Camden (1551-1623). Camden published various editions of his *Britannia* in the sixteenth and early seventeenth centuries. He noted that the site of Verulamium had 'ruins of walls, chequered pavements and Roman coins now and then digg'd up there'. In the early eighteenth century William Stukeley visited the settlement at Wall and described walls 1m (3ft) thick and 3.5m (12ft) high running parallel with one another forming

168 A fanciful view of the temple precinct at Bath in the fifth century and later. In fact the nature of the decay here is documented in Anglo-Saxon poetry and supported by archaeological excavation

square rooms. Even at Verulamium he was still able to prepare a map showing *Umbra Strati* ('shadow of a street') and *Vestigia cavitas* ('traces of hollows'), the latter probably being the sites of cellars of ruined houses. None are visible now except those excavated in modern times.

Stukeley also visited Hadrian's Wall and graphically described the desecration of the remains during the construction of the Military Road.

> The overseers and workmen . . . demolish the Wall, and beat the stones in pieces, to make the road withal. Every carving, inscription, altar, milestone, pillar etc., undergoes the same vile havoc, from the hands of these wretches.

Stone from the Wall was also re-used by local people. In 1801 William Hutton travelled the Wall and recorded his horrors, though further along at Brunton he was successful in pleading for the curtain's preservation.

169 The fort bathhouse, known as 'Walls Castle', at Ravenglass on the Cumbrian coast. Only part of this building is visible but the visible remains are amongst the best-preserved in Britain, and still stand to a height of 3.8m. It lies just outside the north-east corner of the fort and owes its preservation to its remote location, and substantial stone construction

Had I been some months sooner I should have been favoured with a noble treat; but now that treat was miserably soured. At the twentieth milestone I should have seen a piece of Severus's Wall [the real date of the Wall was still unknown] 7 feet high and 224 yards long, a sight not to be found in the whole line: but the proprietor, Henry Tulip, esq., is now taking it down to erect a farmhouse with the materials . . .

But it seems that antiquarians began to take an interest in Britain's past centuries of stone-robbing long before, and the depredations of weather and farming had already exacted a huge toll. There is practically no evidence for any houses remaining in a maintained state after the early fifth century. An arch in the crypt of All Hallows-by-the-Tower, built by the early eighth century, is made entirely of re-used Roman brick and tile. In fact many early churches (being amongst the few Saxon structures built of stone) seem to have been made out of material taken from Roman buildings. Much further north the builders of the eighth-century church at Escomb, county Durham, made use of the remains of the fort at nearby Binchester. The town of Verulamium was gradually abandoned as the settlement moved south-east to cluster round the *martyrium* of St Alban. Subsequently the abbey church was built largely from stone and brick taken from the Roman town. This is even recorded as being due to the abbots Ealdred and Eadmar who lived around the middle of the tenth century, and ransacked the ruins for building materials. Silchester was almost completely abandoned after the Roman period and the site remains open fields today. But despite this, and its comparative remoteness, the site was almost completely robbed out by the time any serious archaeological attention was paid to it in the nineteenth century.

Many other Romano-British towns like London, Lincoln and York had never really been abandoned and there was very little chance of Roman structures enduring indefinitely, apart from the city walls and gates. The earliest map of London dates from about 1559 and shows nothing which can be related to the Roman city save the Guildhall Yard which is now known to have originally formed the arena of the amphitheatre. Even the site of the huge basilica and forum was split in half by Gracechurch Street running south from Bishopsgate towards London Bridge. At York the great Minster was built over the remains of the headquarters of the legionary fortress.

The consequence of this kind of activity, quite apart from the depredations of nature, sets Britain apart from, say, the west coast of Turkey where the retreat of the sea due to silted rivers has left many of the greatest and richest cities of Asia Minor, like Ephesus, Miletus and Priene, high and dry. Their sites serve no useful purpose any more and their remoteness has ensured that they have largely suffered only from earthquakes and undergrowth. For Romano-British archaeology the challenge has been a huge one — to make sense of the rather undistinguished remains of buildings revealed in modern construction works, by the plough or rabbits scattering fragments of mosaic from their burrows. Apart from city walls, forts and a few rare instances like the 'Mint Wall' in Lincoln or the bathhouse at Ravenglass, almost nothing of Roman Britain has been found without having to dig it up (**169**).

The result has been that a very wide range of buildings has been excavated over the years, and throughout this book as many different types of building as possible have been looked at with a view to recreating some of the sense of form. Most of the drawings are fairly rigorous orthographic projections retaining relative dimensions. This has the advantage of retaining much of the original plan yet dispensing with the lifelessness of solid black lines. They are highly subjective and can never be definitive, but equally it would be futile to claim that 'more work needs to be done' in order to produce more reliable reconstructions. No amount of work will ever undo the work of generations of rabbits and stone-robbers, and no amount of discussion about wall strengths (or lack of) will ever supply certain evidence for an alternative reconstruction, especially as not a single one stands to prove its viability. There are countless ancient buildings scattered around the Mediterranean, which defy gravity and make such arguments beyond fairly general observations quite pointless. A centuries-old bathhouse in the outskirts of the old Ottoman capital of Bursa in north-west Turkey must surely be one of the most rickety looking constructions ever erected. Its teetering roofs lean on each other covered with ancient tiles, some broken, held together with liberal daubs of cement and judiciously placed struts of wood. Yet it has served as a bathhouse for longer than most Romano-British buildings would have ever had to serve, and despite its crumbling plaster it serves still.

So these neat geometric drawings are unrealistic in the sense that they can never record the myriad of unrecorded instances and imperfections caused by rotting wood, cracked tiles, stones flung by drunken youths, and errors of an architect who had no idea that the ditches of an early fort would cause his basilica's wall to subside. From a structural sense they may be wrong or they may be right — we can never know, and the question is unanswerable.

There are very few cases amongst the buildings discussed in this book where we can associate the structures with testified events. This is a shame but it remains an unavoidable fact. In most respects archaeological and historical evidence are incompatible because archaeology merely dates periods of occupation. Without inscriptions or other written evidence to associate a site with historically testified events or people, such associations are pure supposition. The 'palace of Togidubnus' at Fishbourne is probably the best-known example where a supposition has become something of a fact with the passage of time.

Nevertheless there is no harm in occasional flights of fancy — throughout the preparation of this book it was very hard to avoid the feeling that some places in Roman Britain must have been amongst the most beautiful, or at least striking, ever created in this island. The temple precinct at Bath was, in its final form, a triumph of cluttered intimacy combining the symmetry of classicism with the irregularity of the site and the Celtic presence of the god of the spring. The valley of Nettleton Shrub is a quiet, isolated place today; the octagonal shrine and its attendant buildings must have seemed almost grotto-like to the visitors approaching from the slopes on either side. Even Hadrian's Wall was built into the landscape, rather than over it. All this seems particularly poignant when one considers the controversy surrounding architecture in Britain today. So this book is an attempt to recreate a little of the lost spirit of the buildings and their nameless builders in and amongst which the Romano-British passed their lives.

Appendix 1:
Orthographic projections

Many of the numerous drawings forming the basis of this book depend on the various techniques of perspective and orthographic projection. Orthographic projection is the presentation of a three-dimensional, i.e. solid, object in two dimensions. There are a number of different ways of doing this and they all depend on an accurate ground plan. Representing an upstanding building, of whatever age, is made much easier simply because all the other dimensions and details of the structure are there to be seen and measured. The only consistent feature of Romano-British buildings is, unfortunately, that none of them are upstanding and very few survive above their foundations.

Despite this it is still possible to use the ground plan, along with better-preserved parallels from elsewhere and common sense, to create a reconstruction which is at least founded on known details. Sometimes the simplicity of a plan makes a reconstruction almost certain. In other cases, like the temple at Nettleton, the remains are so complex that a reconstruction can be no more than an educated guess.

Perspective projection

Perspective drawing creates an illusion of natural depth and realism. The technique is a complex one and the result is not always entirely satisfactory for a variety of reasons. Firstly a good drawing depends on selecting a suitable viewpoint. Secondly the distortions involved in using straight lines to represent the effect of what in reality are curves may produce a drawing which is 'accurate' but simply 'does not look quite right'. The reasons for this are very complicated but in short it can often be more effective to exaggerate, or subdue, the effects of perspective in order to produce the desired effect.

For the purposes of this book perspective is not always suitable simply because the relative dimensions of the structure are not evident. They are necessary to produce the drawing but do not appear in it. Although perspective sketches and paintings can create a considerable sense of mood and time it can be very easy to fudge details. The end result can be very hard to reconcile exactly with the known plan, if at all. In addition it is not usually very easy to find a way of showing a building in such a way that all its various features can be seen. For this reason orthographic projections and elevations have been preferred. They can provide the raw material for perspective reconstructions, as well as supplying exact detail.

170 *Reconstructions. The two illustrations show how an axonometric and an isometric reconstruction are developed from the same ground plan. In the former case the plan (based on the Romano-Celtic temple at Maiden Castle; see* **129** *and* **colour plate 25***) is retained in its original form. In the latter the opposing angles are altered to 120° and 60° respectively*

Orthographic projection

The most important techniques used in this book are axonometric and isometric projection (**170**). The terms are occasionally transposed in error so it is worth discussing them in detail, particularly as they are used so frequently in archaeological books.

Axonometric projection
This technique retains the true plan of the building and is actually drawn straight from it. The precise orientation of the plan is only important insofar as the building is presented in such a way that all its features can be appreciated. Once the relative heights of the walls have been decided on (if they are unknown), vertical lines are drawn from all the angle changes in the plan to the chosen heights. The angles of corners remain as they appear in the plan. The roof can then be added but the technique is especially suitable for illustrating interiors. A single scale then suffices for the whole drawing because the proportions reflect those of the real structure.

Isometric projection
Isometric projection is similar but distorts the plan in order to create an effect, which is more realistic for some shapes. Generally these are rectangles and squares. Either shape contains four right angles at 90°, 360° in total.

In isometric projection the plan is tilted 30° to the horizontal. Within the plan the two pairs of opposite right angles are converted so that one pair becomes two angles at 60°, and the other pair becomes two angles at 120°. The total is obviously still 360° but what started out as a rectangle has now become a parallelogram, and a square a rhombus. The villa at Great Witcombe (**114**) is a particularly suitable subject for this technique but even the

235

octagonal temple at Nettleton can be shown effectively (**135**). As with axonometric projection all the dimensions are in correct proportion, the only difference being the alteration of the angles to emulate some of the effect of perspective.

Elevation

The plan of a building can also be described as a 'vertical view'. An elevation is a horizontal view and is a very good way of depicting monumental buildings, which were designed to impress. The technique allows a single facade to be shown in accurate proportion. There were very few such buildings in Roman Britain and hardly any are known in detail. However, so many monumental buildings have survived in other parts of the Roman world that even the barest outline of a plan can provide enough information to create a reconstruction which will be true to the spirit of the original. Adding detail is not always advisable unless there are enough traces to make an accurate restoration. The precinct of the Temple of Sulis-Minerva is a case in point (**126**). On the other hand, a non-committal outline sketch is unlikely to be stimulating, so where the building type is well-known it seems quite reasonable to embellish the elevation with likely accessories. This was done with the elevations of the Temple of Claudius at Colchester and the *quadrifons* monument at Richborough. The effect is quite satisfying but it should not be forgotten that both structures survive only in the form of their foundations (**79**, **122**).

Appendix 2: Recommended sites

There are numerous Romano-British sites where remains can still be seen today. However, most of these are of military origin and consist of little more than denuded fortifications. This gazetteer lists the best of Roman Britain's sites by type where the remains are reasonably informative and well worth a visit. Outstanding examples are indicated with an asterisk (★). Those keen to explore more widely are advised to consult books under the heading of **Guides to Roman Britain** in the bibliography where far more information than can be given here is available. However, sites mentioned in the text with visible remains of any sort are indicated in the bibliography.

1 Military buildings

a) Fort defences

★ Birdoswald	NY 6166 (86)
Brecon y Gaer	SO 0029 (160)
Burgh Castle	TG 4704 (134)
Caerleon	ST 3490 (171)
Hardknott	NY 2101 (89)
High Rochester	NY 8398 (80)
Housesteads	NY 7968 (86/7)
★ Lunt (Baginton)	SP 3475 (140)
Pevensey	TQ 6404 (199)
★ Portchester	SU 6204 (196)
Richborough	TR 3260 (179)
★ South Shields	NZ 3667 (88)

b) Internal buildings

Caernarvon	SH 4862 (115)
★ Chesters	NY 9170 (87)
★ Corbridge	NY 9864 (87)
★ Housesteads	NY 7968 (86/7)
Lunt (Baginton)	SP 3475 (140)
South Shields	NZ 3667 (86)
Vindolanda	NY 7766 (86)
York	SE 6052 (105)

c) Military baths

★ Binchester	NZ 2031 (93)
★ Caerleon	ST 3490 (171)
★ Chesters	NY 9170 (87)
★ Ravenglass 'Walls Castle'	SD 0895 (96)
★ Wallsend	NZ 3066 (86)
(operational replica bathhouse)	

d) Amphitheatres (*ludus*)

★ Caerleon	ST 3490 (171)
Chester	SJ 4066 (117)

e) Frontiers

Hadrian's Wall curtain:

Benwell (vallum)	
Brunton	
(turret 26b)	NY 9269 (87)
Black Carts	
(turret 29a)	NY 8871 (87)
Limestone Corner	
(ditch/vallum)	NY 8771 (87)
★ Housesteads west	
(milecastle 37)	NY 7968 (86/7)
★ Poltross Burn	
(milecastle 48)	NY 6366 (86)
Antonine Wall:	
Watling Lodge	NS 8679 (65)

2 Towns

a) Basilica
★ Lincoln 'Mint Wall'	SK 9771 (121)
★ Wallsend	NZ 3066 (86)

(operational replica bathhouse)

b) Amphitheatres/theatres
Cirencester	SP 0201 (163)
Silchester	SU 6462 (175)
★ Verulamium	TL 1307 (166)

c) Public baths
★ Bath	ST 7564 (172)
Leicester 'Jewry Wall'	SK 5804 (140)
Wall	SK 1006 (139)
Wroxeter 'Old Work'	SJ 5608 (126)

d) Gates and Defences
★ Caerwent	ST 4690 (171)
★ Colchester	TL 9925 (168)
★ Lincoln	SK 9771 (121)
Silchester	SU 6462 (175)

3 Houses

a) Town houses
Caerwent	ST 4690 (171)
Dorchester	SY 6990 (194)

b) Villas
★ Bignor	SU 9814 (197)
★ Brading (I of Wight)	SZ 6086 (196)
★ Chedworth	SP 0513 (163)
★ Fishbourne	SU 8404 (197)
★ Lullingstone	TQ 5365 (188)

4 Sacred sites
★ Bath	ST 7564 (172)
Benwell	NZ 2164 (88)

★ Carrawburgh	NY 8571 (87)
Colchester	TL 9925 (168),

temple vaults (under Castle), church (on ring road by police station)

5 Others
Ackling Dyke (road)	SU 0116 (195)
★ Chesters (bridge)	NY 9169 (87)
★ Dover (lighthouse)	TR 3141 (179)
High Rochester (tombs)	NY 8398 (80)
(farm)	
Mersea (barrow)	TM 0214 (168)
Piercebridge (bridge ?)	NZ 2115 (93)
★ Willowford (bridge)	NY 6266 (86)

Bibliography and references

This is a select bibliography. The first section lists works under a number of general headings; the second follows the chapter headings with a general section for each followed by sites referred to in alphabetical order. The reader is advised also to examine the pages of *Current Archaeology* which is often the only illustrated source of detailed information and illustrations for sites excavated in recent years prior to their formal publication (publishing address: 9 Nassington Road, NW3 2TX). Useful information will also be found in the pages of *Britannia*, a journal published by the Society for the Promotion of Roman Studies under the section headed 'Roman Britain in 19—'.

All sites with visible remains listed in the bibliography are indicated ★ along with a four figure National Grid reference. Many are in private ownership (though most of the outstanding sites are in the guardianship of official bodies or the National Trust) and the reader should not assume that access is freely available.

General background works

Romano-British history and background
de la Bédoyère, G., 1999, *The Golden Age of Roman Britain*, Stroud
Esmonde Cleary, A.S., 1989, *The Ending of Roman Britain*, London
Frere, S.S, 1987, *Britannia*, London, third edition
Henig, M., 1995, *The Art of Roman Britain*, London
Jones, B., and Mattingly, D., 1990, *An Atlas of Roman Britain,* Oxford
Millett, M., 1990, *The Romanization of Britain*, Cambridge
Salway, P., 1993, *The Oxford Illustrated History of Roman Britain*, London

Guides to Roman Britain
Clayton, P., 1980, *A Companion to Roman Britain*, Oxford
Clayton, P., 1985, *A Guide to Archaeological Sites*, London
Ottaway, P., and Cyprien, M., 1987, *A Traveller's Guide to Roman Britain*, London [excellent photographs but lacking in precise detail]
Wilson, R.J.A., 1988 (3rd edition), *A guide to the Roman Remains in Britain*, London [this book is outstanding and indispensable for anyone seriously pursuing sites as it supplies exact descriptions of locations down to the last field gate, as well as serving as a universal site guide book]

H.M. Ordnance Survey, 1978 (4th edition), *Map of Roman Britain*, Southampton

Architecture and reconstruction
Drury, P.J., 1982, *Structural reconstruction*, B.A.R. 110 (British Series), Oxford
Johnson, P., and Haynes, I., (eds), 1996, *Architecture in Roman Britain*, CBA Research Report 94, London
Sorrell, A., 1981, *Reconstructing the Past*, London
Ward-Perkins, J.B., 1981, *Roman Imperial Architecture*, Pelican History of Art series, Harmondsworth
Ward-Perkins, J.B., 1988, *Roman Architecture*, History of World Architecture series, London

Archaeology
Frere, S.S., and St. Joseph, J.K.S., 1983, *Roman Britain from the air*, Cambridge
Wacher, J.S., 1966, *The Civitas Capitals of Roman Britain*, Leicester
Wacher, J.S., 1995 (2nd edition), *The Towns of Roman Britain*, London

Sources
Collingwood, R.G, and Wright, R.P, 1965, *The Roman Inscriptions of Britain*, Oxford
de la Bédoyère, G., 2000, *Companion to Roman Britain*, Stroud
Rivet, A.L.F., and Smith, C., 1979, *The Place-Names of Roman Britain*, London

1 Techniques

References to sites mentioned in this chapter will be found under the relevant chapter headings below; for example Caerleon will be found under chapter 2 for Military buildings, Bignor villa will be found under chapter 4 for Houses and so on.

General

Barry, R., 1980, *The construction of buildings. Volume I: Foundations, Walls, Floors, Roofs*, Oxford

Chapman, H., 1979, 'A Roman mitre and try square from Canterbury', *Antiq. J.*, 59, 403-407

Ling, R., 1985, 'The mechanics of the building trade' in Grew, F., and Hobley, B., (eds) 1985, *Roman Urban Topography in Britain and the Western Empire*, CBA Res. Rep. 59, London

Surveying

Dilke, O.A., 1971, *The Roman Land Surveyors*, Newton Abbot

Walthew, C.V., 1978, 'Property Boundaries and the Sizes of Building Plots', *Britannia* 9, 335-50

Walthew, C.V., 1987, 'Length-Units in House-Planning at Silchester and Caerwent', *Britannia* 18, 201 ff

Timber

McCarthy, M.R., 1986, 'Woodland and Roman Forts' in *Britannia*, 17, 339-343

Richmond, I.A., 1961, 'Roman Timber Building' in E.M. Jope (ed.), *Studies in Building History*

Stone, brick and tile

Blagg, T.F.C., 1976, 'Tools and Techniques of the Roman Stonemason in Britain' in *Britannia* 7, 152-72

Brodribb, G., 1987, *Roman Brick and Tile*, Gloucester

Darvill, T., and McWhirr, A., 1984, 'Brick and tile production in Roman Britain', *World Archaeology*, 15, 239-61

Greene, K., 1986, *The Archaeology of the Roman Economy*, London, 149-56

Dunning, G.C., 1949, 'The Purbeck Marble Industry in Roman Britain' in *Archaeological News Letter*, 1, 11, 15 ff

McWhirr, A., and Viner, D., 1978, 'The Production and Distribution of Tiles in Roman Britain with particular reference to the Cirencester region', *Britannia*, 9, 357-77

McWhirr, A., 1979 (ed), *Roman Brick and Tile. Studies in Marketing, Distribution and Volume in the Western Empire*, B.A.R. (International Series) No.68, Oxford

Peacock, D.P.S., 1977, 'Brick and tiles: petrology and origin', *Britannia*, 8, 235-247

Pritchard, F.A., 1986, 'Ornamental Stonework from Roman London' in *Britannia*, 17, 169-89

Williams, J.H., 1971, 'Roman Building-materials in South-East England', *Britannia*, 2, 166-195

Williams, J.H., 1971, 'Roman Building-Materials in the South-West', *TBGAS*, 90, 95-119 Woodfield, P., 1978, 'Roman Architectural Masonry from Northamptonshire', *Northamptonshire Archaeology*, 13, 67-87

Mosaics

Johnson, P., 1982, *Romano-British Mosaics*, Shire Archaeology No.25, Aylesbury

Ling, R., 1997, 'Mosaics in Roman Britain: discoveries and research since 1945', *Britannia*, 28, 259-96

Neal, D.S., 1981, *Roman Mosaics in Britain*, Society for the Promotion of Roman Studies, London

Rainey, A., 1973, *Mosaics in Roman Britain*, Newton Abbot

Wall-painting

Davey, N., and Ling., 1982, *Wall-Painting in Roman Britain*, Society for the Promotion of Roman Studies, London

Ling, R., 1985, *Romano-British Wall-Painting*, Shire Archaeology No.42, Aylesbury

2 Military building

General works

Breeze, D.J., 1983, *Roman Forts in Britain*, Shire Archaeology No.37, Aylesbury

Campbell, D.B., 1984, '*Ballisteria* in first to mid-third century Britain: a reappraisal', *Britannia*, 15, 75-84

Evans, E., 1994, 'Military Architects and Building Design in Roman Britain', *Britannia*, 25, 143-64

Frere, S.S., and St Joseph, J.K.S., 1983, *Roman Britain from the air*, Cambridge

Gentry, A.P., 1976, *Roman Military Stone-Built Granaries in Britain*, B.A.R. (British Series) No. 32, Oxford

Holder, P.A., 1982, *The Roman Army in Britain*, London

Jarrett, M.G., 1969 (ed), *The Roman Frontier in Wales*, Cardiff

Johnson, A., 1983, *Roman Forts*, London

Lepper, F., and Frere, S.S., 1988, *Trajan's Column*, Gloucester

Manning, W.H., and Scott, I.R., 1979, 'Roman Timber Military Gateways in Britain and on the German Frontier', *Britannia* 10, 19-61

Webster, G., 1985 (3rd edition), *The Roman Imperial Army*, London

Webster, G., 1988 (ed), *Fortress into City. The Consolidation of Roman Britain*, London

Welsby, D.A., 1982, *The Roman military defence of the British province in its later phases*, B.A.R. (British Series) 101, Oxford

Wilson, D.R., 1984, 'Defensive Outworks of Roman Forts in Britain', *Britannia*, 15, 63-74

Wilson, R., 1980, *Roman Forts*, London

Sites

ANTONINE WALL ★

Breeze, D.J., and Dobson, B., 1987 (3rd, revised, edition), *Hadrian's Wall*, London, 86-111

Hanson, W.S., and Maxwell, G.S., 1986, *Rome's North-West Frontier, the Antonine Wall*, Edinburgh

Keppie, L.J.F., 1982, 'The Antonine Wall 1960-1980', *Britannia*, 13, 91-111

Robertson, A.S., 1979, *The Antonine Wall*, Glasgow

Woolliscroft, D.J., 1996, 'Signalling and the design of the Antonine Wall', *Britannia* 27, 153-78

BAGINTON (The Lunt) SP 3475 ★

Hobley, B., 1971, 'An experimental reconstruction of a Roman military turf rampart', *Roman Frontier Studies 1967*, Tel Aviv, 21 ff

Hobley, B., 1971-3, 'Excavations at the Lunt Roman military site, Baginton, 1968-71', *Trans. Birm. and Warwicks. Arch. Soc.*, 85, 30 ff.

Hobley, B., 1974, 'The Lunt fort, 1966 experimental rampart and ditch: years 1-3' (Appendix 1), *Roman Frontier Studies 1969*, (eds E. Birley, B. Dobson, and M.G. Jarrett), Cardiff, 79 ff

BEATTOCK NS 9915

Maxwell, G.S., 1976, 'A Roman Timber Tower at Beattock Summit, Lanarkshire', *Britannia*, 7, 33 ff

BEAUPORT PARK TQ 7814 ★

Brodribb, G., 1979, 'Tile from the bathhouse at Beauport Park', *Britannia*, 10, 139 ff

Brodribb, G., and Cleere, H., 1988, 'The *Classis Britannica* Bath-house at Beauport Park, East Sussex', in *Britannia*, 19, 217 ff

BIRRENS *Blatobulgium* NY 2175 ★

Robertson, A.S., 1975, *Birrens. Blatobulgium*, Edinburgh

BIRDOSWALD *Banna* NY 6166 ★

Wilmott, T., et al, 1997, *Birdoswald: Excavations of a Roman fort on Hadrian's Wall and its Successor Settlements 1987-92*, London

BRECON Y GAER *Cicutio* SO 0029 ★

Wheeler, R.E.M., 1926, *The Roman Fort near Brecon*, London

CAERLEON *Isca* ST 3390 ★

Boon, G.C., 1987, *The Legionary Fortress of Caerleon-Isca*, Caerleon

Zienkiewicz, J. David, 1986, *The Legionary Fortress Baths at Caerleon, I. The Buildings*, Cardiff

Wheeler, R.E.M., 1928, 'The Roman Amphitheatre at Caerleon, Monmouthshire', *Archaeologia*, 78, 111 ff

CHESTER *Deva* SJ 4066 ★

Mason, D., 2000, 'Chester, the Elliptical Building', *Current Archaeology*, No.167, 405-13

Thompson F.H., 1975, 'The Excavation of the Roman Amphitheatre at Chester', *Archaeologia*, 105, 127-240; see also *Britannia*, 9, 1978, pl. xxiiiB [latrine], *Current Archaeology*, no. 84, 1982, 6-12, *Britannia*, 20, 1989, 283, pl. xxB [cornice stone]

CHESTERHOLM see VINDOLANDA

CHESTERS *Cilurnum* NY 9170 ★

MacDonald, G., 1931, 'The Bath-house at the Fort of Chesters (Cilurnum)', *AA*[4], 8, 219-304

CIRENCESTER *Corinium Dobunnorum* SP 0201 ★

Wacher, J., and McWhirr, A., 1982, *Early Roman Occupation at Cirencester*, Cirencester Excavations I, Cirencester

CORBRIDGE *Coriosopitum* NY 9864 ★

Bishop, M.C., and Dore, J.N., 1988, *Roman Corbridge: the Fort and Town*, London

DOVER *Dubris* TR 3141 ★

Philp, B.J., 1981, *The Excavation of the Roman Forts of the Classis Britannica at Dover, 1970-1977*, Kent Monograph Series No. 3, Dover

EASTER HAPPREW NT 1940

Steer, K.A., 1956-7, 'The Roman Fort at Easter Happrew, Peeblesshire', *PSAS*, 90, 93-101

ELGINHAUGH NT 3267

Hanson, W.S., 1987, 'Elginhaugh', *Current Archaeology*, 104, 268-72; see also *Britannia* 19, 1988, 428-9 [annex]

EXETER *Isca Dumniorum* SX 9192

Bidwell, P.T., 1979, *The Legionary Bath-House and Basilica and Forum at Exeter*, Exeter Archaeological Report No. 1, Exeter

Bidwell, P.T., 1980, *Roman Exeter: Fortress and Town*, Exeter

GELLYGAER ST 1397

Ward, J., 1903, *The Roman Fort of Gellygaer*, London and Derby

GOLDSBOROUGH NZ 8315

Hornsby, K., and Laverick, W.D., 1933, 'Roman Signal Station at Goldsborough, near Whitby', *Arch. J.*, 89, 206 ff

GLOUCESTER *Glevum* SO 8318 ★
Hurst, H.R., 1985, *Kingsholm*, Gloucester Archaeological Report No. 2, Gloucester
Hurst, H.R., 1986, *Gloucester, Roman and Later Defences*, Gloucester Archaeological Report No. 2, Gloucester

GREAT CASTERTON TF 0009
Manning, W.H., and Scott, I.R., 1979, *op. cit.* (under general references above), 31
Todd, M., 1968, *The Roman Fort at Great Casterton, Rutland*, Nottingham

HADRIAN'S WALL ★
Breeze, D.J., and Dobson, B., 1987 (3rd, revised, edition), *Hadrian's Wall*, London
Collingwood-Bruce J., 1853, *The Roman Wall*, London
Collingwood-Bruce J., 1885, *The Hand-Book to the Roman Wall*, London
de la Bédoyère, G., 1998, *Hadrian's Wall. History & Guide*, Stroud
Daniels, C., (ed) 1978, *Handbook to the Roman Wall*, 13th edition, Newcastle
Graham, F., 1984, *Hadrian's Wall in the Days of the Romans*, Newcastle-upon-Tyne
Jones, G.D.R., 1976, 'The western extremity of Hadrian's Wall: Bowness to Cardurnock', *Britannia*, 7, 236-243
Johnson, S., 1989, *Hadrian's Wall*, London
Kendal, R., 1996, 'Transport Logistics associated with the Building of Hadrian's Wall', *Britannia* xxvii, 129ff
Simpson, F. Gerald, 1976, *Watermills and Military Works on Hadrian's Wall. Excavations in Northumberland 1907-1913*, (edited by Grace Simpson), Kendal; see also *Current Archaeology*, 96, 1985, 16-19 [foundations and whitewashing], *Current Archaeology*, 116, 1989 [special edition concerned entirely with recent work on the wall at Carlisle, Birdoswald, Vindolanda, Wallsend and South Shields]

HIGH ROCHESTER *Bremenium* NY 8398 ★
see Daniels, C., 1978, *op. cit.* under Hadrian's Wall above, 295-301

HOD HILL *Dunium?* ST 8510 ★
Brailsford, J.W., 1962, *Hod Hill, I: Antiquities from Hod Hill in the Durden Collection*, London
Richmond, I.A., 1968, *Hod Hill II*, London

HOLT *Bovium?* SJ 4054
Grimes, W.F., 1930, *Holt, Denbighshire: The Works Depôt of the XXth Legion at Castle Lyons*, Y Cymmrodor 41, London

HOUSESTEADS *Vercovicium* NY 7868 ★
Crow, J., 1995, *English Heritage Book of Housesteads*, London

INCHTUTHIL NO 1239
Pitts, L., and St Joseph, J.K., 1985, *Inchtuthil, the Roman Legionary Fortress*, Britannia Monograph Series No. London
Shirley, E.A.M., 1996, 'The building of the legionary fortress at Inchtuthil', *Britannia* 27, 111-28

LINCOLN *Lindum* SK 9771 ★
Webster, G., 1949, 'The Legionary Fortress at Lincoln' in *JRS*, 39, 57-78

LONGTHORPE TL 1597
Dannell, G.B., and Wild, J.P., 1987, *Longthorpe II: the military works depot: and episode in landscape history*, Britannia Monograph Series No. 8, London
Frere, S.S., and St. Joseph, J.K., 1974, 'The Roman Fort at Longthorpe' in *Britannia*, 5, 1-129

LUNT, THE (see BAGINTON)

LYMPNE *Portus Lemanis* TR 1134 ★
Cunliffe, B., 1980, 'Excavations at the Roman fort of Lympne' in *Britannia*, 11, 227-288

MARYPORT *Alauna* NY 0337
Jarrett, M.G., 1976, *Maryport, Cumbria: a Roman Fort and its Garrison*, Kendal

NEWSTEAD *Trimontium* NT 5734
Curle, J., 1911, *A Roman Frontier Post and its People: The Fort of Newstead in the Parish of Melrose*, Glasgow

PORTCHESTER *Portus Adurni?* SU 6204 ★(AM)
Cunliffe, B.W., 1975, *Excavations at Portchester Castle, I: Roman*, RRCSAL No. 32, London

RAVENGLASS *Glannoventa* ST 0895 ★
see Daniels, C., 1978, *op. cit.* under Hadrian's Wall above, 284-86

RICHBOROUGH *Portus Rutupiae* TR 3260 ★
Bushe-Fox J.P, 1949, *Fourth Report on the Excavation of the Roman Fort at Richborough, Kent*, RRCSAL No. 16, London
Cunliffe B.W, 1968, *Fifth Report on the Excavations of the Roman Fort at Richborough, Kent*, RRCSAL No. 23, London

SAXON SHORE (Bradwell, Brancaster, Burgh Castle, Dover, Reculver, Richborough, Lympne, Pevensey, Portchester)
Johnson, S., 1979, *The Roman Forts of the Saxon Shore*, London
White, D.A., 1961, *Litus Saxonicum*, Madison, Wisconsin

SCARBOROUGH (see also GOLDSBOROUGH) TA 0589 ★
Rowntree, A., 1931, *History of Scarborough*, Scarborough, 40-50

SOUTH SHIELDS *Arbeia* NZ 3667 ★
Bidwell, P., and Speak, S., 1994, *Excavations at South Shields Roman Fort*, Newcastle upon Tyne

VINDOLANDA (Chesterholm) NY 7766 ★
Bidwell, P.T., 1985, *The Roman Fort of Vindolanda at Chesterholm, Northumberland*, London
Birley, R., 1977, *Vindolanda: A Roman frontier post on Hadrian's Wall*, London

YORK *Eburacum* SE 6052 ★
Addeyman, P.V. and Black, V.E., 1984, *Archaeological Papers from York presented to M.W. Barley,* York. Arch. Trust
Ottaway, P., 1996, *Excavations and Observations on the Defences and Adjacent Sites, 1971-90,* The Archaeology of York, Vol. 3, The Legionary Fortress, Fasc. 3, York
RCHM, 1962, *Eburacum — Roman York*, Volume I, London, 15 fig.8 [Multangular Tower]

3 Public buildings

General Works
de la Bédoyère, G., 1992, *Roman Towns in Britain*, London
Duncan-Jones, R.P., 1985, 'Who paid for public buildings in Roman cities?', in Grew, F., and Hobley, B., (eds) 1985, *op. cit.*
Esmonde Cleary, S., 1987, *Extra-Mural Areas of Romano-British Towns*, B.A.R. (British Series) 169, Oxford
Frere, S.S., 1987, *Britannia*, London, 229-256
Grew, F., and Hobley, B., (eds) 1985, *Roman Urban Topography in Britain and the Western Empire*, CBA Res. Rep. 59, London
Johnson, S., 1973, 'A Group of Late Roman City Walls', *Britannia*, 4, 210-223
Mackreth, D.M., 1987, 'Roman public buildings' in Schofield, J., and Leech, R., 1987, *Urban Archaeology in Britain*, CBA Res. Rep. No. 61, London
Maloney, J., and Hobley, B., (eds) 1983, *Roman Urban Defences in the West*, London
Sorrell, A., 1976, *Roman Towns in Britain*, London
Wacher, J.S., 1966, *The Civitas Capitals of Roman Britain*, Leicester
Wacher, J.S., 1995, *The Towns of Roman Britain*, London
Wacher, J.S., 1985, 'The functions of urban buildings: some problems' in Grew, F., and Hobley, B., (eds) 1985, *op.cit.*
Yegül, F. K., 1986, *The Bath-Gymnasium at Sardis*, Archaeological Exploration of Sardis Report 3, Harvard University Press [a fascinating account of the excavation and partial reconstruction of a monumental public building in Turkey]

Sites
CAERLEON *Isca* ST 3390 ★
for *ludus*/amphitheatre see reference under chapter 2

CAERWENT *Venta Silurum* ST 4690 ★
Ashby, T., 1906, 'Excavations at Caerwent, Monmouthshire, on the site of the Romano-British City of Venta Silurum, in the year 1905', *Archaeologia (second series)*, 10, 112-17 (South Gate)
Frere, S.S., 1989, 'Roman Britain in 1988', *Britannia*, 20, 264
Nash-Williams, V.E., 1953, 'The Forum and Basilica and Public Baths of the Roman Town of *Venta Silurum* at Caerwent in Monmouthshire ', *BBCS*, 15, 159, ff

CAISTOR-BY-NORWICH (also Caister St Edmunds) *Venta Icenorum* TG 2303 ★
Atkinson, J., 1931, *Caister Excavations*, London
Frere, S.S., 1970, 'Caistor-by-Norwich forum and basilica' in *Britannia*, 1, 1 ff

CANTERBURY *Durovernum Cantiacorum* TR 1457 ★
Bennett, P., 1984, 'The Topography of Roman Canterbury: a brief reassessment', *Arch. Cant.*, 100, 47-56
Frere, S.S., Stow, S., and Bennett, P., 1982, *Excavations on the Roman and Medieval Defences of Canterbury*, Maidstone, Canterbury Arch. Trust (Arch. of Canterbury vol. II)

CASTOR TL 1296
Mackreth, D., 1984, *Durobrivae: A Review of Nene Valley Archaeology*, ix, Peterborough

CHARTERHOUSE ST 5056 ★
Campbell, Elkington, D., Fowler, P., and Grinsell, L., 1970, *The Mendip Hills in Prehistoric and Roman times*, Bristol Arch. Research Group

CIRENCESTER *Corinium Dobunnorum* SP 0201 ★
McWhirr, A., 1981, *Roman Gloucestershire*, Gloucester, 28-36
McWhirr, A., 1988, 'Cirencester' in Webster, G., *op.cit.* above (general), 81-83

COLCHESTER *Camulodunum* TL 9925 ★
Crummy, P., 1977, 'Colchester: the Roman Fortress and the Development of the Colonia', *Britannia*, 8, 65-105 [Balkerne Gate revision]
Crummy, P., 1982, 'The Roman theatre at Colchester' in *Britannia*, 13, 299-302
Hawkes, C., and Hull, M.R., 1947, *Camulodunum*, RRCSAL No. 14, London

Hull, M.R, 1958, *Roman Colchester*, RRCSAL No. 20, Oxford [Balkerne Gate, Duncan's Gate, defences general]

DORCHESTER (Dorset) *Durnovaria* SY 6990 ★
Bradley, R., 1975, 'Maumbury Rings, Dorchester: The Excavations of 1908-13', *Archaeologia*, 105, 1-97

GOSBECKS (near Colchester) TL 9622
Dunnett, R., 1971, 'The Excavation of the Roman Theatre at Gosbecks', *Britannia*, 2, 27-47

LEICESTER *Ratae Corieltauvorum* SK 5804 ★
Hebditch, M., and Mellor, J., 1973, 'The Forum and Basilica of Roman Leicester', *Britannia*, 4, 1 ff
Kenyon, K.M., 1948, *Excavations at the Jewry Wall site, Leicester*, London
Wacher, J.S., 1974, *The Towns of Roman Britain*, London

LINCOLN *Lindum* SK 9771 ★
Jones, M., Gilmour, B., and Camidge, K., 1982, 'Lincoln', *Current Archaeology*, 83, 366-9
Jones, M., 1988, 'Lincoln', in Webster, G., (ed), *Fortress into City*, London, 145-65
Thompson, F.H., and Whitwell, J.B., 1973, 'The Gates of Roman Lincoln' in *Archaeologia*, 104, 129-207

LONDON *Londinium* TQ 3881 ★
Bateman, N.C.W., 1997, 'The London amphitheatre: excavations 1987-1996', *Britannia*, 28, 51-86
Fuentes, N., 1986, 'Some Entertainment in Roman London', *London Archaeologist*, volume 5, no.6, 144-6 [theatre]
Hill, C., Millett, M., and Blagg, T., 1980, *The Roman Riverside Wall and Monumental Arch in London, Excavations at Baynard's Castle, Upper Thames Street, London, 1974-76*, LAMAS Special Paper No. 3, London
Johnson, T., 1975, 'A Roman Signal Tower at Shadwell, E1', Interim Note, *LAMAS*, 26, 278-80 [see also Merrifield, 1983, below, 192-4]
Marsden, P., 1975, 'Excavation of a Roman Palace Site in London, 1961-72' in *LAMAS*, 26, 1-102
Marsden, P., 1976, 'Two Roman public baths in London', *LAMAS*, 26, 1-102 [Huggin Hill and Cheapside]
Marsden, P., 1978, 'The discovery of the civic centre of Roman London' in *Collectanea Londiniensia*, LAMAS Special Paper No. 2, 89 ff
Marsden, P., 1980, *Roman London*, London
Marsden, P., 1987, *The Roman Forum Site in London — Discoveries before 1985*, London

Merrifield, R., 1983, *London, City of the Romans*, London
Perring, D., 1985, 'London in the 1st and early 2nd centuries' in Grew, F., and Hobley, B., (eds) 1985, *Roman Urban Topography in Britain and the Western Empire*, CBA Res. Rep. 59, London
Philp, B., 1977, 'The forum of Roman London' *Britannia*, 8, 1 ff
Royal Commission on Historical Monuments (England) 1928, *An Inventory of the Historical Monuments in London, Volume III, Roman London*, London
see also *Current Archaeology*, 109, 1988, 49-50 [amphitheatre]; *Current Archaeology*, 115, 1989, 244-45 [Huggin Hill baths]

RICHBOROUGH *Rutupiae* TR 3260 ★
Cunliffe B.W, 1968, *Fifth Report on the Excavations of the Roman Fort at Richborough, Kent*, RRCSAL No. 23, London

ST ALBANS see VERULAMIUM

SILCHESTER *Calleva Atrebatum* SU 6462 ★
Boon, G.C., 1974, *Silchester: The Roman Town of Calleva*, Newton Abbot
Fulford, M., 1985, 'Excavations on the sites of the Amphitheatre and Forum-Basilica at Silchester, Hampshire. An Interim Report' in *Antiq. J.*, 65, 39-81

STONEA GRANGE TL 4493
Jackson, R.P.J, and Potter, T.W., 1996, *Excavations at Stonea, Cambridgeshire 1980-85*, London

VERULAMIUM (St Albans) TL 1307 ★
Kenyon, K.M., 1934, 'The Roman Theatre at Verulamium' in *Transactions of the St Albans and Hertfordshire Architectural and Archaeological Society*
Frere, S.S, 1983, *Verulamium Excavations II*, RRCSAL No. 41, London
Wheeler, R.E.M., and Wheeler, T.V., 1936, *Verulamium, a Belgic and two Roman Cities*, RRCSAL No. 11, Oxford
Richardson, K.M., 1944, 'Report on Excavations at Verulamium, Insula XVII, 1938' [Macellum], *Archaeologia*, 90, 81

WALL *Letocetum* SK 1006 ★
Webster, G., 1958, *The Roman Site at Wall, Staffordshire*, London [site booklet]
see also various references in the "Roman Britain in..." section of *Britannia*, vols 3 (1972), 6 (1975), 7 (1976), 8 (1977), 9 (1978)

WROXETER *Viroconium Cornoviorum* SJ 5608 ★
Atkinson, J., 1942, *Excavations at Wroxeter 1923-27*, Oxford
Barker, P., 1985, 'Aspects of the topography of Wroxeter (Viroconium Cornoviorum)' in

Grew, F., and Hobley, B., (eds) 1985, *Roman Urban Topography in Britain and the Western Empire*, CBA Res. Rep. 59, London

Barker, P., White, R., Pretty, K., Bird, H., and Corbishley, M., *The Baths Basilica, Wroxeter: Excavations 1966-90*, London

Bushe-Fox, J.P., 1913, *First Report on the Excavations on the Site of the Roman Town at Wroxeter, Shropshire, 1913*, RRCSAL No. 1, Oxford

Bushe-Fox, J.P., 1914, *Second Report on the Excavations on the Site of the Roman Town at Wroxeter, Shropshire, 1914*, RRCSAL No. 2, Oxford

White, R., and Barker, P., 1998, *Wroxeter: Life and Death of a Roman City*, Stroud

YORK *Eburacum* SE 6051 ★
Royal Commission on Historical Monuments (England) 1962, *An Inventory of the Historical Monuments in the City of York, Volume I, Eburacum, Roman York*, London

4 Houses

General works

Black, E.W., 1987, *The Roman Villas of south-east England*, B.A.R. (British Series) 171, Oxford

Branigan, K., 1976, *The Roman Villa in South-West England*, Bradford-on-Avon

Branigan, K., and Fowler, P.J., 1976, *The Roman West Country. Classical culture and Celtic society*, Newton Abbot

Casey, J., 1985, 'The Roman housing market' in Grew, F., and Hobley, B., (eds) 1985, *Roman Urban Topography in Britain and the Western Empire*, CBA Res. Rep. 59, London

de la Bédoyère, G., 1993, *Roman Villas and the Countryside*, London

Ellis, P., 1995, 'Classical reception rooms in Romano-British houses', *Britannia* 26, 163-78

Friendship-Taylor, R.M. and D.E., 1997, *From Round House to Roman Villa*, Northampton

Johnston, D.E., 1988 (3rd edition), *Roman Villas*, Shire Archaeology No. 11, Aylesbury

Neal, D.S., 1981, *Roman Mosaics in Britain*, London

Percival, J., 1976, *The Roman Villa. An Historical Introduction*, London

Rainey, A., 1973, *Roman Mosaics*, Newton Abbot

Rivet, A.L.F., 1969 (ed), *The Roman Villa in Britain*, London

Smith, J.T., 1963, 'Romano-British Aisled Houses' in *Arch. J.*, 120, 1 ff

Smith, J.T., 1997, *Roman Villas: A Study in Social Structure*, London

Smith, R.F., 1987, *Roadside Settlements in Lowland Roman Britain*, B.A.R. (British Series) 157, Oxford

Todd, M., 1978 (ed), *Studies in the Romano-British Villa*, Leicester

Walthew, C.V., 1975, 'The Town House and the Villa House in Roman Britain', *Britannia*, 6, 189-205

Walthew, C.V., 1978, 'Property Boundaries and the Sizes of Building Plots in Roman Towns', *Britannia*, 9, 335-50

Walthew, C.V., 1987, 'Length-Units in House-Planning at Silchester and Caerwent', *Britannia*, 18, 201 ff

Wilson, D.R., 1974, 'Romano-British villas from the air', *Britannia*, 4, 251-262

For references to house ownership elsewhere in the Empire and the Columella passage the simplest source of information is Lewis, N., and Reinhold, M., 1966, *Roman Civilisation, Sourcebook II: The Empire*, New York City, 167-75, 213-14

Sites

ASHTEAD (Surrey) TQ 1760
Lowther, A.W.G., 1928, 'Excavations at Ashtead, Surrey' in *Surrey Arch. Coll.* 37, 144-63
Lowther, A.W.G., 1929, 'Excavations at Ashtead, Surrey. Second Report' in *Surrey Arch. Coll.*, 38, part 1, 1-17

BANCROFT (Bucks) SP 8240 ★
Williams, R.J., and Zeepvat, R.J., 1994, *Bancroft. The Late Bronze Age and Iron Age Settlements, Roman Villa and Temple-Mausoleum*, Buckinghamshire Archaeological Society Monograph 7, Aylesbury

BARNSLEY PARK (Gloucestershire) SP 0806
Webster, G., 1967, 'Excavations at the Romano-British Villa in Barnsley Park, Gloucestershire', *TBGAS*, 86, 74-87
Webster, G., and Smith, L., 1985, 'The Excavation of a Romano-British rural settlement at Barnsley Park: Part III', *TBGAS*, 103, 73-100

BASTON MANOR, HAYES (Kent) TQ 4064
Philp, B., 1973, *Excavations in West Kent 1960-1970*, Dover, 80-93

BIGNOR (West Sussex) SU 9814 ★
Applebaum, S., 1975, 'Some Observations on the Economy of the Roman Villa at Bignor, Sussex', *Britannia*, 6, 118-132
Frere, S.S., 1982, 'The Bignor Villa', *Britannia*, 13, 135-96

BRISLINGTON (Avon) ST 6170
Branigan, J., 1972, 'The Romano-British Villa at Brislington', *Som. Arch. Nat. Hist.*, 116, 78-85

BRIXWORTH (Northants) SP 7471
see *Britannia*, 3, 1972, 322 and figure 7

CAERWENT (*Venta Silurnum*) ST 4690 ★(Cadw)
Martin, A., and Ashby, T., 1901, 'Excavations at Caerwent', *Archaelogia*, 57(ii), 301-310

CHALK (Kent) TQ 6773
Johnston, D.E., 1972, 'A Roman building at Chalk, near Gravesend', *Britannia*, 3, 112-48

CHEDWORTH (Gloucestershire) SP 0513 ★(NT)
Goodburn, R., 1986, *The Roman Villa: Chedworth*, National Trust
Webster, G., 1983, 'The Function of the Chedworth Roman Villa' in *TBGAS*, 101, 5-20

CHEW STOKE/PARK (Avon) ST 5751
Rahtz, P., and Greenfield, E., 1976, *Excavations at Chew Valley Lake*, London, 63 and pl.xxviii

CIRENCESTER (*Corinium Dobunnorum*) SP 0201
McWhirr, A., 1986, *Houses in Roman Cirencester*, Cirencester Excavations III, Cirencester Excavation Committee, Cirencester
McWhirr, A., 1988, 'Cirencester', in Webster, G., *op.cit.* (see general bibliography for chapter 3), 85-7

CLANVILLE (Hants) SU 3148
Victoria County History Hants, (i), 1900, 296

COLCHESTER (*Camulodunum*) TL 9925
Crummy, P., 1977, 'Colchester: the Roman Fortress and the Development of the Colonia', *Britannia*, 8, 65-105
Crummy, P., 1988, 'Colchester' in *Webster, G., (Ed) 1988, Fortress into City*, London, 42-3

COMBE DOWN (Avon) ST 7662
Branigan, K., 1976, *op.cit.* above (general), 45

DITCHLEY (Oxon) SP 3290
Ralegh Radford, C.A., 1936, 'The Roman Villa at Ditchley, Oxon', *Oxoniensia*, 1, 24-69

DORCHESTER (*Durnovaria*) SY 6990 ★
Drew, Lt Col C.D., and Collingwood Selby, K.C., 1939, 'Colliton Park Excavations: Second Interim Report', *Proc. Dorset Nat. Hist. Arch. Soc.*, 60, 51-65

DOVER (*Dubris*) TR 3141 ★
Philp, B., 1989, *The Roman House with Bacchic Murals at Dover*, Kent Monograph Series, Volume V, Dover

ECCLES (Kent) TQ 7260
Detsicas, A., 1983, *The Cantiaci*, Gloucester, 120-6

FISHBOURNE (West Sussex) SU 8304 ★
Cunliffe B.W., 1971, *Excavations at Fishbourne, Vols. I & II*, RRCSAL No. 26, London

Cunliffe, B.W., 1971a, *Fishbourne, a Roman Palace and its Garden*, London (reissued by Tempus, 1999)

FROCESTER (Gloucestershire) SO 7703
see *Current Archaeology*, no. 88, 139-145, no. 169, 11-18, and
Price, E., 2000, *Excavations at Frocester Court*, Stonehouse

GADEBRIDGE PARK (Herts) TL 0508
Neal, D.S., 1974, *The Excavation of the Roman Villa in Gadebridge Park, Hemel Hempstead, 1963-8*, RRCSAL No. 31, London

GLOUCESTER *Glevum* SO 8318
Hurst, H.R., 1988, 'Gloucester' in Webster, G., (ed) 1988, *Fortress into City*, Gloucester, 56-60

GREAT WITCOMBE (Gloucestershire) SO 8914 ★(AM)
Leach, P., 1998, *Great Witcombe Roman Villa, Gloucestershire. A Report on Excavations by Ernest Greenfield 1960-1973*, BAR British Series no. 266, Oxford

HOLCOMBE (Devon) SY 3193
Pollard, S., 1974, 'A Late Iron Age and a Romano-British Villa at Holcombe, near Uplyme, Devon', *Proc. Devon Archaeol. Soc.*, 32, 59-161

HUCCLECOTE (Gloucestershire) SO 8617
Clifford, E.M., 1961, 'The Hucclecote Roman Villa', *TBGAS*, 80, 42-9

KEYNSHAM (Avon) ST 6469 ★
Bulleid, A., and Horne, E., 1926, 'The Roman House at Keynsham, Somerset', *Archaeologia*, 75, 109-38

LEICESTER SK 5804
Wacher, J.S., 1974, *Towns of Roman Britain*, London, 352, pl. 70

LITTLECOTE (Wiltshire) SU 2970 ★
Toynbee, J.M.C., 1981, 'Apollo, Beasts and Seasons: Some Thoughts on the Littlecote Mosaic', *Britannia*, 12, 1-5
Walters, B., 1981, 'Littlecote', *Current Archaeology*, 80, 264-68
see also *Britannia*, 15, 1984, 322-3 and fig. 26 for plans of the whole complex

LLANTWIT MAJOR (South Glamorgan) SS 9569
Hogg, A.H.A., 1974, 'The Llantwit Major Roman Villa: a reconsideration of the evidence' in *Britannia*, 5, 225-50
Nash-Williams, V.E., 1945, 'The Roman Villa at Llantwit Major' in *Arch. Camb.*, 102, 21 ff

Webster, G., 1969, in Rivet, A.L.F., 1969, *op.cit.* (general section), 238-43

LOCKLEYS (Herts) TL 2316
Ward-Perkins, J.B., 1938, 'The Roman Villa at Lockleys, Welwyn', *Antiq.J.*, 18, 339-76

LONDON *Londinium* TQ 3281 ★
Marsden P., 1980, *Roman London*, London, 151-155
Merrifield, R., 1983, *London, City of the Romans*, London, 47, fig. 5
Perring, D., 1985, 'London in the 1st and early 2nd centuries' in Grew, F., and Hobley, B., (eds) 1985, *Roman Urban Topography in Britain and the Western Empire*, CBA Res. Rep. 59, London
see also *Britannia* 15, 1984, 309 & pl.xixB for Lime Street damp course (chapter 1)

LUFTON (Somerset) ST 5118
Hayward, L.C., 1952, 'The Roman Villa at Lufton, near Yeovil, Somerset' [baths], *P. Som. Arch. Soc*, 97, 91-112
Hayward, L.C., 1972, 'The Roman Villa at Lufton, near Yeovil, Somerset' [house], *P. Som. Arch. Soc*, 116, 59-77

LULLINGSTONE (Kent) TQ 5365 ★(AM)
Meates Lt-Col G.W, 1979, *The Lullingstone Roman Villa, Kent, Volume I - the Site*, Maidstone
Meates Lt-Col G.W., 1987, *The Lullingstone Roman Villa, Kent, Volume II - The Wall Paintings and Finds*, Maidstone

NORTH LEIGH (Oxon) SP 3915 ★(AM)
Ellis, P., 1999, 'North Leigh Roman villa, Oxfordshire: a report on excavation and recording in the 1970s', *Britannia* 30, 199-246

PARK STREET (Herts) TL 1403
O'Neil, H.E., 1945, 'The Roman Villa at Park Street, Near St Albans, Hertfordshire', *Arch. J.*, 102, 21-110

PIDDINGTON (Northants) SP 7954
see *Current Archaeology*, 117, 1989, 316-321; and *Britannia*, 20, 1989, 290 for summaries

ROCKBOURNE (Hants) SU 1217 ★
RCHM, 1983, 'West Park Roman Villa, Rockbourne, Hampshire', *Arch. J.*, 140, 129-50

QUINTON (Northants) SP 7753
Taylor, R.M., 1973, 'Quinton' in *Bulletin of the Northamptonshire Federation of Archaeological Societies*, 8, 15-17. See also *Britannia*, 3, 1972, 322

RIVENHALL (Essex) TL 8217
Rodwell, W.J., and Rodwell, K.A., 1986, *Rivenhall: investigations of a villa, church, and village, 1950-77*, Chelmsford Archaeology Trust Report No. 4; CBA Research Report No. 55

ST ALBANS see VERULAMIUM

SILCHESTER *Calleva Atrebatum* SU 6462
Boon, G.C., 1957, *Roman Silchester*, London
Boon, G.C., 1974, *Silchester: The Roman Town of Calleva*, Newton Abbot

SPARSHOLT (Hants) SU 4130
See Johnston, D.E., 1988 *op.cit.* (general section), fig. 23 and plate 5

STANWICK (Northants) SP 9771
Neal, D.S., 1989, 'The Stanwick Villa, Northants.: An Interim Report on the Excavations of 1984-88', *Britannia*, 20, 149-68

STROUD (Hants) SU 7223
Morley Watson, A., 1909, 'The Romano-British Settlement at Stroud, near Petersfield, Hants', *Arch. J.* 66, 33 ff

VERULAMIUM (St Albans) TL 1307 ★
Frere, S.S, 1972, *Verulamium Excavations I*, RRCSAL No. 28, London
Frere, S.S, 1983, *Verulamium Excavations II*, RRCSAL No. 41, London
Wheeler, R.E.M., and Wheeler, T.V., 1936, *Verulamium, a Belgic and two Roman Cities*, RRCSAL No. 11, Oxford

WINTERTON (Lincs) SE 9118
Stead, I.M., 1977, *Excavations at Winterton Roman Villa and other Roman sites in North Lincolnshire, 1958-67*, Department of the Environment Archaeological Reports no. 9

WOODCHESTER (Gloucestershire) SO 8303 ★(very occasionally)
Clarke, G., 1982, 'The Roman Villa at Woodchester' in *Britannia*, 13, 197 ff.
Lysons, S., 1797, *An Account of the Roman Antiquities discovered at Woodchester*, London

5 Sacred sites

General works

Barley, M.W., and Hanson, R.P.C., (eds) 1968, *Christianity in Roman Britain 300-700*, Leicester
Green, M.J., 1986, *The Gods of the Celts*, Gloucester
Henig, M., 1984, *Religion in Roman Britain*, London
Henig, M., and King, A., (eds) 1986, *Pagan Gods and Shrines of the Roman Empire*, Oxford University Committee for Archaeology Monograph No.8, Oxford

Horne, P.D., 1981, 'Romano-Celtic Temples in the Third Century' in Henig, M., and King, A., 1981, *The Roman West in the Third Century*, B.A.R. (International Series) 109, Oxford, 21-26,

Horne, P.D., 1986, 'Roman or Celtic Temples?' in Henig and King, 1986, *op. cit.*

Lewis, M.J.T., 1965, *Temples in Roman Britain*, Cambridge

Milburn, R., 1988, *Early Christian Art and Architecture*, Aldershot

Morris, R., 1983, *Churches in British Archaeology*, CBA Res. Rep. 47, London

Muckelroy, K.W., 1976, 'Enclosed Ambulatories in Romano-Celtic Temples in Britain' in *Britannia*, 7, 173-191.

Rodwell, W. (ed), 1980, *Temples, Churches and Religion in Roman Britain*, B.A.R. (British Series) 77, Oxford [contains a number of useful papers discussing various related topics]

Thomas, C., 1981, *Christianity in Roman Britain to AD500*, London

Webster, G., 1986, *The British Celts and their Gods under Rome*, London

Wheeler, R.E.M., 1928, see reference under Harlow below for a survey of Romano-Celtic temples

Wilson, D.R., 1975, 'Romano-Celtic Temple Architecture', *J. Brit. Arch. Assoc.* 38, 2-27

Sites

BATH *Aquae Sulis* ST 7564 ★

Blagg, T.F.C., 1979, 'The Date of the Temple at Bath' in *Britannia*, 10, 101 ff

Cunliffe, B., 1986, 'The Sanctuary of Sulis-Minerva at Bath: a brief review' in Henig and King

Cunliffe, B.W., 1984, *Roman Bath Discovered*, London, 1971, revised edition, London

Richmond, I.A., and Toynbee, J.M.C., 1955, 'The Temple of Sulis-Minerva at Bath' in *JRS*, 45, 97 ff

Cunliffe, B., and Davenport, P., 1985, *The Temple of Sulis Minerva at Bath, Volume 1: The Site*, Oxford University Committee for Archaeology Monograph No. 7, Oxford

BENWELL *Condercum* NZ 2164 ★

Simpson, F.G., and Richmond, I.A., 1941, 'The Roman Fort on Hadrian's Wall at Benwell', *AA⁴*, 19, 37 ff

BOWES MOOR (Scargill Moor; Durham) NY 9910 ★

Hanson, W.S., and Keppie, L.J.F., 1980, *Roman Frontier Studies, 1979*, B.A.R., Oxford, 233-54

BURHAM (Kent) TQ 7262

Ward, J., 1911, *Romano-British Buildings and Earthworks*, London, 245-6, fig. 70

CAERNARVON *Segontium* SH 4862

Boon, G.C., 1960, 'A Temple of Mithras at Caernarvon-Segontium', *Arch. Camb.*, 109, 136-72

CAERWENT *Venta Silurum* ST 4690 ★(AM)

Ashby, T., Hudd, A.E., and King, F., 1910-11, 'Excavations at Caerwent, Monmouthshire, on the Site of the Romano-British City of Venta Silurum in the year 1908', *Archaeologia*, 62, 4

CARRAWBURGH *Brocolitia* NY 8571 ★(AM)

Richmond, I.A., and Gillam, J.P., 1951, 'The Temple of Mithras at Carrawburgh', *AA⁴*, 29, 1-92

Smith, D.J., 1962, 'The Shrine of the Nymphs and the Genius Loci at Carrawburgh', *AA⁴*, 40, 59-81

CARRON (Arthur's O'on; Central) NS 8782

Henig, M., 1984, *op.cit.* above (general section) 208-9, 227

Steer, K.A., 1958, 'Arthur's O'on: A lost shrine of Roman Britain', *Arch. J.* 115, 99-110

Steer, K.A., 1976, 'More light on Arthur's O'on', *Glasgow Arch. J.* 4, 90-2

COLCHESTER *Camulodunum* TL 9925 ★

Crossan, C., and Crummy, N., forthcoming, *Butt Road cemetery and church*, Colchester Archaeological Reports, Colchester

Crummy, P., 1988, *Secrets from the Grave*, Colchester [Butt Road 'church' and cemetery booklet]

Drury, P.J., 1984, 'The Temple of Claudius at Colchester Reconsidered', *Britannia*, 15, 7-50

Fishwick, D., 1995, 'The Temple of Divus Claudius at *Camulodunum*', *Britannia*, 26, 11-28

Hull, M.R., 1958, *Roman Colchester*, London, 160 ff (Temple of Claudius)

Simpson, C.J., 1993, 'Once Again Claudius and the Temple of Colchester', *Britannia*, 24, 1-6

FARLEY HEATH (Surrey) TQ 0544 ★

Goodchild, R.G., 1947, 'Farley Heath' in *Antiq. J.*, 27, 83

FRILFORD (Oxon) SU 4396

Bradford, J.S.P., and Goodchild, R.G., 1939, 'Excavations at Frilford, Berks', *Oxoniensia*, 4, 1-70

Hingley, R., 1982, 'Recent Discoveries of the Roman Period at the Noah's Ark Inn, Frilford, South Oxfordshire', *Britannia*, 13, 305-9

GODMANCHESTER *Durovigutum* TL 2470

Green, H.J.M., 1986, 'Religious Cults at Roman Godmanchester' in Henig and King, *op. cit.*, 1986, 29 ff

HARLOW (Essex) TL 4612 ★
France, N.E., and Gobel, B.M., *The Romano-British Temple at Harlow, Essex*, Gloucester, 1985
Wheeler, R.E.M., 1928, 'A "Romano-Celtic" temple near Harlow, Essex, and a note on the type', *Antiq. J.*, 8, 300-26
see also *Current Archaeology* 112 for a summary of recent work

HAYLING ISLAND (Hants) SU 7202
Downey, R., King, A., and Soffe, G., 1980, 'The Hayling Island Temple and Religious Connections across the Channel' in Rodwell, W., (ed) 1980, *Temples, Churches and Religion in Roman Britain*, B.A.R. (British Series) 77 (vol.i), Oxford

HEATHROW (Middlesex) TQ 0574
Grimes, W.F., 1961, 'Draughton, Heathrow and Colsterworth' in Frere, S.S. (ed.), *Problems of the Iron Age in Southern Britain*, 21-3

HINTON St. MARY (Dorset) ST 7816 ★ (British Museum)
Painter, K.S., 1966, 'The Design of the Roman Mosaic at Hinton St Mary', *Antiq. J.*, 56, 49-54

HOUSESTEADS *Vercovicium* NY 7868
Bosanquet, R.C., 1904, 'The Roman Camp at Housesteads', *AA²*, 25, 255-63 [mithraeum] ff

ICKLINGHAM (Suffolk) TL 7872
West, S., 1976, 'The Roman Site at Icklingham', *East Anglian Arch.* 3, 63-126

JORDON HILL (Dorset) SY 7982 ★
Drew, C.D., 1931, 'Jordon Hill', *Proceedings of the Dorset Natural History and Archaeological Society*, 53, 265 ff

LAMYATT BEACON (Somerset) ST 6636
Leech, R., 1986, 'The excavation of a Romano-Celtic Temple and a Later Cemetery on Lamyatt Beacon, Somerset' in *Britannia*, 17, 259-328

LONDON *Londinium*
Grimes, W.F., 1968, *The Excavation of Roman and Mediaeval London*, London [Mithraeum]
Hill, C., Millett, M., and Blagg, T., 1980, *The Roman Riverside Wall and Monumental Arch in London, Excavations at Baynard's Castle, Upper Thames Street, London, 1974-76*, LAMAS Special Paper No. 3, London
Merrifield, R., 1983, *London: City of the Romans*, London, 179-180 [Isis altar], 183-7 [Mithraeum]
Shepherd, J., 1997, *The Temple of Mithras: Excavations by WF Grimes and A Williams at the Walbrook, London*, London

LULLINGSTONE (Kent) TQ 5365
Meates Lt-Col G.W., 1987, *The Lullingstone Roman Villa, Kent, Volume II — The Wall Paintings and Finds*, Maidstone

LYDNEY PARK (Gloucestershire) SO 6102 ★
Wheeler, R.E.M., and Wheeler, T.V., 1932, *Report on the Excavation of the Prehistoric, Roman and Post-Roman site in Lydney Park, Gloucestershire*, RRCSAL No. 9, London
see also Henig, M., 1984, *op.cit.* (general section), 253, note 16

MAIDEN CASTLE (Dorset) SY 6688 ★(AM)
Wheeler, R.E.M., 1943, *Maiden Castle, Dorset*, RRCSAL No. 12 Oxford

NETTLETON (Wilts) ST 8276
Wedlake W.J., 1982, *The Excavation of the Shrine of Apollo at Nettleton, Wiltshire, 1956-1971*, RRCSAL No. 40, London

PAGANS HILL (Avon) ST 5562
Rahtz, P., 1951, 'The Roman Temple at Pagans Hill, Chew Stoke, North Somerset', *P. Som. Arch. Soc.*, 96, 112 ff

RICHBOROUGH *Rutupiae* TR 3260 ★
Brown, P.D.C., 1971, 'The Church at Richborough', *Britannia*, 2, 225-31

RUDCHESTER *Vindobala* NZ 1167
Gillam, J.P., 1954, 'The Temple of Mithras at Rudchester', *AA⁴*, 32, 176-219

SILCHESTER *Calleva Atrebatum* SU 6462
Ford, S.D., 1994, 'The Silchester Church: a Dimensional Analysis and a New Reconstruction', *Britannia*, 25, 119-26
Fox, G.E., and Hope, W.H. St. John, 1892-3, 'Excavations on the site of the Roman city at Silchester, Hants, in 1892' [church], *Archaeologia*, 53, 563
Frere, S.S., 1975, 'The Silchester Church: the Excavation by Sir I. Richmond in 1961', *Archaelogia*, 105, 277-302
King, A., 1983, 'The Roman Church at Silchester Reconsidered', *Oxford J. Archaeol*, 2, 225-237

ST ALBANS see VERULAMIUM

SOUTH CADBURY (Somerset) ST 6325
Alcock, L., 1970, 'Excavations at South Cadbury Castle, 1969', *Ant. J.*, 50, 14-25

SPRINGHEAD *Vagniacae* TQ 6172
Detsicas, A.P., 1983, *The Cantiaci*, Gloucester, 60 ff
Penn, W.S., 1959, 'The Romano-British settlement at Springhead', *Arch. Cant.*, 73, 24 ff
Penn, W.S., 1964, 'Springhead: the temple ditch site', *Arch. Cant.*, 79, 170 ff

STANWICK (Northants) SP 9771
Neal, D.S., 1989, 'The Stanwick Villa, Northants.: An Interim Report on the Excavations of 1984-88', *Britannia*, 20, 156-7

ULEY (Gloucestershire) ST 7899
McWhirr, A., 1981, *Roman Gloucestershire*, Gloucester, 156-8
Woodward, A., and Leach, P., 1990, *The Uley shrines: excavation of a ritual complex on West Hill, Uley, Gloucestershire, 1977-9*, London

VERULAMIUM (St Albans) TL 1307
Lowther, A.W.G., 1935, 'Verulamium: Insula XVI', *Trans. St. Albans and Herts. Arch. and Arch. Soc.*, 166-72
Wheeler, R.E.M., and Wheeler, T.V., 1936, *Verulamium, a Belgic and Two Roman Cities*, RRCSAL No. 11, Oxford

WANBOROUGH (Surrey) (withheld)
Williams, D., 2000, 'Wanborough Roman Temple', *Current Archaeology* no. 167, 434-7

WOODEATON (Oxon) SP 5312
Goodchild, R., and Kirk, J.R., 1954, 'The Romano-Celtic Temple at Woodeaton', *Oxoniensia*, 19, 15 ff

WOOD LANE END (Herts) TL 0807
Neal, D.S., 1983, 'Unusual buildings at Wood Lane End, Hemel Hempstead', *Britannia*, 14, 73-86
Neal, D.S., 1983, 'A Sanctuary at Wood Lane End, Hemel Hempstead', *Britannia*, 15, 193-216

WROXETER *Viroconium* SJ 5608
Bushe-Fox, J.P., 1913, *First Report on the Excavation on the Site of the Roman Town at Wroxeter, Shropshire, 1913*, RRCSAL No. 1, Oxford

6 Other Buildings

Roads
Bagshawe, R.W., 1979, *Roman Roads*, Shire Archaeology No. 10, Aylesbury
Davies, H.E.H., 1998, 'Designing Roman Roads,' *Britannia* 29, 1-16
Margary, I.D., 1973 (revised edition), *Roman Roads in Britain*, London
see also the *Ordnance Survey Map of Roman Britain*, 4th edition, 1978

Bridges
Bidwell, P., and Holbrook, N., 1989, *Hadrian's Wall bridges*, London [Chesters NY 9170 ★ (AM); Willowford NY 6266 ★ (AM)]
Fitzpatrick, A.P., and Scott, P.R., 1999, 'The Roman bridge at Piercebridge, North Yorkshire-County Durham', *Britannia* 30, 111-22

Kackson, D.A., and Ambrose, T.M., 1976, 'A Roman Timber Bridge at Aldwincle, Northants', *Britannia*, 7, 39-72
Milne, G., 1982, 'Further Evidence for Roman London Bridge?', *Britannia*, 13, 271-276 (see also Milne G., under Quays and wharfs below, p44-54)
Selkirk, R., 1983, *The Piercebridge Formula*, Cambridge [NZ 2115 ★]

Quays and wharfs
Boon, G., 1978, 'Excavations on the site of a Roman quay at Caerleon', in Boon, G. (ed), 1978, *Monographs and Collections, I, Roman Sites*, Cambrian Arch Assoc., 1-24
Dillon, J., 1989, 'A Roman Timber Building from Southwark', *Britannia*, 20, 229-231
Dyson, T., (ed) 1986, *The Roman Quay at St Magnus House, London: Excavations at New Fresh Wharf, London 1974-78*, LAMAS Special Paper No. 8, London
Milne, G., 1985, *The Port of Roman London*, London

Aqueducts and water supply
Clarke, G., 1982, 'The Roman Villa at Woodchester' in *Britannia* 13, 217
Forster, R.H., (ed) 1908, 'Corstopitum: Report of Excavations in 1907', *AA³*, 4, 272
Richardson, K.M., 1940, 'Excavations at Poundbury, Dorset', *Ant. J.*, 20, 435
Stephens, G.R., 1985, 'Civic Aqueducts in Britain', *Britannia* 16, 197 ff
Thompson, F.H., 1954, 'The Roman Aqueduct at Lincoln', *Arch. J.* 111, 106
Wacher, J.S., 1978, *Roman Britain*, London, pl. 27 [Catterick]
Whitwell, J.B., 1976, 'The Church Street Sewer and an Adjacent Building', *The Archaeology of York. Volume 3: The Legionary Fortress*, York

Mills
Simpson, F. Gerald, 1976, *Watermills and Military Works on Hadrian's Wall. Excavations in Northumberland 1907-1913*, (edited by Grace Simpson), Kendal
Spain, R.J., 1985, 'Romano-British Watermills', *Arch. Cant.*, 100, (for 1984), 101-128

Glass-making, kilns and ovens
Atkinson, D., 1930, 'Caistor Excavations', *Norfolk Arch.* 24, 93-139
Hull, M.R., 1963, *The Roman Potters' Kilns of Colchester*, RRCSAL No. 21, London
Pitts, L.F., and St Joseph, J.K., 1985, *Inchtuthil*, Gloucester, 195-200
Rudling, D.R., 1986, 'The Excavation of a Roman Tilery on Great Cansiron Farm, Hartfield, Sussex' in *Britannia* 17, 191-230
Swan, V.G., 1984, *The Pottery Kilns of Roman Britain*, RCHM Supplementary Series No. 5, London

Wild, J.P., 1973, 'A fourth-century Potter's Workshop and Kilns at Stibbington, Peterborough' in Detsicas, A.P., (ed), 1973, *Current Research in Romano-British Coarse Pottery*, CBA Research Report No. 10, London

Woods, P.S., 1974, 'Types of Late Belgic and Early Romano-British Pottery Kilns in the Nene Valley', *Britannia*, 5, 262-289

Lighthouses

Brodribb, G., 1982, 'Graffito drawing of a Pharos', *Britannia*, 13, 299

Wheeler, R.E.M., 1930, 'The Roman Light-houses at Dover' in *Arch. J.*, 86, 22ff TR 3141 ★

Tombs

Bancroft (Bucks): 'Roman Britain in 1983', *Britannia* 14, 302

Harpenden (Herts): *JRS* 28, 1938, 186

High Rochester (Northumberland): *A History of Northumberland*, 15, 1940, 105 NY 8398 ★

Keston (Kent): *Archaeologia* 22, 1829, 336 TQ 4163★

Lullingstone (Kent): Meates, Lt Col G.W., 1979, *The Roman Villa at Lullingstone, Kent, Volume I — The Site*, Maidstone, 122-32

Welwyn (Herts): Rook, T., Walker, S., and Denston, C.B., 1984, 'A Roman Mausoleum and Associated Marble Sarcophagus and Burials from Welwyn, Hertfordshire', *Britannia* 15, 143 ff

West Mersea (Essex): Clapham, A.W., 1922, 'Roman Mausolea of the Cart-Wheel Type', *Arch. J.*, 79, 93 TM 0214 ★

Gerald of Wales [Giraldus Cambrensis], *The Itinerary through Wales and the Description of Wales*, edited by W. Llewellyn Williams, London, 1908 [or trans. by L. Thorpe in the Penguin Classics Series]

Gildas, *The Ruin of Britain and Other Works*, edited and translated by M. Winterbottom, London, 1978

Hutton, W., 1801, *The History of the Roman Wall*

Mackreth, D.F., 1996, *Orton Hall Farm: A Roman and Early Anglo-Saxon Farmstead*, East Anglian Archaeology No. 76, Nene Valley Archaeological Trust, Manchester

Stukeley, W., 1723, *Itinerarium Curiosum*, 1759, *Carausius*, and 1776, *Iter Boreale*

William of Malmesbury, *Gesta Regum Anglorum*, ed. W. Stubbs, 1887-9, Rolls Series

Conclusion

Some of the sources referred to in this short chapter are difficult to find though a small number are available in the Penguin Classics series. Modern general works which include them are also mentioned here.

Anonymous Anglo-Saxon poet in Kershaw, N., 1922, *Anglo-Saxon and Norse Poems*, Cambridge [also quoted in Cunliffe, B., 1984, *Roman Bath Discovered*, London, 213-4

Bede, *A History of the English Church and People*, trans. Leo Sherley-Price, 1968, London [Penguin Classics series]

Bede, *The Life of St Cuthbert*, trans. by L. Sherley-Price, 19—, London [Penguin Classics Series]

Camden, W., 1586, *Britannia*

Davies, D.G., and Saunders, C., 1986, *Verulamium*, St Albans [the museum guide which supplies a useful synopsis of references to Verulamium]

Embleton, R., and Graham, F., 1984, *Hadrian's Wall*, Newcastle-upon-Tyne

Index

All figure references are in **bold**